ONE CANADA
MEMOIRS OF THE RIGHT HONOURABLE
JOHN G. DIEFENBAKER

ONE CANADA

MEMOIRS OF THE RIGHT HONOURABLE

JOHN G. DIEFENBAKER

✳

THE TUMULTUOUS YEARS
1962-1967

MACMILLAN OF CANADA

TORONTO

Canadian Cataloguing in Publication Data

Diefenbaker, John G., 1895-
One Canada

Includes indexes.
Contents: [1] The crusading years 1895-1956. —
[2] The years of achievement 1956-1962. — [3] The
tumultuous years 1962-1967.

ISBN 0-7705-1331-X (v.1).   ISBN 0-7705-1443-X (v.2).
ISBN 0-7705-1569-X (v.3).

1. Diefenbaker, John G., 1895-   2. Canada –
Politics and government—1935-   * I. Title.

FC616.D53A36   971.06′42′0924   C75-10480-5
F1034.3.D5A36

Grateful acknowledgement is made to Longman Canada Limited, Toronto,
for permission to reprint the passage on p. 89
from *Vision and Indecision* © Patrick Nicholson, 1968.

Printed and bound in Canada by Hunter Rose
for The Macmillan Company of Canada Limited
70 Bond Street, Toronto M5B 1X3

TO THE MEMORY
OF MY DEAR WIFE
OLIVE

LIST OF ILLUSTRATIONS

✳

PREFACE

✳

Throughout the preparation of my memoirs, I have been fortunate to have had available to me the remarkable historical and literary skills of historian John A. Munro, and I am much indebted to him. To Dr. John H. Archer, whose contribution to these memoirs has been most beneficial, and who has written the tribute to the memory of my dear late wife, Olive, I owe a special debt. To those of my other friends and associates who gave of their valued advice and counsel, I also give my warmest thanks. I acknowledge the generous support of the Canada Council in continuing to provide former Prime Ministers with the support services necessary in the preparation of projects of this magnitude.

FOREWORD

The Right Honourable John Diefenbaker, like Britain's former Prime Minister, the Right Honourable Arthur Balfour, is a conservative because he is "absolutely certain that no community in this world has ever flourished, or could ever flourish, if it was faithless to its own past." His memoirs, *One Canada*, stand as a personal testament to the worth of our heritage and institutions, and to the solubility of our problems as a nation. Nowhere within these pages the craven apologies of contemporary Canadian pontificators, so often offered, for the essentials of our very existence! Mr. Diefenbaker, throughout his three volumes, shows concern with what Canadians have built, and how further to build upon this. Indeed, his second volume ends with Burke's admonition that "it is with infinite caution that any man ought to venture upon pulling down an edifice, which has answered in any tolerable degree for ages the common purposes of society."

It is the wisdom of Proverbs 29:18 that "Where there is no vision, the people perish." Today, when the Canadian sun seems resting in eclipse, when Canadian men and women of every age and origin are asking: "Where are we going?" the Diefenbaker memoirs serve as a beacon to those who seek the confidence to stand four-square and proudly Canadian. It is nearly a full twenty years since a majority of Canadians last caught the vision of a national greatness. Within the pages of these volumes, the reader will discover, or rediscover, the alchemy of this experience.

The third volume of *One Canada, The Memoirs of the Right Honourable John G. Diefenbaker*, covers the tumultuous years of his leadership from 1962 until 1967, years that saw three general elections and three minority governments, and were perhaps the most exciting five-year period in Canadian politics. Mr. Diefenbaker provides his readers with a full picture of the reasons for the devaluation of the dollar in 1962, the Cuban missile crisis (and, indeed, the whole defence–nuclear arms question during the whole period of his government), the Cabinet crisis and the defeat of his government in 1963, and the intervention of the administration of United States President Kennedy before and during the general election that followed. The battles for control of the Conservative Party from 1963 to 1967 are treated directly and in detail, but with an overview of men and events that places the fundamental questions in clear view. Mr. Diefenbaker's One Canada philosophy finds forceful and convincing articulation, making this volume much more than another memoir. It is a powerful national statement.

If one is prepared to accept, as George Grant does in his *Lament for a Nation*, the existence of a relatively common world view among Canadian managers of international business, journalists, and other purveyors of establishment thought, the elections of 1962, '63, and '65 may be taken as measures of the division of Canada, particularly its English-speaking areas, into nationalist and international constituencies. The Conservative Party Annual Meetings in 1964 and 1966 and the Leadership Convention that followed may be seen in the same light. Quebec was never cast as the villain in John Diefenbaker's Canada. So far as there was a villain, it existed in the forces of continental homogenization, which he believed would destroy the Northern Vision and the One Canada dream. The power brokers, the principal anti-nationalist forces in Canada, the big-business interests and their establishment Liberal and Conservative Party spokesmen, whose well-being did not necessarily relate to the continuance of the Canadian nation, saw John Diefenbaker as a dangerous man.

Mr. Diefenbaker's "One Canada" involved the conceptual embrace of all that was Canadian, institutionally, territorially, and historically. More important, it sought the redirection of the average Canadian's dreams to new horizons of achievement and adventure, one that would counter the popular fixation with goals established south of the 49th parallel. Quebec was important in this, for its own sake as an essential part of Canada, and as a bulwark against the homogenizing influence of American culture. Thus, Mr. Diefenbaker implemented the concept of two official languages as provided for in the Constitution and took important initiatives to make this a reality by simultaneous translation in the House of Commons (which made the House effectively bilingual for the first time), bilingual cheques, the first French-Canadian Governor General, and a more equitable distribution of diplomatic and senior bureaucratic positions. The Liberal Party's co-operative federalism, its Two Nations theory, and the Lesage-Lévesque concept of *maîtres chez nous* were not acceptable to him. Without a strong central government, Canada would not be able to withstand the pressures, external and internal, that mitigated against her continuance as an independent nation. It was Mr. Diefenbaker's final battle as Leader of the Progressive Conservative Party of Canada at the National Leadership Convention in September 1967 that prevented his party, the party of Sir John A. Macdonald, from embracing the disastrous Two Nations expedient. With that act, he saved Canada from Balkanization by default. There is more to be written, but it will await another day.

John A. Munro

OLIVE EVANGELINE DIEFENBAKER
1902-1976*

She will do him good and not evil all the days of her life.

*Give her of the fruit of her hands; and let her own works
praise her in the gates.*

*She openeth her mouth with wisdom; and in her tongue is the
law of kindness.*

Each and all of these verses from Proverbs 31 could be
applied to Olive Evangeline Diefenbaker and still much
would have been left unsaid. Olive Diefenbaker was
much more than a faithful wife and helpmate, a home-
maker, a tactful companion, and the wife of a great man.
She was a whole person in herself, a resourceful, cul-
tured woman who made a conscious choice of role and
unfalteringly pursued and developed that role.

Olive Diefenbaker had family roots in Nova Scotia and
these she never forgot. Indeed, her family roots go back
to the Pilgrim Fathers who landed as part of the
Mayflower company at Plymouth Rock in 1620. She was
directly descended from Richard Warren and Elder Wil-

---

* So many have written to ask for a short biography of the late Mrs.
Diefenbaker that Mr. Diefenbaker requested that this essay be prepared for
inclusion in his third volume of Memoirs, to serve until such time as a full
biographical study is undertaken.

liam Brewster, the latter being one of the authors of the Mayflower Compact. Loyalist to the core, her people later moved to Nova Scotia as United Empire Loyalists during the American War of Independence.

Her grandfather, the Reverend David Freeman of Harmony, Queens County, was one of the founders of Acadia University. Historian Edward M. Saunders records him as "unselfish, self-sacrificing, highly honoured and beloved". Another historian, George Levy, noted that Mr. Freeman was the first secretary of the Associated Alumni of Acadia, which was the first organization of its type in Canada.

The Reverend Dr. Charles B. Freeman, Mrs. Diefenbaker's father, was born in Canning, Nova Scotia, and he married Angie Alicia Eaton, a member of another distinguished U.E.L. family, in 1897. Dr. Freeman attended Acadia University, obtaining his Bachelor of Arts in 1891. Years later, he was to receive an Honorary Doctorate of Divinity from Acadia. Before his death in 1942, he served Baptist pastorates throughout Ontario and the West.

Olive Freeman, one of five children, was born in Roland, Manitoba, in 1902. As a child of the parsonage, she grew up in a family atmosphere closely associated with church and church life. Here, she learned much of the ordinary joys and anxieties of parish family life and very early came to understand the plight of those in need. It was this experience that led her to become a teacher, so that she might help people to help themselves through the medium of education.

Olive received her public and high school education in a variety of schools as the family moved from one charge to another. One of these moves, to Saskatoon, brought about the first meeting of Olive Freeman with John G. Diefenbaker in 1917. He was a young officer invalided home from overseas. She was a pig-tailed student. There was interest enough for them to see each other at church and at school. Mr. Diefenbaker remembers that they once debated on the subject of capital punishment at a gathering in the basement of the First Baptist Church. Olive Freeman first attended the University of Saskatchewan, but when she moved to Brandon, Manitoba, to join her parents, the lives of John and Olive parted until many years later.

Olive graduated in 1923 from Brandon College, a Baptist liberal arts centre of education on the prairies. She was one of a distinguished number of alumni including T. C. Douglas, M.P., and Stanley Knowles, M.P. After college she followed her family to Ontario and earned a high school teaching diploma at the Ontario College of Education in Toronto. Subsequently, she taught at Huntsville High School in 1926 and at Guelph Collegiate Institute for the period 1929-32.

While at Guelph she met Harry Palmer, a lawyer and a musician. They were married in 1933 and Olive gave up teaching. A daughter, Carolyn, was born the following year. When her husband died in 1936, she returned to teaching.

She taught high school at Arthur, Ontario, and then at Owen Sound Collegiate Institute. She was a sensitive high school teacher, imposing a discipline of the mind and communicating well with young people. She was good at sports both as a player and as a coach in field sports and basketball. She had the ability to listen, and this gained her the confidence of the young. She inspired students with a wish to achieve, a gift essential to a leader in educational counselling. She became one of the pioneers on guidance, and as a recognized authority was invited to give lectures to educational groups in both Canada and the United States. As her stature in this field grew, she became Assistant Director of Vocational Guidance for the Province of Ontario, a position she held from 1945 to 1953. In this role, she became an inspiring confidante to thousands of young Canadians as she visited schools in every part of Ontario. She was offered the Directorship in November 1953. Her answer to the Minister of Education, who tendered the position, was that she was about to become Mrs. John Diefenbaker. Earlier she had been offered the position of headmistress of two prestigious girls' schools.

Many writers have commented on the change in Olive Palmer after her marriage to John Diefenbaker. Up to that time she had been easy to interview about herself. Afterwards, it was claimed, this became impossible as she channelled her resources and activities to the support of her husband's well-being and career. It was difficult to separate his interests and hers, and she stated with candour and fervour, "The whole direction of my life is that I am John's wife."

Mrs. Diefenbaker accompanied her husband on his campaign tours, watching over his health, looking after the social chores that are a part of any campaign, and generally acting as a balance wheel for her husband. She was fond of meeting people and loved to talk about prairie pioneers who brought the wilderness under the plough, having taught for a year out of University in the early 1920s at Paddockwood, an area north of Prince Albert opened for soldier settlers after the First World War. She bravely went through lobster dinners in the Maritimes, for she admired and respected the people even if allergic to lobster. Although she rarely talked politics in public, she corresponded with hundreds of friends across the country. She wrote "thank-you" notes to those who put themselves out for her or her husband. She dropped in on groups of students. She visited people in hospitals and homes for the aged and the poor. It was said by scores of people that she gained more support for her husband than was gained by all the signs and slogans, printed or spoken. But she was far more than a great election asset, she was her husband's full partner and counsellor. Mr. Diefenbaker fondly remembers that when it was suggested that he and Olive move immediately into Stornoway, the Leader of the Opposition's official residence, following his Convention victory in December 1956, she objected on the grounds that it would be foolish to move twice in so short a period.

Olive Diefenbaker was discreet and diplomatic in public life. She was quick to accept the further need for discretion as the Prime Minister's wife. When John Diefenbaker gained the leadership of the Progressive Conservative Party in 1956, party officials told her that it was traditional for the wife to say a few words at the convention. "I decided I had to, but that was it. After that, I made up my own mind." She departed from this course only on rare occasions—a school reunion in Huntsville, a graduation address at Owen Sound, a CBC interview in 1963, and an address when she was awarded an honorary degree at Brandon University.

When the Diefenbakers moved into the Prime Minister's residence on Sussex Drive in June 1957, Olive's heavy round of official functions commenced. She found herself entertaining numerous groups. She began the practice of holding teas for M.P.s' wives. She was hostess to many world leaders, and she became the friend of Prime Ministers and Presidents (Churchill, Eisenhower, Eden, de Gaulle, Macmillan, and Adenauer to name a few). She took part in organizations for the aged and for crippled children. She travelled in Canada and abroad. In all this she was charming, poised, gracious. Her charm was not superficial but was the product of a genuine interest in people. Her poise stemmed from her naturalness, the fact that she was herself a calm island of good sense in a troubled sea. She was gracious because she had been well brought up. Although she walked by choice in the shadow of her husband, the Prime Minister, she was not anonymous, for she shone with an inner radiance all her own.

Olive Diefenbaker believed in the monarchy, and she shared her husband's love for Canada. She shared, also, his belief in the good sense of people, his belief in Parliament, and his rapport with the man on the street. Throughout his vigorous march to power, during the hectic days of prime-ministership, during the troubled months of party upheavals, and in the bleak days of the leadership convention in 1967, she was that constant support that enables a man in political life in a high place to cope with each day's crises. The election campaigns of 1957 and 1958 were boisterous, exciting days full of hope and anticipation. The elections of 1962 and 1963 were turbulent; the threats of violence, the jostlings, and the disturbances are described in the text of this volume.

Olive Diefenbaker was an omnivorous reader of English and French literature. She had been a teacher of French and spoke the language flawlessly. Years later, she recalled how she would sit for hours when her husband was Prime Minister, knitting and reading on the bed while Mr. Diefenbaker worked into the night. Mrs. Diefenbaker was, by nature, a night person, "an owl" as she called herself, and was never keen to get up early in the morning. Her husband, up with the larks, was always out for this thirty-minute walk shortly after first light. On his return, she would join him for breakfast—he "so cheerful it would kill you". She had a delightful sense of humour. Mr. Diefenbaker enjoys telling of the time he asked his wife to say grace before dinner. She said it in her soft tone and Mr. Diefenbaker said to her, "I didn't hear you." To which she replied, "I wasn't talking to you." On another occasion her husband remarked, "Now you read faster than I do." "I always did!" was her reply.

It was daily routine for Mrs. Diefenbaker to deal with correspondence each morning immediately after breakfast. She wrote an incredible number of letters—all by hand. One day's total reached fifty-three, and each of the messages was different. In addition, there were the household tasks of shopping, crewel work, making cushion covers and wall hangings. She played the piano, and Beethoven was her favourite. She attended luncheons, bazaars, launchings, Quota clubs, Girl Guide jubilees, and those many political and formal occasions already mentioned. During Mr. Diefenbaker's years as Prime Minister, Olive Diefenbaker became known as the hardest-working Prime Minister's wife in Canadian history.

Perhaps nothing better illustrated Olive Diefenbaker's graciousness and composure in public and in private than her bearing during the leadership convention held in Toronto in 1967. When Robert Stanfield was chosen as leader, her husband went to the platform to make one more attempt to unify the party behind the new leadership. Meanwhile, it is reported, Mrs. Diefenbaker went through the whole public ordeal of seeing her husband go down to defeat without losing her composure or dignity. When supporters came to the suite to express their dismay, she went around comforting them. She was, indeed, a lady of dignity.

Few people, hearing the news in 1975 that Olive Diefenbaker had suffered a stroke, realized what a history of pain stoically borne lay behind the smiling face. Her arthritis was intensified in 1957 when the aircraft on which she was travelling with her husband to the Prime Ministers' Conference in London suddenly dropped one thousand feet, crushing three vertebrae. No one would have guessed the pain she experienced as she climbed steps to the dais or stage to sit with and support her husband, except during two election campaigns when she had to have crutches. The news of her stroke in December 1975 brought a flood of mail from admirers. In a single month she received some two thousand letters, and she set about hand-writing replies. She had appeared to be recovering well from the stroke but a serious heart condition forced her to return to hospital. She had spent most of the last three months of 1976 in hospital but was released on Tuesday, 21 December, to spend Christmas at home. The next morning, Mr. Diefenbaker left for Parliament Hill without waking her. He phoned her later and she seemed well. She complained of dizziness at noon and died, peacefully, shortly afterwards.

Mrs. Diefenbaker's death was announced to Members of Parliament by Joe Clark, Leader of Her Majesty's Loyal Opposition. The Prime Minister and the leaders of the NDP and the Social Credit party paid her tribute. Thousands of friends and admirers wrote or telegraphed messages of condolence, including Her Majesty the Queen and the Governor General and Madame Léger, of whom she was very fond. The tremendous void in Mr. Diefenbaker's life is bearable only because of the faith they shared; recently, he said, "Olive is not with me but I know that all is well with her."

Funeral services for Olive Diefenbaker were held at First Baptist Church, Ottawa. The church was crowded with the leaders of the nation and with average Canadians. Mr. Diefenbaker was accompanied by his stepdaughter, Carolyn Weir, and her five children. An eight-man guard of honour from the House of Commons security staff stood outside the church. There has rarely been such a spontaneous outpouring of love and sympathy as was evinced in Ottawa. The Reverend Dr. Ralph Cummings conducted the service assisted by the Reverend Dr. R. Fred Bullen. Among the hymns chosen by Mr. Diefenbaker was Mrs. Diefenbaker's favourite. By John Bunyan, it characterizes the courage and faith of Olive Diefenbaker:

> Who would true valor see,
> Let him come hither.
> One here will constant be,
> Come wind, come weather.

There's no discouragement
Shall make him once relent
His first avowed intent
To be a pilgrim.

John H. Archer

ONE CANADA

MEMOIRS OF THE RIGHT HONOURABLE

JOHN G. DIEFENBAKER

CHAPTER ONE

✳

A T THREE P.M., 5 February 1963, I rose in the House of Commons to speak to a Motion of Non-confidence that had been moved the previous day by the Leader of the Opposition, the Honourable Lester B. Pearson. He had charged that my government, "because of lack of leadership, the breakdown of unity in the Cabinet, and confusion and indecision in dealing with national and international problems, [did] not have the confidence of the Canadian people."

His motion was so general, so widespread, so obviously diffuse, that I could only conclude it was a deliberate attempt by his party to sidle away from the central question of whether Canada would continue as a sovereign state, of whether Canadian policies would be made in Canada by Canadians or by the United States. He had been shrill and nervous as he laid his case before the House, and I was reminded of his performances in 1957 and 1958: the same decayed platitudes, the same single concern, the same cry for office! "Power at any price" was as close as the Pearson Liberals came to having any principles. Indeed, Mr. Pearson has since admitted in his memoirs that from the day of the 1962 election his only concern "was to bring on and win the next election," and that not one of his Members "had any reservations on our tactics of attack without quarter on every front." With a great deal of help from his friends across the border to the south, he was now on the verge of succeeding.

To describe the situation I faced that day: Mr. Pearson had swallowed himself on the question of nuclear arms for Canada, and the Kennedy government, in consequence, had committed itself to aiding and abetting the Liberal Party in its attempt to throw out my government. The chain of public events that began on 3 January 1963 and ended thirty-three days later on 5 February make this conclusion inescapable and virtually irrefutable.

On 3 January, General Lauris Norstad, the newly retired NATO Supreme Allied Commander Europe, visited Ottawa under the guise of paying us a farewell visit. This United States general had held, since November 1956, the most politically sensitive military command in the NATO structure. It is impossible to accept that he innocently wandered into Canada's nuclear debate. His visit to Ottawa could only have been at the behest of President Kennedy. His purpose was to establish a basis for Mr. Pearson's conversion to United States nuclear policy. His message was that my government had not lived up to its commitments in NATO. When asked at his press conference whether Canada would be fulfilling her NATO commitments if she did not accept nuclear weapons, Norstad replied, "not under the terms of the requirements that had been established by NATO. . . . We are depending upon Canada to produce some of the tactical atomic strike forces." Through the medium of a well-rehearsed Canadian press, the United States was taking its case directly to the Canadian public.

It is revealing that Canada's Chairman of the Chiefs of Staff, Air Chief Marshal F. R. Miller, was with Norstad at his press conference, as was the Honourable Pierre Sévigny, Associate Minister of Defence, and that neither took exception to anything that was said. I cannot speak for Mr. Sévigny in this regard but it is certainly true that certain senior officers in the Canadian military had taken my Minister of Defence, the Honourable Douglas Harkness, under their wing. The Honourable Howard Green has always maintained that one of his problems as Secretary of State for External Affairs was the existence of what amounted to a supra-governmental relationship between the Canadian military, in particular the Royal Canadian Air Force, and the Pentagon. Indeed, Air Marshal C. R. Slemon, the Canadian Deputy Commander-in-Chief NORAD, organized visits by Canadian businessmen, journalists, and academics to NORAD headquarters at Colorado Springs, where these leading Canadians were brainwashed with the necessity of Canada's acquiring nuclear weapons for its NORAD forces. The Norstad visit was part of this pattern; it was the Canadian military that organized his press conference. As to Slemon's role in joining the outcry that we should arm the Bomarc, nothing can justify it.

It was, however, the United States State Department that orchestrated the direct intervention of the American government in Canadian politics. Secret lecture courses had been given under United States Ambassador Livingston Merchant in the basement of the United States Embassy in Ottawa, during which Canadian journalists were advised what they could do in order to undermine my government's policy on nuclear weapons. I knew nothing about these machinations until Charles Lynch, Ottawa bureau chief for Southam Press, and one of the "students" in receipt of this American tutelage, revealed all in his newspaper column on 14 July 1965. I confronted him with his own evidence during a nationally televised interview on 7 February 1966. I told him then, and I have not changed my mind since, that I attributed a not insignificant portion of the press activity against my government to this scandalous school. Never will I be able to accept the specious argument that the United States was engaged only in normal lobbying in support of its point of view. Surely none of these select press representatives could seriously contend that he received every day from the ambassadors of other countries arguments to use against the Government of Canada in order to force upon us a policy which we had decided was no longer necessary. Had I known about these activities at the time, the Canadian people would have been given full opportunity to judge their propriety, but not one of the journalists involved said even a "boo" about it in 1962 or 1963, when it might have made a difference.

One of the problems in a democracy is that occasionally leading journalists develop a disproportionate political influence. The result in this case was a campaign to defeat me that began before the 1962 election. The pattern was that, first, few stories of credit to my government received media coverage. Then, despite the fact that we had put more beneficial legislation on the statute books than any previous Canadian government in a comparable period, the line was taken that I could not make decisions. The attacks next centred on whether my word could be trusted. Finally, it reached the point where I was pictured as suffering from a terminal palsy, too ill to be allowed to continue in office, and this despite the fact that I made public the report of a full medical examination by two eminent doctors, Dr. Albert Crowther and Dr. Keith Welsh.

I recall discussing the vicious press coverage of our government at an informal meeting of Cabinet on Saturday, 8 December 1962. I took as examples some of the recent editorials and articles in the Toronto *Telegram* and the Montreal *Gazette*, a major article in the *Financial Times* of the previous week by Michael Barkway, which had been reprinted in the *Hamilton Spectator* and the *Winnipeg Tribune*, and the campaign the *Calgary*

Herald and the *Edmonton Journal* were conducting against the government. It was becoming apparent that no matter what legislation we brought before Parliament certain powerful interests were out to destroy us. I noted that in that very day's *Globe and Mail* there was a feature article stating that there were seven resolutions to be presented to the Conservative Party's annual meeting on 17 January by the YPC organization demanding my resignation. This, I predicted, would be built up out of all proportion by the press in the weeks to come. I reminded my colleagues that at our last annual meeting, the activities of one critical delegate, who was of no particular importance within the party, had been featured in every newspaper in Canada. When I mentioned that no defence had been raised to this ongoing campaign, the Honourable Davie Fulton answered that when he or any of our colleagues defended me or the record of the government, they received no press at all.

Before I leave the subject, I think it only fair that the media be given proper credit for their full role in the events of early 1963. Contrary to popular belief, the resignation of the Honourable Douglas Harkness as Minister of National Defence on 3 February was not of great importance. He had never seemed to recover from being removed from Agriculture in 1960. Further, it was difficult for me to take seriously the alleged reason for his resignation. To me, the revealing aspect involves only the circumstances in which his decision to resign "on principle" was made.

On the night of Saturday, 2 February, I attended the annual Press Gallery dinner in Ottawa. So did Mr. Harkness. It was an evening I will never forget. Indeed, I know of no other press affair to equal it. The Gallery dinner is usually a jocular occasion where press men, in song and skit, poke fun at the politicians and issues of the day. Normally, as Prime Minister, I would have taken part in

these proceedings by delivering a few appropriate remarks. I declined to speak that evening, however, because my friend Chief Justice Kerwin had died earlier in
the day. Now, I have been caricatured thousands of
times, and I doubt if anyone enjoys these things more
than I do; if one cannot laugh at oneself there is little
hope of survival in political life. But on this particular occasion, I had been marked for demolition. In one skit,
they adapted the slander I mentioned earlier — that I was
the victim of an advanced case of Parkinson's disease —
as they sang and acted out my physical and mental suf-
ferings from "Harkness's disease", some actually pro-
nouncing it "Parkinson's". It was so tasteless and offensive that the President of the Gallery, Greg Connolly, who
was always a thorough gentleman, felt obliged to send me
a formal apology.

About two or three o'clock the next morning, I received
a telephone call from a distinguished former member of
the press. He told me that around midnight a prominent
journalist had got to the point of baiting Harkness with
taunts that he had "no guts at all", and that if he had any
he would resign on the Bomarc question. Harkness was
reported in a state of high exhilaration, obviously enjoy-
ing the notoriety accorded him in the evening's celebra-
tions. And after a few more rounds of refreshment he had
agreed: "I'll do it, I will resign tomorrow morning." He
did, but to his surprise it was no surprise to me.

I shall have more to say about Mr. Harkness later. For
the moment, the story of the 1963 Gallery dinner will
serve to give the reader an indication of the extremes of
some of the Fourth Estate's involvement in the events
surrounding the defeat of my government. The exhorta-
tion of the Toronto *Star*'s Val Sears to his Press Gallery
cohorts during the 1962 campaign, "To work gentlemen,
we have a government to overthrow", can be taken as a
literal statement of fact.

The Gallup Poll of 3 January 1963, which indicated a decline in the popularity of my government, and an earlier poll on 27 December, which showed a swing in support of the Canadian acquisition of nuclear arms, revealed that the campaign against me was gaining ground. As a dog-lover, I have said many times I consider that dogs know best the appropriate treatment to give poles, and I believe that any assessment of the record shows my distrust of these samplings of public attitude to be amply justified. More than this, however, I believe that no political party worth its salt would determine its course on the basis of polls. If it does, out goes principle and in come the temporary views of the population as a whole. Leadership does not consist of finding out in which direction the people are going or want to go and then running to the front of the parade to announce: "I'm your leader."

At the time, I could not tell the story now revealed. National security forbade it. The Leader of the Opposition, however, felt no such constraint. Nor, apparently, was he bound by any concepts relating to his proper role as a national leader. One charge that could never be made against him was that of consistency. In August 1960, Mr. Pearson said in the House of Commons:

In my view, we should get out of the whole SAGE-BOMARC operation.

If the United States wishes to continue that kind of protection, let the United States do so—let us withdraw from that direct form of continental defence.

It seems to me that our experience in the last three years has shown that in attempting to participate in continental defence in the way we have, we are becoming nothing more than just the last two knots on the Bomarc tail of the defence kite.

In November 1961, he was quoted in the *Winnipeg Tribune*:

Canada would be "throwing away a great political asset for a very dubious mechanism" if it decided to join the nuclear club. Its position at the UN would be "completely ruined" in the fight to stop nuclear testing.

His position remained the same throughout the 1962 election campaign. Then, on 7 January 1963 he travelled to New York. With whom he met I do not know, but his conversion to the United States State Department's point of view on nuclear arms was an instant one. In a speech in Scarborough, Ontario, on 12 January 1963, he said:

As a Canadian I am ashamed if we accept commitments and then refuse to discharge them. In acting that way we deceive ourselves, we let our armed forces down, and betray our allies. . . . [The Canadian government] should end at once its evasion of responsibility, by discharging the commitments it has already accepted for Canada. It can only do this by accepting nuclear warheads, for those defensive tactical weapons which cannot effectively be used without them but which we have agreed to use. . . .

President Kennedy had achieved his dearest Canadian wish. It was a partnership complete: the Liberals under Pearson had progressed, if one may call it that, from condemning our wheat sales to Communist China ("this government that sells on credit to our enemies and for cash to our friends") to embracing the United States position on arming with nuclear weapons the Bomarcs and, no doubt, yielding to United States demands for the storage of all manner of nuclear devices in Canada. At the time, Pierre Elliott Trudeau described Mr. Pearson as "the unfrocked pope of peace".

On 14 January, the United States Ambassador, W. Walton Butterworth, is alleged to have written Mr. Pearson as follows:

Please accept my sincere congratulations on the excellent and logical speech you made at the Liberal party conference on nuclear weapons on January 12th.

We appreciated your statement which indicated that the points of view expressed by the Liberal party and my government are identical. As the result of your address, no other Canadian politician on record has gained as many devoted friends in my country as you have.

I was delighted with the timing, which I considered perfect, announcing the stand taken by the party. The Conservatives will be forced to repeat what you have already stated. It will be quite evident to the electorate that the policy of the Conservatives is narrow-minded and that they are unfit to continue governing the Country.

At the first opportune moment, I would like to discuss with you how we could be useful to you in the future. You can always count on our support.

I received a copy of the above document, postmarked Acton, England, 20 March 1963, two weeks before the election. I was campaigning in British Columbia at the time and my immediate concern was to establish its authenticity. I suggested to Howard Green that he return to Ottawa at once, call in the Ambassador, and confront him with his letter. Mr. Green was reluctant to do this. I then suggested that he secure samples of Ambassador Butterworth's signature so that a comparison could be made. In a memorandum dated 25 March 1963, I noted that Mr. Green also objected to this on the grounds that such a course "would arouse suspicion". I thus turned the investigation over to the Minister of National Defence, the Honourable Gordon Churchill.

There simply was not time before the election, given the rigours of the campaign and the fact we did not know who had sent us the copy, to determine whether it was a forgery. I have since concluded on the basis of confidential knowledge, which will be revealed in due course, that it was a true copy and that not using it constituted a major political error. Pertinent to my conclusion that Ambassador Butterworth was indeed the author of this letter—his vapid denials to the contrary—are Mr. Churchill's statements on this matter, recorded in Hansard on 27 May 1963 and 8 April 1965.

The *Winnipeg Free Press* revealed on 28 May 1963 that they too had received a copy of the Butterworth letter, but with a covering letter indicating the informant's motives. It read:

Since I am sincerely concerned over the fate of Canada, I brought the contents of a letter, a photostatic copy of which is enclosed, to the attention of some prominent government officials.

However none of them were willing to bring these facts to the attention of the Canadian voters, pointing out to them the unprecedented interference of the Yankees in Canadian affairs and the unbecoming role of Mr. Pearson as their henchman.

I hope you share my indignation.

The *Free Press* didn't. I did. But, as I have explained, I felt bound not to use what I could not then confirm.

On 21 January 1963, I made a statement in the House of Commons, the major part of which is included at the end of Chapter Four, emphasizing my concern over the implications for Canadian defence policy of the December 1962 Nassau Agreement between Britain and the United States. Four days later, in response to Mr. Pearson's explanation in the House of his Scarborough declaration, I reviewed in detail our defence policy considerations. I said, in part:

We are united in NATO. We have never and will never consent to Canada breaking any of her pledged words or undertakings. It is at . . . [the NATO Ministerial Meeting in May] where there will be reviewed the entire collective defence policy, that we shall secure from the other member nations their views, and on the basis of that we will be in a position to make a decision, a consistent decision, first to maintain our undertakings and secondly to execute, if that be the view, the maintenance of our collective defence. In the meantime the training of Canadian forces in the use of these weapon systems can continue.

So far as NORAD is concerned I have said at the beginning of my remarks that Canada's sovereignty must be maintained. We shall continue our negotiations. They have been going on quite forcibly for two months or more. . . .

There was never any concealment of the fact. We will negotiate with the United States so that, as I said earlier, in case of need nuclear warheads will be made readily available. In other words, we will be in a position to determine finally, in the interests of Canada and our allies, the course to be followed in the light of changing circumstances in the disarmament field, which have become encouraging recently through Khrushchev's acceptance of even a minimum observation of nuclear testing. We will discuss with the nations of NATO the new concept of a nuclear force for NATO. If that concept at Nassau is carried into effect, much of our planning in the past will pass out of existence.

. . . It is so easy to say what should be done. Conscientiously and honestly we have tried, in the face of changing conditions, to bring about peace. We do not want to do anything at this time to rock the boat. If in the progress of disarmament it is found that we are beginning to approach that new era that all of us look forward to, the NATO nations meeting together can make that determination in agreement that is best for each and all. If, on the other hand, there is going to be set up a multilateral nuclear force, then all our planning to date, or most of it, will be of little or no consequence. I know they say: "Make decisions. Be concrete; be direct." . . . Recklessness was never evidence of decisiveness. We will, as a result of the fullest discussion and consideration, determine a course which I believe now means a vast alteration in all the defensive techniques that we have accepted in the last few years, and we will come back to Parliament and place before it the considered view of this government.

On 28 January, Mr. Harkness, Minister of National Defence, responded intemperately to press criticism of my speech by issuing a "clarification" of my remarks:

I was surprised and disappointed by the interpretation put on the Prime Minister's speech in the House of Commons on Defence by some of the newspaper reports I have read. Headlines that the nuclear weapons carriers we have secured are to be scrapped and nuclear arms decisions avoided, are completely incorrect.

In the speech nearly all the varying theories and ideas which have been put forward on nuclear arms were mentioned, but the definite policy of the government is contained in a few paragraphs which appear in the right-hand column on page 3136 of Hansard for January 25th. Those paragraphs state a definite policy for the acquisition of nuclear arms in these terms;

First, our obligations to equip certain weapons systems with nuclear arms are reiterated, together with the determination to honour those obligations.

Second, that the strike-reconnaissance role of the F-104s has been placed in some doubt by the recent Nassau declaration, as well as other developments in the defence field; thus it is necessary for Canada to seek, on the part of NATO, a clarification of her role in NATO defence plans and dispositions; this clarification to be provided when the NATO Ministerial Meeting is held in Canada next May. Should NATO reaffirm for Canada a role involving nuclear weapons, Canada will equip her NATO forces to discharge her obligation.

Third, so far as NORAD is concerned, Canada has been negotiating with the United States for the past two to three months in order that nuclear warheads will be made available for our two squadrons of Bomarcs and for the F-101 interceptor squadrons. These negotiations will be continued in order to reach a satisfactory agreement. I believe such an agreement can be arrived at in the near future.

My speech required no interpretation. It had been sufficiently clear, direct, and comprehensive for Mr. Harkness to rush over to shake my hand when I had concluded. I recall him saying, "That covers the situation." There was no disagreement. I do not know who convinced him to issue his press release and thus muddy the waters by lending substance to press rumours that there was a serious division in Cabinet over defence matters.

It was at this point that Mr. Pearson received the help Ambassador Butterworth had promised. (According to Bruce Hutchison's *The Far Side of the Street* (pp. 260-1), there was hardly any limit to the help President Kennedy was prepared to give Mr. Pearson in an effort to defeat me.) On 30 January, the United States State Department issued its unprecedented and infamous four-hundred-and-fifty-word press release contradicting the major points of my 25 January speech. It read:

The Department has received a number of inquiries concerning the disclosure during a recent debate in the Canadian House of Commons regarding negotiations over the past two or three months between the United States and Canadian Governments relating to nuclear weapons for Canadian armed forces.

In 1958 the Canadian Government decided to adopt the BOMARC-B weapons systems. Accordingly two BOMARC-B squadrons were deployed to Canada where they would serve the double purpose of protecting Montreal and Toronto as well as the U.S. deterrent force. The BOMARC-B was not designed to carry any conventional warhead. The matter of making available a nuclear warhead for it and for other nuclear-capable weapons systems acquired by Canada has been the subject of inconclusive discussions between the two governments. The installation of the two BOMARC-B batteries in Canada without nuclear warheads was completed in 1962.

In addition to the BOMARC-B, a similar problem exists with respect to the modern supersonic jet interceptor with which the RCAF has been provided. Without nuclear air defense warheads, they operate at far less than their full potential effectiveness.

Shortly after the Cuban crisis in October 1962, the Canadian Government proposed confidential discussions concerning circumstances under which there might be provision of nuclear weapons for Canadian armed forces in Canada and Europe. These discussions have been exploratory in nature; the Canadian Government has not as yet proposed any arrangement sufficiently practical to contribute effectively to North American defense.

The discussions between the two governments have also involved possible arrangements for the provision of nuclear weapons for Canadian NATO forces in Europe, similar to the arrangements which the United States has made with many of our NATO allies.

During the debate in the House of Commons various references were made to recent discussions at Nassau. The agreements made at Nassau have been fully published. They raise no question of the appropriateness of nuclear weapons for Canadian forces in fulfilling their NATO or NORAD obligations.

Reference was also made in the debate to the need of NATO for increased conventional forces. A flexible and balanced defense requires increased conventional forces, but conventional forces are not an alternative to effective NATO or NORAD defense arrangements using nuclear-capable weapons systems. NORAD is designed to defend the North American continent against air attack. The Soviet bomber fleet will remain at least throughout this decade a significant element in the Soviet strike force. An effective continental defense against this common threat is necessary.

The provision of nuclear weapons to Canadian forces would not involve an expansion of independent nuclear capability, or an increase in the "nuclear club". As in the case of other allies custody of U.S. nuclear weapons would remain with the U.S.

Joint control fully consistent with national sovereignty can be worked out to cover the use of such weapons by Canadian forces.

This was the crowning example of that "adroit statecraft" of the Kennedy government so approved by United States journalists, among them Scripps-Howard columnist Richard Starnes, who were now called in to bring the full weight of American cultural imperialism in Canada against the re-election of my so-called "crypto-anti-Yankee government", and to replace it "with a régime which promises to be faithful to the concept of Canadian-American interdependence." "American intervention," Starnes boasted, "was calculated to do exactly what it did, and it was a brilliant success."

President Kennedy's press release was issued on Wednesday, 30 January. (I cannot accept his attempt to label MacGeorge Bundy as the goat in this affair.) Douglas Harkness resigned as Canada's Minister of National Defence on Sunday, 3 February. (The circumstances of his resignation were described earlier.) On Monday, 4 February, Mr. Pearson moved his amendment of non-confidence. On Tuesday, 5 February, the Government of Canada that I had the honour to lead was defeated in the House of Commons. On Wednesday, 6 February, on my advice, Canada's Twenty-fifth Parliament was dissolved by proclamation of His Excellency the Governor General. The central issue was the determination of the United States government to overthrow my government. Pierre Trudeau described it well in the April 1963 issue of *Cité Libre*. He wrote:

You think I dramatize? But how do you think politics works? Do you think that General Norstad, the former supreme commander of allied forces in Europe, came to Ottawa as a tourist on January 3 to call publicly on the Canadian government to respect its commitments? Do you think it was by chance that Mr.

Pearson, in his speech of January 12, was able to quote the authority of General Norstad? Do you think it was inadvertent that, on January 30, the State Department gave a statement to journalists reinforcing Mr. Pearson's claims and crudely accusing Mr. Diefenbaker of lying? You think it was by chance that this press release provided the leader of the Opposition with the arguments he used abundantly in his parliamentary speech on January 31? You believe that it was coincidence that this series of events ended with the fall of the government on February 5?

But why do you think that the United States should treat Canada differently from Guatemala, when reason of state requires it and circumstances permit? . . .

The full story of my government's defence relations with the United States is told for the first time in the three chapters that follow. The interested reader will have his chance to judge not only the propriety of our policies but the price of Canadian independence. We made it abundantly clear to Washington that while our basic attitude was co-operation ever, we were determined on a course which represented a new stand for Canada: subservience never.

CHAPTER TWO

✳

GENERAL CHARLES FOULKES TESTIFIED, in October 1963, before the House of Commons Special Committee on Defence that, as Chairman of the Chiefs of Staff Committee in 1957, he had "stampeded" the new Conservative government into accepting the North American Air Defence (NORAD) Agreement. Nothing could be further from the facts. I considered the NORAD Agreement a good one, and, for its time, necessary. Indeed, I had no personal consultation with Foulkes on this subject. For him to suggest that we were stampeded in the early weeks of our government is to suggest that I, as Prime Minister, and, more particularly, Major-General George Pearkes, V.C., the Minister of National Defence, had no appreciation of the requirements of North American defence. General Foulkes's admiration for the St. Laurent government was obvious and may explain his decision, following his retirement, to contest a Liberal Party nomination.

Despite the disavowals of Mr. Pearson, the St. Laurent government should be given credit for the origin and development of the NORAD concept. Without diminishing the value of the NORAD Agreement in any way, the fact is that when we came into office NORAD was virtually a *fait accompli.* In 1951, Canada made its initial commitments to NATO for the defence of Europe and North America.

Concomitantly, the St. Laurent government approved plans for the development and co-ordination of the air defence systems of Canada and the United States to provide for mutual protection of contiguous vital areas of the two countries. Further, the St. Laurent administration approved the principle of mutual reinforcement by the air defence forces of Canada and the United States, and agreed that, in the event of war, the Air Defence Commander of each country was to be empowered to authorize the redeployment to bases in his country of air defence forces of the other country.

In June 1954, an official Canadian study recommended the creation of a separate Commander-in-Chief (CINC) for North American Air Defence, with responsibility for planning and an appropriate measure of operational control over air defence forces allocated to the Canada–United States region. It further recommended that Canada take the initiative in discussion with the United States for the appointment of a CINC Air Defence. The Canadian Chiefs of Staff Committee did not accept these recommendations, but did agree that it would be desirable to have personnel from the Royal Canadian Air Force's Air Defence Command stationed at the United States Air Force's Air Defense Command, which had been newly established at Colorado Springs.

In February 1956, a joint Canada–United States study of the CINC NORAD question was initiated by the United States. A report submitted to the Canadian and United States Chiefs of Staff organizations on 19 December 1956 concluded that, in order to provide the most effective air defence of North America, the *operational* control of the air defence forces of Canada and the United States should be integrated. Indeed, a clear and definite distinction was made between "operational control" of the forces and "command" of the forces. The basic command organization, e.g., training, equipment, logistics, etc., would be controlled by national commanders who would be responsible to their respective national authorities. The Commander-in-Chief's task was to defend North America from air attack in accordance with plans approved by the two governments. Provision was to be made for a fully integrated headquarters staffed by Canadian and United States service personnel. The Deputy Commander was to be a Canadian, who, in the absence of CINC NORAD, was to have *full power*. CINC NORAD was to be responsible to the Chiefs of Staff of both countries. This report was approved by the Canadian Chiefs of Staff Committee on 1 February 1957, having already been approved by the United States Chiefs of Staff.

A Cabinet Memorandum on NORAD was prepared for submission to the Cabinet Defence Committee in early April 1957, and again for a meeting scheduled for 13 June 1957, but was not formally considered by the Ministers on either occasion. My understanding is that Mr. St. Laurent did not wish to take action which might lead to controversy during the election campaign, and that later he was not prepared to act because he was leaving office. However, the fact that the Chairman of the Chiefs of Staff had been authorized by the then Minister of Defence, the Honourable Ralph Campney, to intimate to the United States authorities that Canadian approval of the plan could be anticipated following the election must lead to the conclusion that this matter had been discussed by Mr. Campney and Prime Minister St. Laurent, and without doubt Mr. Pearson as well, and that Mr. St. Laurent had indicated his full support for the NORAD Agreement. Mr. Pearson's assertion in the House on 10 June 1958 that the St. Laurent Cabinet had not approved a joint air defence command can be taken as no more than literalism in search of political advantage.

When this agreement was brought to me for decision on 24 July 1957, it had already been approved by the

United States Secretary of Defense, Charles E. Wilson, and the United States Chief of Staff. General Pearkes considered it urgent that we proceed at once to approve NORAD; that any further delay by the Canadian government over matters of procedure might prove embarrassing when the question was of such importance and agreement in substance had been achieved. Ordinarily, General Pearkes would have brought the proposed NORAD Agreement before the Cabinet Defence Committee. As the organization of my government had not been completed, there had not been time in which to create such a committee. The National Defence Act gave authority to the Minister of National Defence to set up military commands. General Pearkes had studied the matter in detail and had taken the best advice available to him. General Foulkes had expressed his view that NORAD was within the NATO concept and therefore should not be difficult to explain to either Parliament or the public. That view made sense. The Canada–United States region was part of the NATO area. The Canadian and United States governments were committed by treaty to the defence of the NATO area. Even if the NORAD Agreement introduced a command structure at variance with those in operation elsewhere in NATO, it was inconceivable that CINC NORAD was to be authorized to take any action not wholly consistent with agreed NATO strategy for the defence of the NATO area.

The purpose of Canada's defence policy was fully established when we came into office. It provided for the security of our nation by means of collective arrangements within the NATO alliance. These arrangements constituted, as far as I was concerned, an effective deterrent to aggression and thus minimized the possibility of a third world war. Furthermore, the government of Mr. St. Laurent had subscribed to the strategic doctrine of deterrent, and until disarmament negotiations resulted in a substantial modification of the "balance of terror", I felt that there was no option to the strategy of preventing war by creating the greatest possible deterrent to war, as well as the means of defending that deterrent. The deterrent consisted of the United States strategical air force, supplemented by the United Kingdom bomber force, and protected by the air defence system of Canada and the United States. NORAD was to be the logical extension of developments and commitments that long predated the year 1957.

Certainly, we were aware of difficulties for Canada in any defence partnership with the United States. The United States had world-wide commitments and responsibilities not shared by Canada. Consequently, United States involvement in armed conflict anywhere in the world might adversely affect Canadian vital interests. This situation was not uniquely Canadian, as each of the NATO partners was to some degree similarly affected. The United States, as a super-power, was obliged, if she wished to maintain this position, to afford the cost of the whole panoply of modern weaponry. Canada, as a middle or small power, had neither the obligation nor the ability to meet such costs.

Yet there was, in our view, no possibility of isolating Canada from the Cold War. Aside from there being reasons enough for opposing the advance of Soviet imperialism in Canada's Western, Christian, and democratic heritage, it is sometimes forgotten that Soviet defence planners had designated Canada and the United States a single target area. Therefore, to take any course other than that of defence co-operation with the United States and with our other NATO and free world partners would be one of national irresponsibility. Technological advances rendered Canadian territory exposed to the possibility of crippling attack. Alone, we were not able to defend our vast territories against the might of a potential aggressor. Furthermore, it was clear that the effectiveness of United States defences would be considerably weakened without Canadian co-operation. Essential to the defence security of the United States were not the nine air defence squadrons that Canada was about to commit to NORAD, but the nearly completed, comprehensive early-warning radar system, the Pine Tree Line, the Mid Canada Line, and the Distant Early Warning Line, stretching from the Canada–United States border to the Arctic Circle. I attached importance to Canada's having a voice in any decisions resulting from information obtained from this early-warning system, a view that I expressed very strongly in my first meeting with the United States Secretary of State, John Foster Dulles, on 27 July 1957 in Ottawa. I agreed that the appointment of a Canadian as Deputy Commander-in-Chief NORAD would give Canada a desirable measure of responsibility in any decisions that might have to be taken to defend North America against Soviet attack.

When General Pearkes and I discussed the proposed NORAD Agreement on 24 July 1957, we agreed to approve the creation of the NORAD Command and to announce this decision without further delay. In making this important decision I was acting as Secretary of State for External Affairs as well as Prime Minister. The Cabinet was apprised of this decision, and at length, when the appointment of Air Marshal Slemon as Deputy Commander of the integrated headquarters was placed before it on 31 July. In approving his appointment, the Cabinet noted and agreed to the proposals regarding the integration of command.

The impression, later created and widely disseminated by the Liberal front bench, that the officials of the Department of External Affairs had not been consulted prior to the agreement to create the NORAD Command is simply untrue. The then Under-Secretary of State for External

Affairs, in a letter to General Foulkes dated 10 September 1957, denied dissatisfaction concerning the Chiefs of Staff Committee's liaison with his department on this matter. The department was also aware that, in the absence of a Cabinet Defence Committee, General Pearkes and I would be making the tentative decisions on NORAD. Further, following our meeting on 24 July, General Pearkes went immediately to the office of the Under-Secretary of State for External Affairs to inform him fully, as he did Robert Bryce, Secretary to the Cabinet. The point is, and this is especially so because I was Secretary of State for External Affairs, that, had the Department of External Affairs had any useful suggestions to make on NORAD either before the decision was taken or before it was announced on 1 August, there was every opportunity for them to do so. What is more, it was their clear duty to do so. None did so.

The Chiefs of Staff advised that an exchange of notes between Canada and the United States was not necessary to the agreement to constitute the organization and operation of NORAD; General Foulkes advised General Pearkes that by suggesting an intergovernmental note, we would be calling into question the authority of the United States Secretary of Defense to set up a joint command with Canada. External Affairs felt strongly to the contrary; their arguments, when finally presented, were convincing enough to cause the initiation of appropriate steps to secure United States agreement to an exchange of notes. I know of no explanation as to why External Affairs waited until mid-October to provide the government with their advice. By itself, however, this failure on the part of External Affairs would have caused little political embarrassment. The integrated headquarters of NORAD had become operational on an interim basis on 12 September. On 8 October, recommendations on the proposed "mission and terms of reference of NORAD" were submitted to the Canadian and United States Chiefs of Staff organizations by CINC NORAD, General Partridge, and his Deputy, Air Marshal Slemon. These terms were approved by the Canadian Chiefs of Staff Committee on 21 November; they had now to come before Cabinet. Two days earlier the United States government agreed in principle to an exchange of notes on NORAD. Cabinet might then consider approving the terms of reference and the public exchange of notes as a single task. At worst, we might be criticized in the House for not having required the intergovernmental note as a first step in finalizing NORAD. Unfortunately, this appears to have been the beginning of a concerted effort by some senior officials in External Affairs to discredit NORAD, National Defence, and the government. Stories began to appear in the press about the lack of consultation with External Affairs over the establishment of NORAD. These press reports could have had only one source. It reached the stage on 4 December where I had to request that the Secretary of State for External Affairs take steps to ensure that his officials do or say nothing that would find echo outside their department.

Further, as explained earlier, we had accepted the view that NORAD was an "effective" part of NATO. It was up to External Affairs to advise us of their views to the contrary before we had taken a public position on this question. We did not see the relationship as hinging on the fact that CINC NORAD was not responsible to the NATO Standing Group and derived no authority from the North Atlantic Council. Canada was not a member of the NATO Standing Group, and the ineffectiveness of the North Atlantic Council as a body ensuring adequate consultation on vital decisions by the member-nations had long since been established. External Affairs, I was to discover, had no sympathy for the perception of the NORAD-NATO relationship advanced by our military advisors;

they sided with the views expressed by the Opposition in the House and took comfort in the fact that Mr. Pearson's old friend, as he described him, Paul-Henri Spaak, NATO Secretary-General, saw fit, during his visit to Ottawa in late May 1958, to question the NORAD-NATO link. The hard fact that NORAD was advancing Canadian interests and making Canadian sovereignty more, not less, secure seemed to escape some paragons of diplomatic virtue.

Also, it would appear that this issue was in some part a departmental conflict involving feelings brewing for some time before the 1957 election within the Department of External Affairs that National Defence was usurping External's "rightful" position as principal advisor to the government on all foreign-policy matters. They now decided to take advantage of the change of government to endeavour to re-establish their pretended "pre-eminence". By definition, no one wins in an internecine battle between departments of government. I might add that had the public debate over NORAD become important enough to cost us victory in the 1958 election, there would have been some happy faces in the Department of External Affairs. The specious Opposition charges, raised by one or two former Ministers, that my government had acted with undue haste, without sufficient information, without proper consideration, and with a recklessness that was synonymous with negligence in bringing Canada into a perilous situation in which war might simply be thrust upon us by our potentially irresponsible partner in NORAD, answer themselves.

One determination that I never departed from in the operation of NORAD was that Canada's sovereignty should be, must be, and would be respected at all times, and that no decision on hostilities or any action approaching hostilities should be made except with the consent of myself as Prime Minister on behalf of the Government of Canada. I will discuss later the events of October 1962. For the moment, suffice it to note that however much the United States President and government, CINC NORAD and his Deputy, and the Canadian military establishment may have wanted a course to the contrary, there was no question of my yielding automatically to their demands for a full NORAD alert.

The interests of Canadian sovereignty clearly had not been upheld or maintained by the Mackenzie King and St. Laurent governments. Since 1947, United States money and Canadian territory had been progressively matched in the name of collective defence. The North, it seems clear, was not important to their concept of national development. For example, in 1955 the St. Laurent government authorized the United States to build, man, and operate the Distant Early Warning (DEW) Line in Canada. In January 1957, they informed United States authorities through the Permanent Joint Board on Defence that the United States Air Force should continue to man and operate that portion of the DEW Line in Canada until 1963. Fortunately, the 1953 authorization contained the proviso that Canada should have the right to review her decision should conditions change. I was concerned, in approving the establishment of NORAD, to change conditions so far as the DEW Line was concerned. Thus, in January 1958, agreement was concluded that on 1 February 1959 the Royal Canadian Air Force would take over the effective manning of all DEW Line stations in Canada.

If one looks back at the pace of technological development in modern weaponry, it is easy to appreciate how impossible it was to know the future demands of continental defence. As the means to meet one threat were developed, a new threat appeared. It had been obvious to me when in Opposition that by the time the DEW Line was operational, weapons developments would have overtaken its effectiveness; something I mentioned when speaking in the House on 22 June 1956. It was important to reverse the Liberal policy with respect to the control of defence installations in Canada before the situation became irretrievable.

On 19 May 1958, an Exchange of Notes, dated 12 May, was tabled in the House of Commons. The detail set out therein on the Canada–United States Agreement on the Organization and Operation of the North American Air Defence Command conformed with what had been revealed about the NORAD Agreement since its first announcement on 1 August 1957. Canada's formal alliance with the United States existed not in NORAD but in the North Atlantic Treaty, signed in 1949, as we were careful to make clear in the Exchange of Notes. I must admit that my government's concern in this regard was not entirely shared by our partner in NORAD. The United States, given its position as the world's most powerful nation, naturally had no cause for apprehension about the effects on American sovereignty of the disproportion in the relative power of our two countries. It was less complicated for them to think of NORAD as one more defensive arrangement in a globe-encompassing network of interlinking alliances and pacts. We felt, however, that Canadian interests would be more fully protected by confining NORAD to a NATO context. Indeed, we insisted upon it.

Thus, the preamble in our ambassador's note to the United States Secretary of State read in part:

In support of the strategic objectives established in NATO for the Canada–United States region and in accordance with the provisions of the North Atlantic Treaty, our two governments have, by establishing the North American Air Defence Command, recognized the desirability of integrating headquarters exercising operational control over assigned air defence forces. The agreed integration is intended to assist the two governments to develop and maintain their individual and collective capacity to resist air attack on their territories in North America in mutual self-defence.

It was further provided that "The North Atlantic Treaty Organization will continue to be kept informed through the Canada–United States Regional Planning Group of arrangements for the air defence of North America." By making certain that NORAD acted at all times in accordance with the strategic objectives of the NATO Council, goals established in common within the North Atlantic community, we were able to limit the further sacrifice of Canadian sovereignty. No other course was acceptable to the government, or to the Canadian people as a whole. I might add that our action here was also in the best interests of our European NATO allies.

There is, of course, no question that my government had troubles over air defence problems. These problems, naturally, have been popularly associated with NORAD. The fault, however, did not lie in this agreement *per se*, but with the very nature of air defence requirements in the period. The advent of the Kennedy administration in 1961 added an extra political dimension to problems that were already difficult. Leaving aside for the moment the antagonism of President Kennedy, I have mentioned earlier the effects of rapid technological change on air defence planning. It was the norm to be always one step behind the new offensive capabilities of potential enemies. Technological changes consequent on meeting the threat of new Soviet weapons often resulted in military hardware within the Western Free World being obsolete by the time it came off the production line. Consequently, and in common with the governments of our allies, we were obliged to take the best advice available (we had perforce to give heed to the views of the Chiefs of Staff), to weigh carefully the expenditure of public monies, and to hope that the decision taken was the right one.

For example, in 1957, the manned bomber was still regarded as the principal Soviet threat to North American

defence. Although it was predicted that within the decade Intercontinental Ballistic Missiles (ICBMs) would replace bombers, our military advisors felt they needed until 1959 to be able to properly assess Soviet plans. In the
meantime, the concern of NORAD was that the Soviet long-
range jet bomber had a performance which exceeded the
capacity of the North American air defence system. Inability to meet this threat was constituted a military emergency. In consequence, the Canadian government was
asked to approve the expenditure, exclusive of new interceptor costs, of from $120 million to $190 million (depending upon cost-sharing arrangements) to modernize
control and data-handling, to extend radar cover in certain areas, and to introduce more effective anti-bomber
weapons.

The United States had recently completed the development of an impressively effective, and expensive, electronic control system (that portion of the air defence network which processed the data gathered by radars and
utilized this information to bring our fighters and missiles
to bear against enemy aircraft) known as SAGE, which
stood for semi-automatic ground environment. Each
SAGE sector (the United States had been divided into a
number of sectors for the purposes of implementing
SAGE) had at its heart an electronic computer that was capable of thousands of computations per second, and
could handle several hundred aircraft interceptions simultaneously. On 23 September 1958, I announced that
the Canadian government had approved the introduction
of SAGE to Canada. No longer would the information from
our radars be transmitted by voice and plotted by hand;
nor, when control officers had worked out a solution to
the intercept problem, would detailed verbal instructions
be communicated to our defence aircraft, indicating the
direction, height, speed, and turns to be adopted through-

out the combat mission. We now acquired a system with the capacity to handle mass bomber attacks, and to control high speed aircraft, like the CF-105, or surface-to-air missiles, like the Bomarc. Further, our technical experts considered that, with improvements, SAGE could be adapted for anti-missile defence.

I announced as well that we had approved the installation of two additional prime radars to extend and strengthen the Pine Tree radar line. Basically the arguments in favour of the installation of SAGE and the new radars were the same: the effectiveness of the weapons systems of NORAD would be greatly improved, enabling the air battle to be engaged farther north than would otherwise be possible. In short, greater protection to assumed Canadian and United States targets would be provided. The defence of Canadian targets depended on engagement of enemy raids as far north as possible with as many weapons as possible. The Defence Research Board considered that the addition of the two radars would allow forty to fifty per cent more weapons to engage in this area and would give a corresponding gain in the defence of Canadian targets. It was agreed that neither the introduction of SAGE nor the Pine Tree Line extension was dependent for its effectiveness on our choice of a particular anti-bomber weapon.

In a briefing to Cabinet on the air defence system in North America on 28 April 1958, it was explained that, to provide flexibility to the system, a family of complementary weapons was required for defence against the manned bomber, consisting of manned interceptors and surface-to-air missiles. The interceptor in such a system had to be capable of flying at speeds in excess of one thousand miles per hour and at altitudes above fifty thousand feet. The CF-100 with which the RCAF air defence squadrons were then armed did not meet these requirements. We had, however, in the development stage a

Canadian aircraft, the CF-105 or AVRO Arrow, the early flight tests of which indicated its ability to meet, within circumscribed limits, these operational demands.

The basic question was whether, given the demands on its defence budget, Canada could afford the continuation of the Arrow program, particularly if the manned bomber threat was disappearing. Up to 31 March 1958, including expenditures under the St. Laurent government, $221 million had been spent on the CF-105 program; we were being asked to approve the expenditure of a further $213 million in 1958-59, followed by another $359 million in 1959-60, with an unspecified balance being spent in the following years. The CF-105 program, taken together with the other air defence items on the Chiefs of Staff agenda, provided for Canadian expenditures of almost a billion dollars in the 1958-60 period to improve our defence against a threat that could disappear shortly after these improvements were operational.

To put this problem into a wider perspective, when we came into office there were serious gaps in the long-range forecast for re-equipping our armed forces. For example, there was no provision made in the Chiefs of Staff forecast of defence expenditures for re-equipping the Air Division in Europe as and when the F-86 Sabre became obsolete, which was near at hand. As part of our NATO contribution, Canada provided an Air Division of eight fighter squadrons of two hundred F-86A aircraft and four defence squadrons of seventy-two CF-100 all-weather fighters. We also provided a brigade group of three infantry battalions, one field regiment, and other supporting troops, to be augmented in 1957 by an armoured regiment. In Canada, we maintained in strategic reserve a division less a brigade group, fully trained and equipped and available for NATO service. The Royal Canadian Navy's commitment was to provide one aircraft carrier and forty-two escort vessels primarily to assist in keeping open the sea lines of communication under the Supreme Allied Commander Atlantic. The RCAF provided forty-eight maritime aircraft to operate with the Navy in this role of maritime control of the Canadian sub area. The threat of missile-carrying submarines in both the Atlantic and the Pacific required the continued provision of long-range maritime aircraft and new escort ships. It was quite obvious that as the expenditures for the defence of North America increased, reductions in expenditures had to be made in other parts of the defence budget. To have proceeded on all fronts with proposed defence expenditures would have meant crippling new taxes or government borrowing to a level where the value of the Canadian dollar would be seriously undermined. It is important to remember that from our first election in 1957 until the middle of 1961, my government was engaged in an all-out battle against an inherited economic recession. It was our duty and our determination to spend our defence dollar as wisely as possible.

In retrospect, the AVRO Arrow should have been cancelled before we came into office. Conceived by Air Force defence planners in 1952, the CF-105 program had begun very modestly, with plans to construct *only* an airframe, to be fitted with a British or American engine and United States fire control, electronics, and weapons systems. Bit by piece, the St. Laurent government assumed the responsibility for underwriting the building of the entire aircraft. First, there was the decision to use a Canadian engine, the Orenda Engines Ltd. "Iroquois", specifically designed and developed for the Arrow. Then, as United States defence planners abandoned one system after another (there had never been any guarantees that suitable United States weapons systems, etc., would be available), Canada picked up the pieces. RCA Victor in Hamilton received the contract for the flight and fire-control system, ASTRA. Canadair in Montreal, in co-operation with Canadian Westinghouse, received the contract for the weapons system, Sparrow. There were sub-contracts let to over four hundred Canadian companies.

The development of an advanced, highly complicated, supersonic aircraft was a financially hazardous venture for both the government and the contractors. It was incumbent upon each and all of them to know the risks involved. That A. V. Roe (AVRO) refused to recognize a risk factor in government contracts of this magnitude does not change the realities involved. When the Cabinet Defence Committee first recommended the production of two CF-105 prototypes in December 1953, the Royal Canadian Air Force estimated its requirements at between five hundred and six hundred aircraft. Their cost was forecast by A. V. Roe at between $1.5 and $2 million per plane. By 1957, the per-unit cost had gone up by $10 million and the number of CF-105s required for RCAF purposes down to roughly one hundred. If the production of the Arrow was to be continued, Canada had to find a market for it either in the United States or in Britain. The Canadian market could no longer supply the necessary demand to make bearable the unit cost of production. The prospect of foreign sales was diminished by the fact that by the time the Arrow was through its pre-production and production phases, substantially cheaper United States interceptors would be available, at end-of-production prices, to meet the operational demands of North American or European defence. One of the major problems in the Arrow's development, no doubt understandable given the way it came into being, was that the length of time between design and prototype had been excessive. Had the election not been looming, I doubt the St. Laurent government would have agreed, on 6 February 1957, to the development and procurement of eight Arrow prototypes. I have it on unchallengeable authority that Mr. St. Laurent and Mr. C. D. Howe had decided that the Arrow was to be cancelled forthwith, after the June election (although this knowledge was not available to my government until 1962).

The officials of A. V. Roe knew that the writing was on the wall for the Arrow, especially if we could find no outside buyers. My government, in effect, gave AVRO a year and one-half's notice for what, in hindsight, was the inevitable. If this were not sufficient, one might have expected that they at least might have glimpsed the future when the first test flight of the Arrow in October 1957 coincided to the day with the Soviet Union's successful launching into space of its *Sputnik*. Apart from making the decision to cancel the Arrow as economically and politically unpleasant as possible, AVRO did nothing in the period from October 1957 until February 1959 to prepare for this eventuality.

There was a foretaste of what was to come when we cancelled the construction of the CF-100 Mark VI in the autumn of 1957. AVRO and Orenda Engines responded vindictively by announcing plans to lay off three thousand employees, more than twice the number actually affected by the CF-100 cancellation. When General Pearkes met with representatives of the companies, he was informed that they were waiting for a decision on the CF-105 and that, given their dependence on defence contracts, if this program were cancelled, they would go immediately into liquidation, putting fifteen thousand skilled men (including four thousand technicians and engineers) on the street, plus as many as ten thousand more in related industries. It was roughly calculated that we would lose five votes for every person whose unemployment was directly attributable to this decision. We were a minority government and might face an election at any time, but we were not willing to be politically blackmailed.

John Pallett, Chief Government Whip and Member for Peel, would be most affected politically by any decision on the Arrow. The AVRO plant and the town of Malton were in his riding. He was an outstanding parliamentarian whose integrity was recognized by all parties in the House. His unselfish advice was that any decision taken by the government must first be for the good of Canada. This was the course that guided our decision. We did not renege on our decision to cancel the CF-100 Mark VI, although we did try to ease the lay-off situation by transferring certain engine repair and overhaul work to Orenda and by procuring an additional twenty CF-100 Mark V aircraft for Mutual Aid purposes. We decided to continue the CF-105 program because it seemed the right thing to do, pending developments: our air defence experts were impressed by its trials and recommended it; the present pre-production phase was covered by the estimates of the previous government; we required an alternative to the CF-100; and we had as yet to receive any authoritative reassessment of Soviet capabilities and intentions.

We went ahead, experimentally. There were doubts in my mind. However, my colleagues and I hoped that some solution might be found that would allow us to proceed to the production of the Arrow. Canadians were air-minded. Canada's airmen in the First World War brought romance and drama to an otherwise horrible conflict; their contribution gave Canada a reputation for greatness and valour in all parts of the world. The Royal Canadian Air Force's altogether magnificent record in the Second World War added to the national lustre. There were times when I felt that the Arrow, as a concept, was an entirely worthy symbol for the proud achievements of flight in Canada. There is no doubt that, from a construction standpoint, the AVRO Arrow was an impressive aircraft, superior to any other known contemporary all-weather fighter, something all Canadians could be proud of as their product. The Arrow's Iroquois engine boasted the highest thrust, the lowest specific weight, the greatest mass flow, and the greatest growth potential of all known engines under development. In all, and as I said at the time, it was a tribute to the high standards of technological achievement and development in the Canadian aircraft industry.

In the end, although we tried hard to secure orders for it in the United States and among our NATO allies in Europe, we had no success. The attitude of the military authorities in those countries paralleled a view that was becoming dominant in our own Chiefs of Staff Committee: that the CF-105 was a fine example of what could be done technologically, but that it was altogether too costly, had too short a range, and would be out of date by the time it got into production. The CF-105 would be able to do nothing but intercept, and that within a very sophisticated ground environment and only within a range of 150 to 200 miles from its base.

In early August 1958, General Pearkes came to me with a report of his visit to Washington to discuss the question of a U.S. market for CF-105s. The United States authorities had made it quite clear that they did not intend to buy any. What had impressed him most, however, was the disparity between the unit cost of the CF-105 and comparable interceptors that might be available for purchase before long in the United States. He felt that it was his duty to recommend to Cabinet against continuance of the Arrow program. I reluctantly agreed. I had listened to the views of various experts; I had read everything I could find on the subject; I thought about it constantly; and, finally, I prayed for guidance. The buck stopped with me, and I had to decide.

It came before the Cabinet Defence Committee on 21 August and before Cabinet on 28 August. My colleagues and I took particular note of that part of the air defence review which read: "Finally the cost of the CF-105 programme as a whole is now of such magnitude that the Chiefs of Staff feel that to meet the modest requirements of manned aircraft presently considered advisable, it would be more economical to secure a fully developed interceptor of comparable performance in the United States." By accepting a recommendation to abandon the Arrow and investigate other aircraft and missile possibilities, the government would have a year to decide whether it would re-equip our air defence fighter force wholly with missiles or with an alternative aircraft or with a combination of both.

We fully appreciated that abandoning the CF-105 would be a shock to the Canadian aircraft industry. We therefore decided to give A. V. Roe and Orenda Engines Ltd. what amounted to a six-month formal notice so that they might adjust gradually to their new situation. On 23 September, I announced that we would not proceed to production but would continue the development phase of the Arrow and the Iroquois engine until March 1959, at which time we would make known our final decision. The Arrow's special flight and fire-control system, ASTRA, and its weapons system, Sparrow, were to be terminated immediately.

The reaction of the A. V. Roe Company was, to say the least, extreme. To begin with, the details of our decisions in Cabinet were leaked to the company, probably by officials in Defence Production who were hostile to my government's decision. A telegram from the President of A. V. Roe, Mr. Crawford Gordon, indicated that they had this information on 12 September. Armed with a detailed brief on why we should continue the Arrow program, he met with me on 17 September. To clear away a misrepresentation of what happened at our meeting, in no sense could it be described as a nasty personal confrontation. I do recall that he began his presentation in a blustering fashion: "Well, I want to tell you," pounding his hand on my desk for emphasis. I stopped him immediately and pointed out that he was liable to do himself serious injury if he kept on banging his hand. That ended his bellicosity.

His brief, however, was strongly worded. The two companies principally involved would be closed down, there would be mass firings, etc. Projects like the CF-105, however, could hardly be considered as primarily a means of promoting employment. I could agree with Gordon's argument that it was important for Canada to have an independent aircraft industry. If AVRO and Orenda went into liquidation, we would still have one: De Havilland would not be affected, nor would the Transport Marine Aircraft Section of Canadair. As to the argument that subsequently became something of a conventional wisdom among critics, that the building of the Arrow had, to use the words of Gordon's brief, "a serious fundamental relationship with Canada's capacity to realize the vast potential of her endowment within today's framework of rapidly developing technology", this was, and is, nonsense. Modern technology is important to the Canadian economy so far as it can contribute to the growth of Canadian industry and the gross national product. A. V. Roe, since the end of the Second World War, had lived and grown rich on Canadian defence contracts. The company seemed horror-struck at the prospect of having ever to compete in a normal market-place situation. As one of the AVRO officials explained to General Pearkes in February 1959, his company was not accustomed to doing business in a "normal commercial way". They apparently had no intention of even trying to do so.

The Minister of Transport and Member of Parliament for Toronto's Broadview riding, the Honourable George Hees, wrote me in this regard on 23 February 1959:

During the past few months, Mr. F. Smye, Vice-president of AVRO, has spoken to me about the possibility of the government giving encouragement to the production of civilian aircraft at the AVRO plant. On every occasion, I have told him that whenever they came up with a positive plan to accomplish this end, the government would give it very serious consideration. I have assured him that I am personally very much in favour of building up a civilian aircraft industry in Canada and would be glad to bring any proposals which he would put forward before my Cabinet colleagues for discussion.

All members of Cabinet were anxious to aid AVRO in any attempt it might make to effect a transition to other work, but we had no opportunity to do so. To the very end, the company had no specific proposals, even in the field of defence production, except those relating to the CF-105. Its long-term development plans centred around the development of a flying saucer!

A. V. Roe's attitude was in stark contrast to those of the companies affected by the termination of the ASTRA and Sparrow systems. For example, on 24 September 1958, the day following the announcement of these decisions, I received this telegram from Mr. G. L. Wilcox, President of Canadian Westinghouse:

I have heard tonight of the momentous decision which you and your Cabinet have made in a most courageous and forthright manner. . . . Canadian Westinghouse will be severely affected as major suppliers of the weapon system and consequent dislocation of a highly trained group of missile engineers and technicians. . . . In listening to your statement with regard to the selection of Bomarc as Canada's air defence weapon may I respectfully suggest that Canadian Westinghouse is uniquely qualified to pursue with your defence staff the orderly incorporation of Bomarc into Canada's defence network. . . .

They were, of course, fully conscious of the financial hardships and dislocations involved, but there was no attempt to challenge the decision involved.

The AVRO airframe and Orenda engine contracts should have been terminated at the same time as the others. The extra six months failed to achieve our purpose to prevent a further wrench in an already sagging economy. The A. V. Roe Company endeavoured to make the Arrow a national political issue. Members of Parliament, especially those whose political futures might be directly affected by the cancellation of CF-105-related contracts, were subjected to most intense lobbying. AVRO hired the public relations firm of Cockfield, Brown and Company (a firm that over the years has been the beneficiary of Liberal Party advertising) to keep the Arrow before the public. Press stories, magazine articles, and finally a feature film (distributed free of charge to television stations across Canada) on the Arrow were produced. AVRO was attempting to take the decision out of the government's hands. Their plans did not succeed. As I stated in the House of Commons on 19 January 1959:

Properly arranged and conducted representation to the government is one thing. Organized pressure and propaganda is another. I should warn any who are tempted to engage in the latter that the results are likely to be in inverse ratio to the effort put forth.

As to AVRO's claim that by substituting existing United States systems for those terminated on 23 September, they had reduced the per-unit cost of the Arrow to $3.5 million, not including the cost of missile armament. The report of the Department of Defence Production to the Cabinet Defence Committee on 5 February 1959 reads in this regard:

At March 31st, 1959, six Arrow aircraft will have been manufactured and an additional three will be more than 75% complete. Twenty Iroquois engines will have been completed, four for development and sixteen for installation, and an additional 12 will be more than 75% complete. Total expenditure on the programme to March 31st, 1959 will be $342.2 million, excluding ASTRA and Sparrow costs. In the event of termination of the programme at that date, cancellation charges are estimated at about $40 million. If cancelled on February 15, 1959 total expenditure would be $325 million, but termination charges would probably increase to about $45 million.

Cost of completing the current 37 aircraft programme is estimated at $257.8 million. . . . Cost of completing the current production programme plus 80 production aircraft would be $769 million. . . .

The government's financial experts calculated the cost of the CF-105 at $7.8 million each, including weapons, spare parts, and the completion of development, but not including any of the $303 million spent prior to September 1958. This was too costly for Canada's defence budget.

However, the issue was decided finally by the inability of the Chiefs of Staff to report any new military developments that would justify the Arrow's production. Thus, I announced to the House of Commons on 20 February 1958:

The government has carefully examined and re-examined the probable need for the Arrow aircraft and Iroquois engine — known as the CF-105 — the development of which has been continued pending a final decision. It has made a thorough examination in the light of all the information available concerning the probable nature of the threats to North America in future years, the alternative means of defence against such threats, and the estimated costs thereof. The conclusion arrived at is that the development of the Arrow aircraft and Iroquois engine should be terminated now.

The A. V. Roe Company fired employees on the spot, without warning, and over their loud-speaker system. A more callous act would be hard to imagine. Yet I was the one who was excoriated and condemned. Every effort was made to place the responsibility entirely on me. I was even reviled for having had the completed Arrow prototypes reduced to scrap when I had no knowledge whatsoever of this action. The press was full of sensational stories about "Malton, the town that died" because of the termination of the Arrow. AVRO proved as uncooperative after the event as it had before. Their main interest apparently was to grind as much as possible out of the government in cancellation charges. The Liberal Opposition demanded that we do something to ease the situation at Malton, but, significantly, no one on their side of the House came forward with so much as a single practical proposal to provide substitute employment for the AVRO plant. One of the very few Liberals who did not play politics with the fate of the AVRO unemployed was Senator W. D. Euler, former Minister of Trade and Commerce in the Mackenzie King Cabinet. He wrote me on 3 March 1959:

May I compliment you on your courage and common-sense in "dropping the Arrow" despite the strong pressure which will probably continue.

The loss of employment is of course regrettable, but I hope we shall not adopt the philosophy which advocates useless and ruinous expenditures merely for the sake of providing employment. That must be dealt with in other ways.

I have mentioned President Truman's observation that over a national leader's desk hangs an imaginary sign, "The Buck Stops Here". Although the decision on the Arrow caused me days of deep concern, it had to be made. Leadership demands doing what is best for one's country and taking responsibility for actions that are not popular. This requires knowledge and infinite patience, combined with a firm conviction that an aroused public opinion is not the surest guide to what is right. No one who has not been honoured with the prime-ministership can ever know the heartaches that he must bear. Churchill, Roosevelt, and Lincoln, in their day and generation, suffered the bitterest and most virulent attacks. Often, it was a sense of humour that carried them through. I think of Churchill in this connection. When the war in Europe was over in April 1945, King George VI offered to confer on him the high honour of Knight of the Garter. Churchill declined. Three months later, this great war leader was overwhelmingly defeated at the polls. With that wit for which he was famous, he commented that although the King had offered him the Garter the people had given him the boot.

Another myth originating with the Liberal Party in relation to our early defence decisions was that we rather hastily adopted the Bomarc as a substitute for the Arrow. Again nothing could be further from the truth. As indicated earlier in this chapter, the Bomarc and the Arrow were conceived by the defence planners as complementary. Again, the origins of the decision to acquire the Bomarc predated my period in office. As early as June 1956, the Cabinet Defence Committee of the St. Laurent government, in considering the need for additional forces for the defence of North America, recognized that circumstances might dictate that two of the three squadrons in a phased build-up of interceptor strength might be equipped with long-range missiles rather than fighter aircraft. Later, the Committee was informed that Bomarc surface-to-air missiles were nearing the operational stage and that both United States and Canadian thinking visualized the introduction of these weapons into eastern Canada within the next few years.

By the time my government began an active examination of whether to introduce the Bomarc into the Canadian air defence system, the United States had already announced plans to build some thirty or thirty-two Bomarc bases along both coasts and across the northern perimeter of the United States. The Chiefs of Staff Committee considered in April 1958 that a similar long-range surface-to-air missile (SAM) would be economical and effective. According to the Defence Research Board, the Bomarc's kill potential in terms of cost was likely to be ten times greater than that of the CF-105. Its range permitted large areas to be covered from a single base and so enabled it to destroy enemy bombers before they were near enough to do serious damage. It was made clear that the Bomarc could be armed with either conventional or atomic warheads and its control requirements were compatible with SAGE.

A joint Canada–United States study on weapons deployment demonstrated the need for two Bomarc bases in Canada in the general vicinity of North Bay and Ottawa, each consisting of one squadron of one hundred and twenty missiles. These bases were to form part of a Canada–United States plan for a continuous system of missile defence from coast to coast designed for the protection of the principal United States targets in North America, with only incidental protection to Canadian targets. It was argued, however, that the two Bomarc bases proposed for Canada would serve to increase the effectiveness of the entire North American air defence system by closing an important gap in key areas. In addition, they would provide substantial defence to nearby Canadian targets. We agreed that it was important for Canada to participate if she were going to do her part in making NORAD more effective.

Our decision to introduce the Bomarc did not work out well. To begin with, the Bomarc was very soon proven to be virtually obsolete, even before it was set up. The day of the bomber was over. The Bomarc was ineffective against Intercontinental Ballistic Missiles. Further, no information was given us that the United States would abandon, or had abandoned, its plans to manufacture a conventional warhead for this missile. Had I had even an inkling of what was to come, there would have been no announcement, on 23 September 1958, of our decision to introduce the Bomarc, because no such decision would have been taken.

CHAPTER THREE

※

B Y MUTUAL AGREEMENT, Canada shared responsibility with the United States for the joint defence of the North American continent. Through NORAD, both governments were determined to erect defences against the most diversified attack of which the Soviet Union was capable. As noted in the previous chapter, this was conceived in 1957 and 1958 as primarily a bomber threat; increasingly thereafter, it was conceived in terms of a mixed bomber and missile attack; before we ceased to be the Government, missiles had become the principal threat—the day of the bomber was thought to be over.

It was to defend against bomber attack that the Cabinet, on 8 September 1958, authorized negotiation with the United States on sharing the costs of two Bomarc squadrons for Canada. On 23 September, I made public that we were giving consideration to employing Bomarc ground-to-air missiles for air defence purposes. Although I announced no detail about the arrangements under which this weapon would be acquired, I did make it clear that it had an atomic capability. On 15 October 1958, the Minister of National Defence proposed opening negotiations with the United States for "the acquisition and storage of defensive nuclear weapons and warheads in Canada". My colleagues and I agreed, and this proposal was discussed with the United States authorities in Washington in November. We hoped that agreement in principle could be reached at the meeting of the Ministerial Committee on Joint Defence in December 1958. From the very beginning, it was clear to the United States that we would open the issue to public debate in Canada by making a general statement regarding these negotiations. At the December ministerial-level meeting, a Canadian draft statement for possible use in Parliament regarding the acquisition and control of nuclear weapons was discussed.

On 20 February 1959, I informed the House of Commons:

The government is . . . examining with the United States government questions connected with the acquisition of nuclear warheads for Bomarc and other defensive weapons for use by the Canadian forces in Canada, and the storage of warheads in Canada. Problems connected with the arming of the Canadian brigade in Europe with short-range nuclear weapons for NATO's defence tasks are also being studied.

We are confident that we shall be able to reach full agreement with the United States on appropriate means to serve the common objective. It will, of course, be some time before these weapons will be available for use by Canadian forces. The government, as soon as it is in a position to do so, will inform the House, within the limits of security, of the general terms of understanding which are reached between the two governments on this subject.

I added, "We must reluctantly admit the need in present circumstances for nuclear weapons of a defensive character."

That statement was intended to give an indication of certain basic considerations in the government's thinking on the question of the acquisition and control of nuclear weapons. We had reached with the United States government the basic understanding that (a) custody and ownership of the warheads would remain with the United States, and (b) control of use of the warheads would be a joint responsibility of the two governments. I realized that there was no immediate necessity to acquire nuclear warheads for use by Canadian forces. The Bomarc sites, for example, had yet to be constructed and Canadian forces concerned had yet to be trained in the use of the weapons. Further, we did not at that time have an exact statement of the technical terms and conditions under which the United States government was prepared to make these weapons available. Therefore, it would be some time before an intergovernmental agreement would be necessary to cover the actual equipping of the weapons with nuclear warheads. Although I did not expect that the nuclear debate thus initiated would last for the next four years, we were prepared for a lengthy examination of this most critical question.

The point should be made here, however, that we never allowed a gap in arrangements whereby the most modern air-to-air weapons would be employed in the continental air defence system. As a result of the Cabinet decision of December 1956, there had been an Exchange of Notes between Canada and the United States on 19 February 1957, setting out the terms and conditions under which the United States Strategic Air Command might overfly Canadian territory with interceptor aircraft carrying the MB-1 atomic rocket. This Exchange of Notes covered only an interim period to 1 July 1957. The United States had indicated a wish to enter into negotiations for more permanent arrangements, and it had been hoped that in the interim they would be able to work out comprehensive arrangements for the greater integration of atomic capabilities in the defence of the two countries.

When we came into office, the necessary amendments to Canada's Atomic Energy Act and Customs Act to make the existing Exchange of Notes legal had yet to be considered by appropriate departments. In these circumstances, the best we could do was to extend this overflight arrangement for a further twelve-month period and take the required steps to eliminate any conflict with Canadian law. We annually extended this arrangement. To underline the point, *nothing* in the defence relations of Canada with the United States during the period of my government in any way reflected negatively on the primary commitment of Canada to the defence of North America, NATO, and the Free World.

As noted above, the discussions begun in 1958 had established general principles only, and we anticipated that the actual agreement would take many months and prove difficult in negotiation. Further, even when completed, it would not necessarily commit Canada to the acquisition of nuclear weapons, since, before this could come about, we would have to work out supplementary agreements covering each type of weapon. The problem of controls was extremely complex, and fundamental to the terms under which Canada might acquire nuclear weapons.

Essentially, this was a question of how to reconcile the requirements of the United States Atomic Energy Act with the respective responsibilities of the Canadian and United States governments to exercise controls through consultation in situations likely to give rise to the possible use of nuclear weapons, and to the need for the responsible military commander to respond to an emergency situation. As I stated in the House on 14 July 1960, United States law required that ownership of the United States warheads must remain with the United States and that the warheads could not be used by non-American forces unless released for that purpose by the President. It could be argued that if the United States government was prepared to enter into an arrangement whereby it shared its responsibility for the defence of the North American continent, why should it be politically so difficult for that government to share control of the weapons to be used? Logical as this argument might be, the reality of United States requirements remained unchanged. We could only hope to balance this with a counter-reality: if and when nuclear weapons were acquired by Canadian forces, they would be used only in the manner approved by the Canadian government, and arrangements for safeguarding the stockpiles would be strictly subject to Canadian approval and consent. These two elements taken together would create, irrespective of the United States Atomic Energy Act, a situation requiring certain responsibilities to be shared by both governments. The controls so exercised jointly would vary, of course, depending upon the weapons and their location. In the same way, these controls would not necessarily be exercised simultaneously in point of time.

At the risk of labouring the point, joint control over use was the most important of all the different aspects of this nuclear question. As applied to the air defence of North America, our position was clear. Canada exercised with the United States joint responsibility for the operations of NORAD, including the weapons placed at NORAD's disposal. In the event that defensive nuclear weapons were made available to NORAD forces in Canada, they could be used only in accordance with agreed procedures, approved by both governments, governing NORAD's operations. Thus, in Canada, such weapons could only be used in Canadian territory or air space under conditions agreed to by Canada. The United States was able to exercise control over use by withholding presidential authority for the release of these weapons. Canada could exercise its share of responsibility only when the weapons were released. But, even so, the weapons could not be used if the Canadian government did not see fit to permit this. What we required amounted virtually to the power of a qualified veto.

The close co-operation between Canada and the United States in defence matters would continue as long as we were mutually threatened. Geography and the nature of modern weapons made it essential; our common viewpoints and mutual confidence made it possible. Inevitably, there were differences on certain aspects, and, of course, the two governments confronted different problems in carrying out their joint programs. Therefore, consultation on general policies as well as on particular questions was always necessary.

The four principal bodies which together constituted the machinery for defence-related discussions between Canada and the United States were as follows:

1) *The Canada–United States Committee on Joint Defence.* Formally established at our initiative in August 1958, its purpose was to ensure an appropriate measure of political consultation over the operation of NORAD. It was to "consult periodically on matters affecting the joint defence of Canada and the United States" and "in particular, to exchange information and views at the ministerial level on problems that may arise with a view to strengthening further the close and intimate cooperation between the two governments on joint defence matters". The committee did not confine itself to purely military questions but reviewed as well the political and economic aspects of joint defence problems.

2) *The Permanent Joint Board on Defence.* Established in 1940, its essential function was to "consider in the broad sense the defence of the north half of the Western Hemisphere". Each of the two national sections was made up of representatives of the three services and civilian members. Its broad terms of reference permitted a wide variety of matters to be discussed, although it possessed only the power of recommendation. As it met at regular intervals (on average, every

three months), and as these meetings were usually conducted in an informal atmosphere, the Board proved to be a flexible instrument for exchanging information, testing out ideas, and negotiating and expediting action on defence matters at a level somewhere between the ministerial and the official. Although the Board had lost some of its earlier influence by the time we came into office, its recommendations still benefited from the considerable prestige built up over its lengthy existence.

3) *Meetings of consultation.* These were established under the terms of the Agreed Minute of 14 June 1951 as an integral part of the procedures to govern the use of Canadian air space by Strategic Air Command (SAC) bombers carrying nuclear weapons. Their purpose was to examine periodically both the international situation, with a view to spotting developments which might lead to the use of nuclear weapons, and the military threat to North America and problems related thereto. In consequence, if the Canadian government were faced with a sudden request for the use of Canadian air space for an immediate United States strike with nuclear weapons, then Canada's response, presumably, would be based on an adequate knowledge of the United States government's views and intentions. Meetings of consultation were designed to provide for a free-flowing exchange of views, not tied too closely to written briefs, in order that senior United States officials and their Canadian opposite numbers might exchange appreciations of situations likely to threaten peace seriously.

4) *Military Cooperation Committee.* The MCC was composed of a Canadian and a United States section, each of which reported to its respective Chiefs of Staff Committee. It was made up of military officers and was charged with the "preparation and continuing revision

of the Canadian–United States basic security plan" and with making "recommendations as to the nature and scope of cooperative measures to be adopted by the armed services of the two countries". The foregoing were, of course, supplementary to the frequent and regular consultations which took place in both the diplomatic and military channels, more especially by the Canadian Embassy in Washington, the Canadian Joint Staff in Washington, and the United States Embassy in Ottawa.

One of the complicating factors in our negotiations was that the initial United States request was that we should discuss ways and means whereby certain nuclear weapons could be stored in Canada for United States use, as well as ways and means whereby nuclear warheads could be provided for Canadian forces. The United States requirements related to the storage at Goose Bay and Harmon Air Force Base of nuclear air-to-air defensive weapons for use by United States interceptor aircraft under the operational control of NORAD. Washington also sought our agreement to the storage of nuclear anti-submarine weapons at the United States Naval Station at Argentia for use by United States naval forces operating under the control of the Supreme Allied Commander Atlantic. Finally, they sought the use of existing storage facilities at Goose Bay for the storage of nuclear weapons for the Strategic Air Command. The United States approach was to regard every item and aspect as part of a single package to be negotiated. We rejected this in favour of approaching each item separately, as portions of the American package had profound implications for our future.

The international tension between the United States and the Soviet Union, both being super-powers, and with Moscow becoming increasingly menacing, threatened not only ultimate destruction by global nuclear war but, more immediately, the jeopardizing of the national political and economic objectives of Canada and the other nations that stood against the Communist evil. Increasingly, we were called upon to commit more and more to the common defence of North America, the North Atlantic, and the European NATO area. Canada's resources were not unlimited; we could not so commit ourselves financially that we would wreck what we were attempting to protect and advance. We had to guard against the steadily developing diminution of Canadian sovereignty which had taken place under preceding governments. We had to maintain as much room for manoeuvre internationally as was possible, lest we lose our image as a small and "disinterested" power capable of making significant political contributions to the solution of international problems through the United Nations and the Commonwealth.

Accordingly, the Cabinet approached United States requests with appropriate care and caution. We gave our approval in principle, this being within the NORAD concept, to United States storage of nuclear air-to-air defensive weapons at the two locations requested, Goose Bay and Harmon, subject to the conclusion of a satisfactory Exchange of Notes. The State Department was given our draft of an Exchange of Notes in October 1959; a second draft, revised in the light of United States comments, was approved by Cabinet and conveyed to the State Department in March 1960. In each, the Canadian principles were:

1) Arrangements for storage would be the joint responsibility of the two governments;
2) The responsibility for the removal of these weapons from the base would be shared; and
3) Responsibility would be shared for the use of the weapons.

In July 1960, the United States Ambassador, Livingston Merchant, made known the American objections to our

1. Chatting with a group of admirers at Castlegar, British Columbia, during the 1962 election campaign.

2 & 3. (*Left*) Whistle-stopping at St. Lambert, Quebec, May 1962. The swearing-in of the new Cabinet Ministers and those who had changed portfolio, August 1962.

4. (*Above*) With Governor General and Madame Vanier at the opening of Parliament on 27 September 1962.

5 & 6. (*Left*) Queen Elizabeth and the Commonwealth Prime Ministers at the September 1962 Conference in London. At a break in the meetings Prime Minister Diefenbaker chats informally with Duncan Sandys, Secretary of State for Commonwealth Relations, President Makarios of Cyprus, Prime Minister Menzies of Australia, and Prime Minister Nehru of India.

7. (*Below*) Relaxing with Prime Minister Harold Macmillan during their talks at Nassau, Bahamas, in December 1962.

8. Whistle-stopping across
the nation during the hectic
1963 election campaign.

9 & 10. Treasured mementoes of meetings with President Charles de Gaulle and Chancellor Konrad Adenauer.

second draft. He explained that the United States required provision that the weapons could be returned to the United States at any time at the request of the United States government. We thought this unreasonable, especially as our acceptance of this provision might establish an intolerable precedent for such nuclear defensive weapons as might be provided Canadian forces in Canada. In consequence, Cabinet decided that the Exchange of Notes "should not be concluded until after discussion with the United States on other matters had been concluded", that is to say, until the position with respect to the acquisition of nuclear warheads for the use of Canadian forces had been resolved. The United States authorities were informed of this decision at the January 1961 meeting of the Permanent Joint Board on Defence.

There were no formal negotiations concerning the storage of nuclear weapons at Argentia for use by the United States Navy. It was, however, discussed in a general way at both the Camp David meeting of the Ministerial Committee on Joint Defence in November 1959, and at the Montebello meeting of the same committee in July 1960. At the former meeting, the discussion centred mainly around the question of control. The United States expressed the view that nuclear weapons carried on board United States Navy ships would not be regarded as having been removed from land storage sites. The Canadian representatives pointed out that, under these circumstances, the Canadian government would not be able to exercise control over release from storage of weapons stored in Canada, a matter to which we attached importance. The United States representatives urged that an attempt be made to avoid imposing such conditions, as these would render the use of the weapons more difficult. Therefore, the question of controls was left in abeyance, to be further explored. It was generally agreed at the Montebello meeting that the principles embodied in the proposed agreement on Goose Bay and Harmon could be applied to storage at Argentia, but that the manner in which Canada could exercise joint control over the nuclear weapons once they had left Canadian territorial waters would also require further study.

As to storage at Goose Bay for SAC, again there were no formal negotiations. This too was discussed by the Ministerial Committee on Joint Defence. The United States stressed the importance they attached to storage at Goose Bay of nuclear weapons for use by the Strategic Air Command on "reflex-strike" missions. Their formal request had originally been made as part of the policy of dispersing SAC forces and SAC weapons, a policy which, in the United States' view, became increasingly valid with the growth of the Soviet missile threat. The Canadian representatives argued that storage for SAC in Canada would present great difficulties politically, as it was clearly beyond the defensive scope of NORAD. We made it understood that we would take no decision on this matter in the immediate future.

There was no mention in the House of Commons or elsewhere of the United States' requests with regard to Argentia or SAC storage at Goose Bay. As there were no negotiations, there was nothing to report. However, I did make note of the negotiations to permit the storing, under joint Canada–United States control, of nuclear weapons at Goose Bay and Harmon Field on 4 July 1960. These negotiations were, as I informed the House, part of our endeavour and determination to ensure "to the maximum degree the security of the Canadian people".

The question of nuclear weapons for the use of Canadian forces centred on the provision of nuclear warheads for the Bomarc missile squadrons to be established at North Bay and La Macaza. Also involved were nuclear warheads for the Lacrosse short-range, ground-to-ground missiles to be provided the Canadian Brigade in Europe.

(In 1960, we replaced this system with the "Honest John" system because of its greater reliability, greater simplicity, and substantially lower cost—some $18 million less.) Nuclear armament for any new interceptors purchased for the RCAF squadrons in NORAD or our Air Division in Europe was in our list of considerations. So too was the possibility of acquiring nuclear devices for the Royal Canadian Navy's anti-submarine force. Bomarc, however, epitomized the question in the public mind.

Certainly, the Bomarc serves as a fitting example of why governments are not more decisive on defence issues; the British Blue Streak program might serve as another. The point is that no matter how effectively governments may plan the various aspects of their defence programs, changing circumstances and requirements often necessitate cancellations and adjustments which could not have been foreseen in the planning stage. Exact future needs cannot always be predicted, and major expenditures on defence weaponry from time to time turn out to be wasted in the light of changes in the threat and in the response required. This applies to all arms programs in general, and to nuclear weapons in particular. For Canada, the Bomarc was a rather special example because we were dependent on the United States, not simply for the necessary warheads but for the development of the entire system. Further, we had come under criticism over the financing of the system.

Mr. Pearson, for the Liberal Party Opposition, argued that in accepting the Bomarc missiles Canada had for the first time taken "lend-lease" assistance from the United States. This might not seem very important today, but twenty years ago it was a serious charge. Ever since lend-lease was invented in 1940 or 1941, Canada had endeavoured to avoid having to acquire arms for Canadian forces from the United States free of charge. It had become a matter of national pride, a symbol of our proud record in the defence of freedom. It was also axiomatic that the more Canada could do for its own defence (by way of paying its share of continental air defence), the greater its freedom of action in the defence field would be. The problem was that of confusing freedom of action with the concept of sovereignty. Canada, and every other nation in the Western alliance, accepted a diminution of sovereignty when it entered into commitments designed to provide collective security for the like-minded nations in NATO. The Bomarc and SAGE installations in Canada were for the collective defence of the NORAD area, and the financial responsibility was shared in accordance with the same one-third/two-thirds formula adopted by the previous government for the financing of the Pine Tree radar installations. We were satisfied that the acceptance of considerable aid with respect to the air defence projects under consideration, including the acceptance of the Bomarc weapons, was reasonable. This was not "Mutual Aid", nor did we ever make a Mutual Aid agreement with the United States, as her other allies were obliged to do.

While the Opposition might rail to its political heart's content about the cost-sharing formula for the Bomarc, the Government had to worry about whether the Bomarc was actually going to come into being. We soon enough had reason to suspect that our acquisition of the Bomarc was a mistake. In June of 1959, the various defence systems and strategies of the United States, including the Bomarc, came under vigorous questioning in Congressional Committee hearings, where United States Secretary of Defense Neil McElroy recommended a new deployment plan for the Bomarc which would substantially reduce the number of Bomarc sites in the United States. When questioned by General Pearkes, McElroy assured him that the new plan did not prejudice or have any effect on the arrangements for the defence of Canada that had been agreed to by our two countries. Indeed, he went further and stated: "On the contrary, the plans are for the development of the Bomarc in the United States in a way which will be fully coordinated with the Bomarc batteries which are scheduled for siting in Canada." He said there was no doubt in his mind that this would receive congressional sanction and represented the position of the administration; he had checked it with President Eisenhower himself.

In March 1960, however, the United States Department of Defense proposed to Congress that the planned expenditure on the Bomarc program for the fiscal year 1961 be reduced from $421.5 million to $40.4 million, and that the number of Bomarc sites be further reduced from eighteen to ten. The two Canadian sites were included in this new figure. On 27 April, the Committee on Appropriations of the United States House of Representatives decided to eliminate all financing of the Bomarc program, including funds previously approved for the fiscal year 1960, except $50 million for future tests.

The government had already let a contract for $3 million for the construction of the site at North Bay. When questioned in the House of Commons, the Minister of National Defence stated that work would continue until a final decision was reached by the United States Congress. We had agreed, on the recommendation of our Chiefs of Staff, to accept the Bomarc; it behooved us not to panic on the first evidence that we had acted on poor technological advice. Furthermore, as General Pearkes observed, the issue had still to be decided.

On 29 June, President Eisenhower wrote me to allay any fears about the possible demise of the Bomarc program:

Dear John:

I thought that you would like to know that the conferees appointed by the House of Representatives and the Senate to consider appropriations for the Defense budget have recommended the appropriation of $244 million of the $294 million which had been requested by the Executive Branch for the Bomarc-B missile program.

While this is, of course, not final since further legislative action must be taken, I hope that you will be as pleased as I was to know of this favorable development for the further improvement of continental defense.

With warm regard,
Sincerely,
Ike

I could only reply:

Dear Ike,

. . . It was kind of you to write, and I shall follow the further legislative course of this appropriation with optimistic interest.

With warmest regard,
John

The Eisenhower administration eventually won what turned out to be a very temporary victory for the continuation of the Bomarc.

The inaugural year of the Kennedy administration brought new developments to increase doubts about Bomarc. President Kennedy's State of the Union message on 30 January 1961, however, directed that there would be a complete review of United States defence policy. He said: "I have instructed the Secretary of Defense to reappraise our entire defense strategy—our ability to fulfil our commitments—the effectiveness, vulnerability and dispersal of our strategic bases, forces and warning system—the efficiency and economy of our operation and organization—the elimination of obsolete bases and installations—and the adequacy, modernization and mobility of our present conventional and nuclear forces and weapons systems in the light of present and future dangers." For the Bomarc, it was, retrospectively, only a matter of time. Until the United States decided to scrap it, however, we had little choice but to continue with our part of the program, especially when we were assured by the Kennedy administration that steps were being taken to make the Bomarc system more effective. Thus, the agreement between Canada and the United States of 27 September 1961, providing for improvements in the continental air defence system, included the establishment of the two Canadian Bomarc squadrons. I emphasize that this agreement contained no specific reference to the armament to be provided for these Bomarc squadrons.

Although there were suggestions in the American Congress in March 1962 (the month in which the first missiles were emplaced at North Bay) that the Bomarc was completely inadequate, we were to wait a further year before Secretary of Defense Robert McNamara publicly pronounced it so in testimony released to the press on 29 March 1963 (see p. 107). By that time it had served President Kennedy's purpose, in that it had brought about the defeat of my government. For the record, Philip Deane, in his book *I Should Have Died*, quotes General Nathan Twining, Chairman of the United States Joint Chiefs of Staff, as describing the Bomarc as "scrap" and "not good for anything" as early as June 1960.

With regard to the acquisition of nuclear warheads for the Bomarc, discussions at the military level had begun, with the approval of Cabinet, in early 1959. On 1 May 1959, the United States made known through service channels that they envisaged a government-to-government Exchange of Notes covering in general terms the broad questions of custody, control, provision of storage facilities, and security and safety requirements. A preliminary technical draft agreement was discussed informally and was subsequently reviewed and revised by our officials in an attempt to provide a formula to meet United States legislative requirements and my Cabinet's wishes regarding Canadian control over release from storage and use.

The broad policy framework was laid down by the Cabinet on 6 December 1960. At that time, it was decided the discussions with the United States government "concerning arrangements for the essential acquisition of nuclear weapons *or warheads* for use by the Canadian forces . . . may proceed as soon as they can be usefully undertaken with the acceptance of joint control to be a basic principle"; the Cabinet also decided that "preparation should also continue to enable the Canadian forces to have the vehicles, missiles, bases, training and other requirements to enable them to be able to use nuclear weapons to be acquired from the United States under joint control arrangements, *if and when the adoption of these weapons is considered necessary.*"

As to the claim that the lack of an appropriate agreement with the United States prevented Canadian forces from receiving training and information about the operation and maintenance of the nuclear delivery systems already acquired by the Canadian armed forces from the United States, we had in May of 1959 signed the same agreement as other NATO members had signed with the United States to permit training and exchange of information on nuclear weapons to proceed on a bilateral basis. I tabled the Canada–United States agreement for cooperation on the use of atomic energy for mutual defence purposes in the House of Commons on 25 May 1959. If it was true, and it was, that the United States armed forces were withholding some training facilities and information from the Canadian armed forces, this was as a form of pressure to bring about the acquisition of nuclear warheads by Canada, and not for the lack of a proper enabling agreement between the two countries. I shall leave the remainder of the Bomarc story until the next chapter.

In July of 1959 the question of the re-equipment of the Canadian Air Division came before Cabinet. (If the reader has begun to think that these defence questions were never-ending, it is well to remember that we lived in dangerous days when war seemed imminent and sleepless were many nights.) In background, Canada's Air Division had since 1951 an air defence role in Europe as part of the Fourth Allied Tactical Air Force. With increasing nuclear and missile capabilities of the Soviet Union and the corresponding emphasis placed on the use of atomic weapons by NATO, General Lauris Norstad, Supreme Allied Commander Europe (SACEUR), recommended in 1957 that our Air Division, along with the United States and the United Kingdom air forces in Europe, assume a strike role. The Cabinet was concerned about the basic implications of this change in role, although our military advisors were not. A change from the established air defence role to a strike role meant a switch from the essentially defensive task of intercepting enemy bombers to the task of attacking with tactical nuclear bombs special targets in Eastern Europe. In other words, the Canadian aircraft would have a tactical bombing assignment and would rely essentially on atomic weapons to accomplish their mission. While it was true that Canadian aircraft would only carry out these responsibilities in the event of a Soviet attack against the NATO area, it would prove difficult to explain Canada's new role to the Canadian public. Further, the problem of reorganization and the cost of re-equipping the Division were of such magnitude that they warranted very careful consideration in themselves.

Apart from the question of armament, there were certain associated questions affecting the assignment of these aircraft to NATO and our bilateral relations with Germany and France. Regarding assignment to NATO, we had to consider the possibility of a new NATO sub-command, a sort of inter-allied nuclear force. In the field of bilateral relations, in the case of France, amendment of the existing agreement between our two governments would be necessary to make provision for stationing the new aircraft in France. Since a change in the RCAF's role from interception to nuclear strike was involved, the French authorities could object. We had to assume that the French government would continue its prohibition of storage of foreign-controlled nuclear weapons on French soil and that as a result there would be no question of Canada's obtaining the right to have warheads available in France for RCAF aircraft there. For an emergency, arrangements would have to be made whereby the CF-104 squadrons stationed in France would pick up their nuclear bombs at RCAF bases in Germany. Indeed, for routine stand-by alert duty the French-based aircraft would have to serve in rotation at the RCAF fields in Germany. We would have to negotiate with SACEUR and the host country, Germany, for the provision of storage for our weapons. Finally, if we went ahead, we would add yet another item to our negotiations with the United States with regard to the control and use of nuclear weapons.

We had to balance the above considerations against the fact that a negative decision on the part of Canada could have unfortunate military and political repercussions in NATO. The Canadian Air Division consistently and rightly had been regarded as a highly important element in NATO's air strength. A decision not to re-equip would in effect mean that the alliance would be deprived of what many considered the most valuable part of the Canadian military contribution. In political terms, such a decision might be interpreted by those of our allies already somewhat lukewarm about meeting their commitments to NATO as a decision on the part of Canada to withdraw. This could have started a chain reaction in diminishing support for the alliance. Also, a decision not to re-equip would undoubtedly result in some considerable weakening of Canadian influence in the alliance. It was argued that a decision to re-equip the air division would place us in good stead with our allies and particularly with the NATO military authorities. It would strengthen the hands of the Canadian government in NATO generally, with the consequent ability to exercise a greater influence on NATO policies. For example, in the atomic field, Canada might have a role to play in trying to formulate a more generally acceptable control system.

While there was considerable pressure from General Norstad and NATO authorities to undertake the new strike role, it was our commitment to the alliance that proved the deciding factor. The nuclear weapons aspect would require long negotiation. There was time. The proposed new aircraft, the CF-104s, would not arrive in Europe until the beginning of 1963. Even then, it was possible that stand-by arrangements would not prove too difficult to arrange, in the event that the necessary permanent agreements had not been completed. Finally, we decided to re-equip, and in July 1959 General Pearkes announced Canada's new strike reconnaissance role in NATO. There was to be, as I stated at the Michigan State University Convocation on 7 June 1959, "no weakening in our support of NATO".

In the meantime, we had been considering other steps to provide for our share of North American air defence. The need for a new interceptor had been on our books since the cancellation of the Arrow. This took on an added importance when the Bomarc system began to collapse. On 13 June 1960, General Pearkes wrote me in this regard:

The present plan for Bomarc deployment has reduced the number of missiles very considerably below that which was originally intended and in a heavy and sustained attack the first waves may very well result in the expenditure of all missiles, leaving the Bomarc defences ineffective. The availability of a limited number of interceptor aircraft therefore provides diversity of defence and ability to continue a sustained effort against an attack.

In addition, if there are no Canadian interceptors provided, the necessary diversity of defence can only be provided by U.S. aircraft patrolling Canadian skies and Canada would not be capable of exercising sovereignty over her own air space. . . .

He proposed the procurement by Canada of sixty-six F-101B interceptor aircraft from the United States. The aircraft were immediately available and could be deployed on Canadian bases within six months to a year. Under his proposal, these fighters could be obtained by trading Canadian-made aircraft for them; he anticipated that the adoption of this program would lead to approximately one hundred million more American dollars being spent in the Canadian aircraft industry than Canada would be required to pay for the new interceptors. Such was the origin of the SWAP deal.

The military integration embodied in the NORAD Agreement was incomplete if it did not extend to defence production. Thus, in my public statement of 23 September 1958, I said:

It now seems evident that in the larger weapons systems now required for the air forces, Canadian work in the design, development and production of defence equipment will have to be closely integrated with the major programmes in the United States. The United States government recognizes this and they are now prepared to work out production sharing arrangements with us. To accomplish effective integration of defence production resources of Canada and the United States will require time and continuing efforts in cooperation.

On 21 September 1960, the Cabinet agreed that the

Minister of National Defence propose to the United States Secretary of Defense that Canada take over the manning and the operation and maintenance of the eleven Pine Tree radar sites in southern Canada then operated by the United States Air Force and assume the costs thereof; that Canada assume forthwith the operating and maintenance costs of the five Pine Tree radar sites currently manned by the RCAF but paid for by the United States Air Force; and that these arrangements become effective as soon as a government-to-government agreement should be reached and continue through the period of the NORAD Agreement, i.e., to 1968 or for such longer period as would be mutually agreed; that the United States make available to Canada sixty-six F-101B aircraft, with supporting equipment, for the use of the RCAF; that the costs of the spares and other related United States equipment for the F-101Bs be shared in the manner agreed at the July meeting of the Canada–United States Joint Committee on Defence (approximately one-third Canada and two-thirds United States); and finally that the United States undertake to procure Canadian CL-44 aircraft to a value of $155 million.

This offer was conveyed to Secretary of Defense Thomas Gates, Jr., on 22 September. Mr. Gates told our Ambassador, Arnold Heeney, that the matter would have to go to the President. When the Honourable Donald Fleming, Minister of Finance, and our Ambassador saw the United States Secretary of the Treasury, Robert B. Anderson, about our proposal on 26 September, Mr. Anderson made reference to the political difficulties which would be involved in the proposal at that time and thought that final decision in Washington would have to be delayed until after the presidential election. When I took this up with President Eisenhower on 27 September, at his suite in the Waldorf Astoria Hotel in New York, however, I was surprised to discover that he had no knowledge whatever about the SWAP proposal. I noted in a letter to Mr. Heeney on 8 October 1960 that the President had said this, "in the presence of Mr. Herter [Secretary of State] and seemed most surprised that this question had not been brought to his attention." This was even more surprising considering that I had discussed the matter at length with the United States Ambassador to Canada, Mr. Richard B. Wigglesworth.

When it did come, the Eisenhower administration's response to the CL-44s–F-101BS–Pine Tree offer was negative. Their counter-suggestion, conveyed to me by Ambassador Heeney on 30 November 1960, was the American fighters (F-101BS) against Canadian manning of the Pine Tree Line, without any purchase of Canadian aircraft. This was not acceptable, but there was no point in pursuing the matter until the new President, John F. Kennedy, and his Cabinet had taken over.

On 31 January 1961, my colleagues and I agreed that we should approach the United States again on the SWAP arrangements as originally proposed. We thought that our case was sound. The history of economic co-operation between Canada and the United States was of long duration. In defence matters, it went back to the Hyde Park Agreement of 20 April 1941 and the statement of principles for economic co-operation of October 1950, wherein it was agreed by the two governments, *inter alia*, that "the economic efforts of the two countries be coordinated for the common defence and that the production and resources of both countries be used for the best combined results." Throughout the NATO alliance there was a surplus of aircraft production capacity, and some rationalization was necessary. It was in the defence interests of the alliance as a whole and North American defence in particular that at least one major plant should be maintained in Canada. Canada's second-largest manufacturer of aircraft had already been obliged to leave the field because production of the Arrow had to be abandoned in view of the high cost to Canada and the absence of orders from the United States. Because of the history of the Arrow, we considered that it would be exceedingly difficult to justify procurement of a United States interceptor in the absence of countervailing orders for Canadian aircraft, the design of which was tailored to a publicly acknowledged United States requirement and which could be provided at a competitive price. Furthermore, the balance of defence expenditures remained substantially in favour of the United States, something the acceptance of our plan would tend to rectify.

We instructed our Ambassador to emphasize that although the Canadian government was fully in accord with the principle that the defence of North America was a joint responsibility, many of the United States defence activities in Canada were primarily related to that country's global responsibilities. If these activities were to continue to demand the support of the Canadian people, there was a public need to demonstrate that mutual co-operation in the field of defence production was a reality. We had to fight continually to assure an equitable deal for Canada. This was because of the fact that Canada, over the years, had been taken for granted in Washington.

Mr. Heeney presented our proposal to Mr. McNamara on 3 February 1961. Subsequently, the United States informally advised us that they were not interested in procuring the CL-44 transport aircraft from Canada but outlined in a general way certain other possibilities involving American procurement in Canada of the F-104 aircraft. Although this would fit in with our manufacture of these aircraft to re-equip our Air Division in Europe, it was not entirely satisfactory because, while our policy was to ensure the maximum Canadian content in the production for Canadian purposes of the CF-104, it was an

American-designed aircraft built under licence in Canada. The CL-44 transport was all Canadian. The refusal of the United States to purchase military aircraft that were not of its own design was disturbing, but the advantages of the United States offer outweighed the disadvantages. The problem of a replacement aircraft for the CF-100 would be solved. The Canadian aircraft industry would gain a substantial production order involving thousands of jobs. But most important, Canadians would now be in physical possession of all the radar stations on Canadian territory. This was, in my opinion, essential to Canadian sovereignty, and to an effective partnership in NORAD.

Agreement in principle was reached on 28 March 1961, whereby:

1) the United States would provide sixty-six F-101B interceptor aircraft for the RCAF squadrons assigned to NORAD;

2) the United States would procure from Canadian sources F-104G interceptor aircraft for NATO to the value of $150 million with Canada contributing a further $50 million;

3) Canada would assume responsibility for the cost of manning Pine Tree radar installations now carried by the United States.

Order-in-Council P.C. 1961-843 of 12 June 1961 authorized the conclusion of this agreement. The success of these negotiations constituted, in my view, an important contribution to the effective defence relations of Canada and the United States.

I should add that the F-101B aircraft were to be equipped with conventional armaments but were capable of being fitted with nuclear weapons if and when the Canadian government decided that our air force should have such weapons. To make certain there were no misunderstandings, towards the end of May, following President Kennedy's visit to Ottawa, I saw the American Ambassador, Mr. Merchant, and obtained from him assurance that the United States government did not require the acceptance of nuclear weapons by Canada for the F-101B aircraft as a condition of proceeding with the deal.

The one consideration fundamental to all defence considerations by my government was our constant commitment to disarmament. Over and over again, I explained our policy. For example, on 24 November 1960, in speaking to the Canadian Club of Ottawa, I said:

We live under a continuing nuclear threat. It touches the hearts of Canadians. The question is asked: are you going to provide nuclear weapons for Canadians? Gentlemen: the responsibility resting on those who have authority, as a trust from the people, knows no greater or more trying problem than this.

We have taken the stand that no decision will be required while progress towards disarmament continues. To do otherwise would be inconsistent. When and if such weapons are required, then we shall have to take the responsibility. The future of Canadians requires that we make that decision which, in the light of the best information we have, represents the maximum security for our country. We have made it equally clear that we shall not, in any event, consider nuclear weapons until, as a sovereign nation, we have equality in control—a joint control. In other words this problem is not one requiring immediate decision. The course to be taken will be determined in the light of what happens in connection with disarmament and in the light of events as they transpire and develop in the months ahead.

This was at a time when Western governments generally, and Canada in particular, were urging in the United Nations that every effort be made to get disarmament discussions going again. The ten-nation Disarmament Committee, of which Canada was a member, had been disrupted when the East European delegations walked out on 27 June 1960. There was some doubt whether the committee would ever be reactivated. The very uncertainty of the situation heightened our determination to pursue vigorously the goal of disarmament. We felt obliged to resist the pressures from our own defence establishment and those emanating from NATO to proceed with the adoption of procedures to facilitate the spread of atomic weapons and to make their use even easier. We fully expected the Canadian resolution on disarmament to be approved by the General Assembly in the second week of December, and we considered that it would be inconsistent, even hypocritical, for us at the same time to adopt policies which could only have the effect of compounding the nuclear problem. We were painfully familiar with the difficulties and frustrations besetting disarmament negotiations, but contemplation of the dangers of an unchecked arms race encouraged us to go on trying.

Also, as we awaited the inauguration of the Kennedy administration, the government considered that we should do nothing, either in NATO or bilaterally, which might hamper the ability of the United States and the Soviet Union to reach a détente and to effect some progress in disarmament. Our substantial interest in progress towards disarmament stemmed from very practical considerations of the consequences for Canada and the world of a possible thermonuclear war, or the political and economic problems we would face in sustaining a modern military program indefinitely (and incidentally the strains such a program would impose on our relations with the United States).

Pursuant to an agreement reached between the United States and the Soviet Union at the resumed session of the twenty-fifth UN General Assembly, these two countries held discussions during the summer of 1961 with a view to reaching agreement on the composition of an effective disarmament negotiating body, and on basic principles to guide further negotiations. On 20 September 1961, the United States and the Soviet Union announced agreement on a statement of basic principles. Canada had been in close and continuing consultation with the United States and the other Western powers concerned during these negotiations, and fully endorsed the agreed principles. Also during the summer of 1961, the five Western members of the old ten-nation committee (Canada, France, Italy, United Kingdom, United States) conducted a series of discussions on the new disarmament proposals which the Kennedy government was then engaged in preparing. On 25 September 1961, President Kennedy submitted a disarmament plan to the United Nations General Assembly. Although this was submitted in the name of the United States only, the Kennedy plan fully reflected our views.

On 26 September 1961 I was asked by the Honourable Lionel Chevrier whether the government had been consulted about the third principle for disarmament put forward by the President, which read as follows: "Prohibiting the transfer of control over nuclear weapons to states that do not now own them." He asked, appropriately, "How can this be reconciled with joint control?" I replied:

The Canadian government has continued to be in favour of a comprehensive system of disarmament which will include measures for stopping the further spread of nuclear weapons. Last year at the General Assembly the Canadian representative said this: " . . . we believe that the spread of nuclear weapons to an ever increasing number of countries would pose a threat to mankind. We consider that the only satisfactory way to dispel the dangers inherent in the possibility is through international agreement on a comprehensive and carefully verified system of disarmament." Consistent with this policy the Secretary of State for External Affairs and all Canadian representatives have worked for the recognition of the importance of including measures to prohibit the spread of these weapons as part of a disarmament programme. I am glad that they form part of these new proposals.

In my view, President Kennedy's third principle represented a pronounced change in the United States' position as compared with the position that the President had taken in his talks with me earlier in the year. I considered that it effectively ended the prospect of joint control and with it the prospect of nuclear weapons in Canada, unless there was war. Of course, I was aware that it would be argued that as ownership of the weapons involved would remain with the United States in any agreement for their use by Canadian forces under a system of joint control, this would not constitute an extension of the Nuclear Club. I, however, judged that argument a mere play on words. I also considered that unless a satisfactory form of NATO control was worked out to govern the use of nuclear weapons, the arming of our Air Division and Brigade in Europe with other than conventional weapons would breach our commitment not to expand the Nuclear Family. Only after war had started might nuclear warheads be moved to Canadian bases. The Minister of National Defence, Mr. Harkness, was informed of my views on the significance of the Kennedy plan during the second week of October, 1961.

During the Sixteenth Session of the UN General Assembly, in the autumn of 1961, Canada continued to press for the earliest possible resumption of disarmament negotiations, and for agreement on a negotiating body whose composition would be representative of geographical areas which had not been represented in previous negotiations. Agreement on a new eighteen-nation committee, composed of the members of the ten-nation committee and eight new members (Brazil, Burma, Ethiopia, India, Mexico, Nigeria, Sweden, United Arab Republic), was eventually reached, and accepted by the General Assembly on 20 December 1961. The General Assembly also endorsed the joint United States–Soviet statement of principles as the basis for negotiations, and recommended that the eighteen-nation committee begin its work as a matter of urgency.

The eighteen-nation committee commenced negotiations in Geneva on 14 March 1962, with representation at the foreign-minister level during the initial period. Without going into the details of the negotiations, the atmosphere in the committee was far more business-like than that at past disarmament conferences, and there was a most encouraging exposition of the position of the two sides to the negotiations.

With respect to general disarmament, which was our principal concern and was emphasized by that sincere and distinguished man of peace, the Honourable Howard Green, Canada's Secretary of State for External Affairs, at the outset of the conference, we sought to identify areas in which it was possible to develop common elements in the proposals of the two major powers into a series of significant agreements. Mr. Green singled out four areas for special consideration within the field of general disarmament: the reduction of conventional armaments; measures to deal with bacteriological and chemical weapons; cessation of production of fissile material for weapons purposes and the transfer of existing stockpiles to peaceful uses; and the reduction of nuclear-weapons delivery vehicles. In the field of *collateral measures*, the main Canadian effort was directed towards seeking out areas in which rapid progress could be made toward agreement. In his opening statement to the conference, Mr. Green noted three such areas which were particularly deserving of ready consideration:
1) prevention of the wider dissemination of nuclear weapons;
2) measures to reduce the risk of war by accident, miscal-

culation, or surprise attack; and

3) measures to prohibit the orbiting of mass-destruction weapons in outer space and to provide for advance notification of satellite launchings.

On the question of non-dissemination of nuclear weapons, Mr. Green stressed, in both his 19 March and his 24 July 1962 statements, the urgent need to reach agreement on effective measures in this field. He strongly emphasized the desirability of proceeding on the basis of the recommendations set forth in the Irish resolution which was unanimously endorsed by the Sixteenth Session of the General Assembly (see Volume Two, page 123).

It was suggested by the Liberal Opposition that we had no policy in regard to nuclear arms. In replying to a question by Mr. Pearson in the House of Commons on 26 February 1962, I said:

I would simply refer the House to what I stated on November 24, 1960, when speaking to the Canadian Club of Ottawa; on August 15, 1961, when speaking in Halifax to the Canadian Weekly Newspapers Association; and again, on October 6, 1961, when Dr. Thomson and those associated with him in the Canadian Committee for the Control of Radiation Hazards made representations to the government.

We take the stand that in the interests of disarmament everything must be done to assure success if it can be attained, and *that the nuclear family should not be increased so long as there is any possibility of disarmament among the nations of the world.* That has been our view throughout. . . .

More and more, the correctness of that stand was brought home to me.

CHAPTER FOUR

✳

MONDAY, 22 OCTOBER 1962, began a week when, to quote Nikita Khrushchev, "the smell of burning hung in the air." Most Canadians and most people the world over went to bed each night without confidence that they would see tomorrow, or even that they would want to if a nuclear war began during their slumbers. This was the week of the Cuban missile crisis.

I was apprised of the impending super-power confrontation some hours in advance when I was advised that Mr. Livingston Merchant, recently retired United States Ambassador to Canada, wished to call on me at five p.m., as a special emissary of President Kennedy, to explain the latest developments concerning the situation in Cuba. We had been informed that President Kennedy would make an announcement of "national" importance at seven p.m. that day. Our Ambassador in Washington, Mr. Charles Ritchie, reported that he had been summoned to the State Department for six p.m., along with the Ambassadors of the United States' other allies. Our Ambassador to the North Atlantic Council in Paris, Mr. George Ignatieff, informed us that the Council would be meeting at ten p.m. (local time) to receive a report brought from Washington by Dean Acheson and Sherman Kent (Deputy Director of the CIA).

We were aware through intelligence channels that as of

16 October, the United States had satisfied itself through photographic and other intelligence media that offensive ballistic missiles with a range of between eleven hundred and twenty-two hundred miles were being installed in Cuba by the Soviet Union. Given this flurry of diplomatic activity on 22 October, and President Kennedy's firm public commitment on 13 September to take preventive action to protect the security of the United States should there be a determination that the USSR had developed in Cuba "an offensive military base of significant capacity", the conclusion was unavoidable that the United States was about to embark on counter-action. Further, at four a.m. on the day of the President's announcement, the United States government had asked us to prohibit, as "a temporary measure", transit stops or over-flights of Czech and Cuban aircraft at Gander. This request strongly indicated United States emergency action to prevent the delivery or further delivery of warheads for the newly discovered launching sites in Cuba; it also suggested that the next forty-eight hours were considered crucial for whatever the United States had in mind.

We were left to speculate whether United States action would take the form of a naval and air blockade of Cuba, a swift invasion and occupation of the whole of Cuba, the destruction of the launching sites by United States military bombing, or a combination of these. We did not know whether the above moves would be preceded by an attempt at private negotiation with the Soviet Union or by a public ultimatum accompanied by a full disclosure of the new Soviet capability in Cuba. We felt reasonably certain, however, that any of these possibilities would lead immediately to counter-measures by the Soviet Union, probably in Berlin, with minimum action in the form of a total blockade of the city as in 1948 and 1949. It was a situation which clearly could escalate rapidly into global war.

Fortunately, the United Nations was in session and we were confident that some international endeavour would be made to avert war and bring about a negotiated settlement, if this became necessary. In this respect, the situation might prove analogous to that at the time of Suez in 1956, when international action to contain and put an end to the fighting was instituted almost simultaneously with the national action taken by France and Britain to protect their vital interests. As I considered all of this in the hours before Mr. Merchant's call, it seemed that the only action which could be taken in a United Nations context to avert measures which could lead to conflict would be a move in the Security Council to have a group of "neutral" nations (perhaps the non-aligned members of the eighteen-nation disarmament committee) conduct an on-site investigation in Cuba of whether that country had permitted the installation on its territory of offensive nuclear missiles. If this move was vetoed in the Security Council or otherwise rejected by the Soviet Union and Cuba, the issue could be taken to the floor of the Assembly, where an overwhelming vote in favour of such a proposal could be expected. Even if such a move failed to result in the admission of an investigation team to Cuba, it would at least have the virtue of confirming and exposing the aggressive designs which the United States maintained the Soviet Union had on North America. Most important, however, reference to the United Nations would prevent any rash and hasty decision by the United States in this crisis situation.

I knew that President Kennedy was still smarting over the 1961 Bay of Pigs fiasco, especially over the charges that he had callously allowed the anti-Castro forces to be sacrificed by failing to provide the umbrella support from the air they had expected. I knew also that the President thought he had something to prove in his personal dealings with Khrushchev after their unpleasant Vienna meeting, where Khrushchev had treated him like a child, referring to him as "the boy". I considered that he was perfectly capable of taking the world to the brink of thermonuclear destruction to prove himself the man for our times, a courageous champion of Western democracy.

Canada certainly had the right to expect notice longer than two hours, if military measures were to be involved. NORAD had worked out, since 1957-58, agreed secret procedures for consultation to be invoked when a threat to North American security was perceived. It was obvious that Canada was not to be consulted but was expected to accept without question the course to be determined by the President. The partnership in continental defence that my government had worked out with the Eisenhower administration could not long survive the strains imposed upon it by President Kennedy.

It is a fact that after I blocked President Kennedy's attempt to interfere with Canada's grain sales to Communist China in June 1961 (see Volume Two, Chapter Seven), his administration went out of its way to cause difficulties for my government. As far as I was concerned, when we received delivery of the necessary grain unloaders, the matter was finished. Not so for John F. Kennedy; he never let go of it. And, short of turning Canada into a state totally subservient to United States wishes, there was nothing I could do, however much I might try, to repair our relations. I will deal in the next chapter with the 1962 exchange crisis for which, I believe, the Kennedy administration was largely responsible. As well, we began in the summer of 1961 to encounter difficulties with the United States over our defence-production sharing under the SWAP Agreement. In August 1962, Kennedy's Secretary of Defense, Robert McNamara, attempted to directly menace all future defence-production-sharing arrangements. On disarmament, President Kennedy's letter to me of 20 October 1962 indicates his extreme displeasure at our attempt to make an independent contribution to the search for world peace:

Dear Mr. Prime Minister:

To my distress, I have learned that your Government intends to support in the General Assembly this year a resolution co-sponsored by the eight new members of the 18 Nation Disarmament Conference and others and calling for an unverified moratorium on nuclear weapons tests. As I wrote you on last April 13, I am convinced that there is no safety in such a proposal and it leads away from the only honest and workable road to arms limitation. . . .

Should Canada cast its vote in favor of a moratorium this year, it will be tantamount to Canada's abandoning the Western position at Geneva on this issue. This will be seen by the Soviet Union as a successful breach of the Western position. In this event, what hope can we hold for pressures on the Soviet Union to take the extremely reasonable step we have proposed? Or to agree even to the limited treaty covering the testing environments of greatest concern, i.e., the atmosphere, outer Space and Oceans. . . .

Mr. Prime Minister, I cannot overemphasize my concern in this matter, and for the reasons I have advanced above, and in the interest of a vital Western solidarity on this testing issue, I hope you will reconsider this decision to cast an affirmative vote for a resolution which can only damage, and damage seriously, the Western position on an essential issue of Western security.

Sincerely,
John F. Kennedy

To return to the Cuban crisis, when Mr. Merchant arrived at my office in the East Block at five p.m. on 22 October, he carried with him photographic evidence of the Soviet missile build-up in Cuba, an advance copy of the President's seven p.m. address, and a description of the President's deliberations and conclusions. The United States planned a naval quarantine of Cuba to prevent any further build-up of Soviet missiles. His purpose was to convey President Kennedy's demand that my government should give *carte blanche* in support of unilateral action by the United States. Specifically, President Kennedy, through Mr. Merchant (as well as through service channels), requested that we immediately and publicly place the Canadian NORAD component on maximum alert. I considered it unacceptable that every agreed requirement for consultation between our two countries should be ignored. We were to be accused by our critics of defaulting on our NORAD commitments. Nothing of the kind! It was the Kennedy government that rendered our joint arrangements ineffective. We were not a satellite state at the beck and call of an imperial master. I telephoned the President.

I asked him why he had not raised United States forces to a level of maximum alert. He said that this would cause international repercussions, but that if Canada did so it would not have the same effect. I told him that our defence forces were alerted and would be ready if a real crisis developed, but that I did not believe that Mr. Khrushchev would allow things to reach that stage. While I hated the Communist system and its philosophy, and while I abhorred Soviet imperialism, I knew something about politicians, whatever their stripe. I saw Nikita Khrushchev as essentially a cautious man, well aware of the strategic superiority of the United States. He could have no interest in a major confrontation with the United States except where the vital security interests of the USSR were at stake. He had been caught fishing in American waters and the President had seized the opportunity to erase the memory of the Bay of Pigs fiasco. It is significant, as has since been revealed, that the majority of the Executive Committee of the United States National Security Council advised the President that the Soviet missiles in Cuba did not alter the balance of power one iota.

President Kennedy objected to my suggestion for a United Nations on-site inspection. I had seen the United States intelligence photographs, so I was not questioning his word. It soon became obvious that while I wanted a UN solution to the Cuban missile problem, he simply wanted UN approval for the course of action he was initiating. When the President again raised the question of a national alert in Canada, I asked, "When were we consulted?" He brusquely replied, "You weren't," as if consultation in North American defence was of no importance to him.

My government's policy with regard to Cuba had been an irritant in our relations with the United States since my first meeting with Kennedy in January 1961. Somehow, I could never get the message through that we were not exploiting, for selfish economic ends, the United States trade embargo against the Castro régime. I have dealt with this at length in Volume Two. This became a tiresome and repetitious exercise which continued through 1962. For example, on 20 February 1962, Walter Rostow, Planning Director of the United States State Department, made the following proposals to the North Atlantic Council:

1) The United States hoped that the NATO countries would agree to deny arms to Cuba, and to prohibit the transshipment of United States-origin goods to Cuba;

2) The United States hoped that the NATO countries would agree to consider Cuba within the COCOM (Coordinating Committee on Export Controls (Paris)) regulations. If the NATO countries agreed to do this, the United States would ask Japan to co-operate (The COCOM members included all NATO countries, less Iceland, plus Japan);

3) The United States hoped that the NATO countries would include Cuba within the NATO system for reporting

credits extended to countries of the Sino-Soviet Bloc.
Even though our policy had been repeated, privately and
publicly, many times, the Canadian delegation, in their
statement on the United States' proposals, once again
pointed out that:

1) The Canadian government had refused to grant export
   permits for the export of United States-origin goods
   from Canada to Cuba since the time of the United
   States embargo of October 1960;
2) The Canadian government had prohibited the export
   of arms, munitions, and military supplies to Cuba for
   over two years and continued to prohibit them;
3) The Canadian government had prohibited and continued to prohibit the export to Cuba of all commodities
   of a strategic nature. This prohibition included all
   items on the COCOM list. The Canadian government's restrictions on trade with Cuba were, in fact, more extensive than the COCOM restrictions;
4) The Canadian government had not been and was not
   granting any credits to Cuba.

There was nothing in our relations with Cuba inconsistent in any sense with our obligations as an ally of the
United States. Nor was there anything inconsistent in our
reluctance in February 1962 to support the United States
suggestion that NATO collectively and publicly adopt a
resolution to extend COCOM controls to Cuba. We felt such
a NATO decision might produce political repercussions
disadvantageous to NATO interests in that this could be interpreted as unwarranted intervention in Latin American
affairs. Although prepared to advance the United States
proposals in other ways, most of our NATO allies agreed
with us. Of course, this added one more item to President
Kennedy's list of grievances with us.

For reasons explained in Volume Two, we continually
refused to yield to United States pressures to break off
all trade with Cuba. When Canada's exports to Cuba

dropped from $31.1 million in 1961 to $8.0 million in the first nine months of 1962, this was not in consequence of any action by my government. Rather, it was because Cuba was suffering a serious shortage of hard currency. We recalled our Trade Commissioner from Havana in the fall of 1962 because there was not sufficient business to keep him there.

President Kennedy's obsession with breaking the Castro government led to United States objections, in September 1962, to the delivery of Soviet Bloc military and economic aid to Cuba in ships of NATO countries. Fortunately, this did not concern us directly, despite press reports that three Canadian companies, Halifax Overseas Freighters Limited, Acadia Overseas Freighters, and Vancouver Oriental Lines Limited, owned eight ships engaged in Cuba–Soviet Bloc trade. As I explained to the House of Commons on 28 September, these ships, although apparently Canadian owned, were under British flag and were operated and managed by British companies. Five of the ships in question had always been under British registry; the other three had been transferred to British registry under an arrangement worked out in 1950. Under Maritime law and general international practice, ships were subject to the laws of the country under whose flag they operated. No doubt this too found misinterpretation in the White House.

Had the missile crisis not intervened, the United States would have closed its ports to the ships of all countries under whose flags arms were carried to Cuba, and closed all United States ports to any ship that on the same continuous voyage engaged in Soviet Bloc–Cuba trade. Canada was not the only country in NATO with which President Kennedy was determined to have his way.

When I told President Kennedy that I did not think the USSR would go to war over Cuba, I had no way of knowing where events might lead. The hesitation and the relative moderation evident in the initial Soviet reaction to President Kennedy's statement, however, suggested that my initial assessment had been correct, although it also may have indicated that the United States action had not come at the time or in the way expected by the USSR. Like ourselves, before Mr. Merchant's briefing, the Soviet Union may have expected, at one extreme, an American armed attack on Cuba or at least a total blockade; or at the other extreme, that the United States would either raise the matter in private discussion with the Soviet leaders or refer it to the United Nations before taking any other unilateral action. Simultaneous reference to the United Nations and the quarantine probably caught the Russians off-stride, for a quarantine designed to prevent only offensive military equipment from reaching Cuba was *per se* less objectionable than a total blockade; and the demand for the dismantling of bases already prepared could be fitted into the developing world's desire to avoid further proliferation of nuclear-weapons sites. Khrushchev's reaction was to buy time rather than precipitate a more severe crisis immediately. Predictably, he used the *tu quoque* argument of United States bases surrounding the USSR, but did not attempt to link the Berlin situation with the Cuban crisis in any way, despite what he could have considered a provocation by President Kennedy in this regard. Indeed, Khrushchev went out of his way to cultivate a moderate and reasonable image.

While my colleagues and I had no intention of doing or saying anything that would add to the seriousness of the Cuban crisis or make the Canadian public more apprehensive than it already was, we were obliged as the Government of Canada to take certain steps. We authorized an increased state of readiness for Canadian Armed Forces (in line with the precautionary measures agreed to by the North Atlantic Council). We delayed the rotation of that third of the Canadian Brigade in Europe sched-

uled for 25 October. Immediately upon receipt of the
United States request, we took steps to ensure that Canadian air space and Canadian air transport facilities were
not used to carry arms to the Soviet bases in Cuba. We
were assured that Canada's Emergency Measures Organization, which we had set up, was at the ready. Appropriate instructions were issued to all departments of government so that they might deal with the types of problems
anticipated in an emergency. I also arranged that the
Leader of the Opposition, Mr. Pearson, meet with Cabinet
to be briefed by the Chiefs of Staff. Throughout, I endeavoured to keep all Canadians informed of what we
were doing and why. On 25 October, I made a major
statement in the House, in which I said:

. . . I wish the house and the Canadian people to know that the
government has taken such precautions as are necessary at this
stage to co-operate with our allies, and to be prepared for con-
tingencies that might arise. As I said a moment ago, the government is seeking to find means by which this dangerous, threatening situation can be settled without recourse to arms. On the
other hand, we recognize the fact that the free world as a whole
cannot afford to permit its essential security to be endangered
by offensive weapons mounted on bases adjacent to North
America. As the Secretary of State for External Affairs said last
evening during the course of his interview on the television facilities of the nation, we shall continue to do everything we can
to avert the dangers to which we are exposed. . . .

I think we may take encouragement from the restraint being
exercised at the moment. However, it would be dangerously
premature to assume that the critical phase of the current situation has passed. There are two pressing needs to be met,
namely not only to avoid conflict but to find a peaceful solution
to this new Soviet challenge.

I think members of the house are in agreement that the greatest hope of finding such a solution lies in the United Nations.

The acting secretary general is to be commended for the speed with which he has acted to discharge the heavy responsibility he bears as the executive head of the U.N. His proposal for a standstill is designed to gain the time that is so urgently needed while the search goes forward for some formula which will provide an acceptable solution. His offer of his personal good offices is in the best tradition of his predecessors in that office. . . .

The fact that we find ourselves in this dire situation may well have some salutary effect. Surely it is not too much to hope that some good will come out of the present dangerous situation. If these facilities were dismantled this would represent a first practical step on the road to disarmament, and if some such suggestion as I made a few days ago were coupled with international inspection of the process then we might well find ourselves taking the first steps away from the dangerous abyss that we have faced for so long in the world.

I came under heavy criticism at the time for not authorizing immediately a full-scale alert for Canada's NORAD squadrons. I have already pointed out that President Kennedy had placed our partnership in NORAD in the breach. In such circumstances, it was up to the Canadian government to decide where its first responsibilities lay. Certainly, we wanted the Soviet missiles removed from Cuba; but not, if there was an alternative, at the price of global destruction. Once we determined that there was no essential role for Canada in finding a United Nations solution to the Cuban crisis, we then authorized that our air defence squadrons be placed at the same alert level as their United States counterparts. As to the popular notion that Canada's Minister of National Defence, Mr. Harkness, under the influence of the Canadian military and the United States Pentagon, engaged in a clandestine authorization of a full alert on 22 October, I do not believe it to be true.

There is one other misapprehension that deserves attention. In Patrick Nicholson's book *Vision and Indecision* the following story appears concerning the role of Senator Joseph A. Sullivan as an intermediary between Cardinal McGuigan and me at the time of the Cuban crisis:

An early visitor who slipped unremarked into the Prime Minister's suite of offices on that morning of crisis was an emissary from the Roman Catholic Church. Senator Joseph Sullivan, lifelong Conservative, honoured man of medicine, honorary surgeon to The Queen, longtime medical adviser to Mr. Diefenbaker, recipient of the highest lay honour in the gift of the Pope, had flown urgently to Ottawa with a message of encouragement.

Immediately after President Kennedy had made his broadcast, the Senator had been invited to call on Cardinal McGuigan in Toronto. The Cardinal asked him to convey to the Prime Minister the assurance of his support for the stand which he would probably take, namely to state publicly at once that Canada, like the other American nations, supported the United States in this crisis. So the Senator flew to Ottawa and called on the Prime Minister to pass on that message, stressing the moral obligation of ally to ally, and indicating that this step would win approval for the Government among the Cardinal's flock.

But this method of encouragement was not welcomed by the Prime Minister. He asserted loudly and forcibly that he did not intend to take instructions from the Catholic Church, and he showed the Senator the door.

Senator Sullivan wrote to one of my associates about this on 12 February 1975:

. . . I refute the remarks in their entirety and unequivocally

deny them in every detail and aspect. . . . *Never* did the late
Cardinal make any such request of me. *Never* did I slip in to
Ottawa quietly. *Never* did Mr. Diefenbaker ever slam the door
on me. He always treated me, as I did him with the greatest degree of respect, friendship, devotion and affection, as I still do.
You are at liberty to quote me in any way you deem appropriate and fit.

It is true that the Cuban crisis brought a new urgency
to the defence debate in Cabinet, in Parliament, and in
the country as a whole. The question of nuclear warheads for our various defence systems had come before
Cabinet in early October and again on the Friday before
the Cuban crisis began. When we once more considered
this question on 30 October, the Soviet Union had agreed
to dismantle its Cuban missile installations. So far as
there was a definite difference of opinion in Cabinet over
our acquisition of atomic warheads, those favouring this
acquisition found their position strengthened by the
events of the previous week. For now there was added to
our deliberations the factor that renewed negotiations
with the Americans would present the best opportunity
to raise questions concerning the working of NORAD,
which, obviously, had been far from satisfactory during
the crisis period of the Cuban affair. Procedures for planning North American defence, taking into account political and economic as well as military considerations, required serious review. Only if Canada could play its full
part in long-range defence planning would consultation
at times of crisis be satisfactory. Also, it was far from
clear what our role in NORAD would be with the phase-out
of the manned bomber. Finally, as I earlier indicated, our
defence-production-sharing arrangements with the
United States seemed far from secure.

To explain this latter consideration, our first difficulties
had begun shortly after our successful negotiation of
SWAP (see Chapter Three). We had agreed, as I stated in

the House when tabling our Exchange of Notes with the United States, that the $200 million worth of F-104Gs to be procured in Canada for NATO (under a 3:1 cost-sharing arrangement) would be disposed of by our two governments "under their respective mutual aid and defence assistance programmes". The details, however, had not been fully settled and were left for separate discussions at a later time. When these discussions began, the United States officials were insistent that Canada must abide by American mutual-assistance legislation, which required title to any military equipment made available to an allied government by the United States to remain with the United States. This was in contrast to Canadian practice, whereby title passed to the recipient government. As we saw it, if the aircraft remained the property of the United States, Canada's contribution to the program would not be clearly identifiable and our contribution would be a source of confusion to recipient governments. We did not find the United States arguments convincing, and our position was strong enough, because of the size of our $50 million commitment, for us to indicate we were prepared to take one-quarter of the production rather than depart from established Canadian policy. This pleased the Kennedy people not at all.

When the United States foreign-exchange conservation measures were announced in August 1962, Kennedy's Secretary of Defense, Robert McNamara, informed us that Canada might be among the countries to which these were applied. His reason was that the United States' balance-of-payments problem has been exacerbated by defence expenditures overseas, and that Canada had had, over the past year, a favourable defence balance with the United States of $240 million. Further, he concluded that we were under-spending on defence between $400 million and $500 million per annum. While we sympathized with the Kennedy administration over their balance-of-payments difficulties and welcomed steps to maintain the strength and integrity of the United States dollar, Canada had its own balance-of-payments difficulties. It was in part these difficulties that had obliged us, in June of 1962, to take temporary emergency measures. The United States was much aware of our situation, and their position with regard to our favourable defence balance was far from helpful when one considered that Canada's current-account deficit with the United States had been running at approximately $1 billion annually. Also, while pressing us to spend $400 million more per annum on defence, they were simultaneously pressing us to adopt long-term fiscal-restraint programs as a condition of our reciprocal currency arrangement with the United States Federal Reserve system and our line of credit from the Export-Import Bank of Washington, two of the emergency steps we had taken in June to stop the run on the Canadian dollar. All this was no more than harassment. What the Kennedy administration actually wanted was Canadian acceptance of nuclear weapons in NORAD and NATO. It did not matter that the Bomarc was useless, or that the threat was now from ICBMS, we were to take the warheads because the President said we must.

The basic problem in any Canadian acquisition of nuclear weapons, however, had not changed. Indeed, it assumed a greater importance after the Cuban crisis than before. Canada had to achieve the maximum degree of political control over the use of the warheads and the means of delivery. It was essential that the Canadian government be in as strong a position as possible to bring its influence to bear on any decision to use nuclear weapons, and perhaps to deter the United States from any possible future ill-considered decisions in this respect. I felt that Canadian public opinion, rightly or wrongly, attached a special significance to nuclear weapons, and that the acceptability of a decision to acquire and use nuclear weapons would be greatly influenced by the degree of control the Canadian government exercised over those weapons. Yet, for this to happen, the United States would have to amend its legislation governing the control of atomic weapons. As I said in the House on 26 February 1962: "So long as the law of the United States is as it is at present, joint control is impossible." President Kennedy gave no indication that he was prepared to initiate the necessary changes in that law.

Personally, I preferred to wait until the NATO ministerial meeting in Ottawa in May 1963 before making definite arrangements, one way or the other, with the United States on the acquisition of nuclear weapons. The issue had assumed such importance, however, that I was open to the negotiation of any necessary stand-by agreements for the interim period. Such agreements would have to ensure that nuclear weapons would not be physically located on Canadian soil in peacetime, but would provide detailed arrangements whereby Canadian forces, either in Canada or in Europe, could rapidly acquire nuclear weapons should war be imminent or have broken out. In Europe, the nuclear weapons could be stored near our Air Division or Brigade, as the weapons themselves were not on Canadian soil. Canadian Voodoo interceptors attached to NORAD would be enabled to acquire nuclear weapons in a short period of time from depots in the United States. The United States had taken the position in the Permanent Joint Board on Defence that stand-by arrangements were impractical in relation to the defence of North America. We sought to re-open this question, and on 30 October 1962, the Cabinet agreed that negotiations be commenced forthwith by Mr. Green, Mr. Harkness, and Mr. Churchill jointly with the Chargé d'Affaires of the United States in Ottawa to work out an agreement or agreements between the two governments under which

1) nuclear warheads would be held in storage for and made available to the Canadian forces in Europe under NATO command for use in CF-104 aircraft and the Honest John rockets; and
2) nuclear warheads would be held in bases in the United

States to be moved to Canada to be available to the RCAF for use in Bomarc missiles and interceptor aircraft, on request by the Canadian government when war appeared imminent.

Meetings were held in Ottawa with a United States negotiating team on 21-23 November to examine studies which had been made by the United States Defense Department on the feasibility of airlifting complete warheads to Canadian bases. As these time factors did not come within the likely warning time of bomber attack, which was estimated at three hours, further studies were carried out by the United States Defense Department of the possibility of airlifting only a part of the warhead, without which the part positioned in Canada would be inoperable. On 4 December, the United States negotiating team presented the results of these studies. They showed that using the "missing part" approach, and using a normal complement of four loading crews, all the Bomarcs in Canada could be made operational within one hour and fifty-five minutes to two hours and ten minutes; and that all the MB-1 missiles for the CF-101s in Canada could be rendered operational in less than two hours, the exact time depending on the nature of the missing part selected. The United States, at a meeting in Paris between Canadian and United States ministers (Howard Green, Douglas Harkness, Dean Rusk, and Robert McNamara) on 14 December 1962, indicated that they were prepared to work out with the Canadian government a stand-by arrangement for the arming of the Bomarcs and the CF-101s in case of need. It seemed then that we had a workable solution at last. The "missing part" approach was reconcilable with all the stated policies of my government and quite capable of meeting the requirements of effective North American defence.

When I first heard of the proposed meeting of President Kennedy and Prime Minister Macmillan in Nassau in mid-December 1962, I invited Harold Macmillan to visit

Ottawa following his meeting with the United States President. On 28 November, I received a message from Macmillan which read: "I am afraid that because of my visit to President de Gaulle [he was meeting with de Gaulle 14-16 December] and the nearness of Christmas it would be very difficult for me to come to Ottawa on this occasion. But I would be delighted to welcome you in the Bahamas on December 21st if you could manage this." He went on to suggest that this would follow the "Bermuda pattern" in 1957 when Mr. St. Laurent went to Bermuda following Macmillan's talks with President Eisenhower. I was pleased to accept.

On 30 November, I received a further message from Prime Minister Macmillan which said: "I have thought that in the light of events of the past few weeks it would be useful to have a personal exchange of views on a number of international problems and in particular to explore the possibilities of negotiations with the Russians in the near future and of progress towards a general détente." He provided me with the agenda for his meeting with President Kennedy. It included: Cuba, nuclear tests, disarmament, Berlin, the Sino-Indian dispute, Anglo-American defence and economic arrangements, negotiations between Britain and the EEC, and Indochina. He further assured me that he would give me a full account of his meetings with both President de Gaulle and President Kennedy. In consequence of that helpful consideration that I experienced over and over again from him, I was able to attend the Nassau meeting fully briefed on every subject under discussion. As things turned out, I was invited as well to join the West's two leaders for luncheon and talks in what might be described as the ninth inning of the Kennedy-Macmillan conference.

As I gave thought to the forthcoming Nassau meeting, I was keenly aware that President Kennedy's appreciation of his apparent success in the handling of the Cuban crisis had very much increased his self-confidence in foreign affairs, as well as that of the key members of his administration (Rusk, McNamara, and brother Robert). They seemed convinced they had shown themselves able to act effectively without any help from their Western allies. Their view did not augur well for Britain's bargaining position, especially the notion that Britain should play some "special role" as advisor to the United States in regard to Western relations with the Soviet Union. In Volume Two, I expressed the view that President Kennedy was at heart anti-British. His lack of self-confidence in foreign affairs prior to the Cuban crisis had generally the effect of preventing any concrete manifestation of this sentiment. However, following the crisis, Dean Acheson, Secretary of State under President Truman and close advisor to Kennedy, gave indication of the new United States approach in a rather insulting speech to the effect that Britain's role in international affairs was "played out". Significantly, when Kennedy's Secretary of State, Dean Rusk, was questioned by the press following Acheson's speech, Rusk reacted unconcernedly and made no effort to salve injured British feelings. The new United States Ambassador to Canada, W. W. Butterworth, was equally bland about the Acheson speech when I questioned him on it during his first call on me on 11 December.

At stake for Britain at the Nassau Conference was her existence as an effective independent nuclear power, and, thus, her ability to continue to meet her world-wide obligations. She was dependent on the United States Skybolt missile project, which the Kennedy administration gave all signs of abandoning. Without these air-to-ground atomic missiles, the British V-Bomber force would be quickly outdated and in any future confrontation with the Soviets, Britain would be unable to act without United States support.

There was some indication that the British knew exactly where they stood vis-à-vis the Kennedy government when they signed, on 29 November, an agreement with the French to produce a supersonic airliner, the Concorde. This major scientific and industrial undertaking, which might or might not provide an economic return, illustrated to me the British determination to maintain an industrial and scientific capability independent of the United States, and was in no small part a consequence of Britain's difficulties with the United States concerning the Skybolt project.

The United States regarded the Skybolt much in the way they regarded the Bomarc, as both expensive and inefficient. President Kennedy seemed aware, however, that to brusquely terminate the Skybolt project would be harmful to the Macmillan government in terms of the internal political situation in Britain. The difference between Prime Minister Macmillan's position and my own (especially after 12 January 1963) was that if the United States acted in such a way as to cause Macmillan's defeat, they would almost certainly bring to power in Britain a government much less sympathetic to United States economic and political objectives.

Olive and I left for Nassau on Friday, 21 December, on board an RCAF Yukon aircraft. My official party consisted of Marcel Cadieux, Deputy Under-Secretary of State for External Affairs, J. H. Warren, Assistant Deputy Minister of Trade and Commerce, my executive secretary, Dick Thrasher, and Miss Bunny Pound, my very able private secretary. We arrived in the Bahamas at twelve noon. In my remarks to the press on arrival I said that I was very pleased to be there in response to Prime Minister Macmillan's invitation and that I attached considerable importance to the talks that we would be having. I noted that the NATO ministers had recently had meetings in Paris to review the position of the North Atlantic Alliance, and that this provided one subject I expected to discuss. I was careful to avoid any of the contentious issues of the conference. I had been forewarned the day before by my executive assistant, Burt Richardson, who had preceded me to Nassau, that the British and the Americans had reached an impasse over the continuation of the Skybolt. Prime Minister Macmillan was getting nowhere by insisting that the United States go ahead with Skybolt, and an element of desperation was developing in the British attitude. In this context, Richardson reported that the British tended to see my arrival as a welcome reinforcement.

Regardless of recent difficulties with the Kennedy government, I expected that I might be called upon to assume a modest role in providing friendly intervention. We were old friends and neighbours of the United States, and bound by Commonwealth and historic ties to Britain. It would not be the first time that Canada had been called upon to serve as the linchpin of the North Atlantic triangle. This might also allow me to advance Canadian interests, particularly as they related to the general defence policies of the West. In the event, however, the Skybolt issue was settled at the eleventh hour.

At lunch with President Kennedy and Prime Minister Macmillan on 21 December, the conversation centred on important issues in Canada–United States relations. On the question of Cuba, the President indicated that the United States had no objection at all to our trade in non-strategic materials. He even volunteered that our Ambassador in Cuba had been particularly helpful to United States interests, and the fact that our Embassy was open during the recent crisis had allowed it to provide services for which the United States was indebted to Canada. (Of interest is the fact that the Cabinet had decided on 23 October that we would not break off diplomatic relations with Cuba because of the missile crisis.)

On the question of defence, I informed the President that there were a number of matters I hoped we soon would have the opportunity to discuss in connection with the defence of North America, and with the provision of nuclear-armed missiles for Canada. Although we did not go into the details of storage in the United States or the joint training there of United States and Canadian squadrons, President Kennedy gave no indication that he was at all dissatisfied with what our ministers had agreed to in Paris the week before. The next day, in conversation with Prime Minister Macmillan, Lord Home, and Lord Amory, it was brought out that something along the line of the proposed Canada–United States arrangement had been discussed regarding the Polaris Plan then being considered by Britain and the United States. I informed them that the plan we had in mind would provide the Canadian armed forces with the necessary defensive weapons but would not thereby extend the Nuclear Family, which I believed should be kept strictly under control.

On the question of Canadian sales to China, I mentioned in my Volume Two that we had encountered and overcome an attempt under United States Foreign Control Regulations to prevent the American parent of a Canadian oil company supplying bunker oil for the ships engaged in the grain trade with mainland China. The issue appeared to be coming to a head once more, in that the United States Treasury Department had written to Standard Oil of New Jersey, the parent company of Canada's Imperial Oil, concerning an alleged violation of regulations under the Trading with the Enemy Act. When I asked President Kennedy during the Nassau meeting if there was any more objection by him to our trade with China, he replied in the negative. When I recalled the difficulties which had earlier arisen concerning bunkering, the President advised that no consideration was being given to any change in the solution that had been worked out. I considered this assurance to be important should the State Department be unsuccessful in its efforts to head off the action of the United States Treasury in connection with the letter to Standard Oil.

In connection with the other matters related to our

sales to China, the President was under the impression that Canadian supplies of wheat had been substantially reduced as a result of the lower 1960-61 crop and increased overseas sales. I advised him that the supply position had much improved as a result of the record 1961-62 crop and that we had some 700 million bushels of wheat available for sale. He was also under the impression that the December 1962 sale to mainland China of an additional 34 million bushels of wheat represented new business. I explained that this was entirely within the existing long-term undertaking announced in 1961. President Kennedy also showed interest in the financing of Chinese grain purchases, and speculated that the sterling used in payments to Canada was being earned by sales of potash to the USSR, which in turn was selling gold. He inquired whether there was anything Canada could do to assist the United States in securing the release of prisoners of war held in China since the Korean conflict. The release of American prisoners of war was a subject so far removed from the normal discussions between Canada and the grain-purchasing agencies of the Chinese government that it was impossible for me to make any commitment, but I was altogether desirous of doing anything that could be of assistance.

On the question of the new United States Ambassador to Canada, the President seemed to hold Mr. Butterworth in high regard. He had been a member of the United States Embassy staff in London at the time the President's father, Joseph Kennedy, had been Ambassador to the Court of St. James. I refrained from mentioning the "Big Boss" impression Ambassador Butterworth had left with Howard Green at their first meeting.

During our luncheon, the President digressed to ask one of the scientific men present for an explanation of radio waves, which he found difficult to understand. The explanation seemed to confuse President Kennedy further, and he stated that he was now certain that he would never understand radio. Yet, from that he moved on to discuss the details of the rocketry necessary for the United States to place a man on the moon by 1967. He said there would be two sections to the moon rocket, and that one portion would revolve around the moon while the other, occupied by an astronaut, would land on the moon surface and, when necessary, be reconnected with the portion remaining in space for the return trip to earth.

In all, I thought it a useful conversation, and pleasant enough. The relations of Canada and the United States were so multifaceted and so important to both countries that I considered it the course of irresponsibility to allow any conflict of personality to encroach for long upon the practical matters that concerned our countries. I could only hope that President Kennedy would see American interests served by a like attitude.

I was very much interested to learn the details of the British–United States discussions on Skybolt and Polaris, as well as the proposed NATO Nuclear Force. This came up in a general way at luncheon when I told President Kennedy that if he was thinking of putting a NATO multi-national crew on board a Polaris submarine, the result would be an explosion beyond any nuclear weapon in his arsenal. He was not amused. It was after the President had left for Washington that afternoon that Prime Minister Macmillan gave me a full account of their discussions.

The Macmillan-Kennedy conversations had taken place against the background that, because of Intercontinental Ballistic Missiles, the era of the manned bomber was over. In the light of the implications for Britain of the United States' discontinuance of the Skybolt missile, a number of options were discussed. The first was the further development of Skybolt on a joint basis, with the United States and Britain each putting up $100 million. A second option offered by President Kennedy was to equip the British V-Bombers with the United States Hound Dog air-to-ground missiles, which had a range of about two hundred miles. With Hound Dog affixed to the bottom of the V-Bombers, there would, however, be only two feet of ground clearance. Even had adaptation of the V-Bombers been possible, this would have left Britain in the outdated manned-bomber stage. Accordingly, this alternative was also rejected. As to other options, because of the vulnerability of fixed missiles in an area as small as Britain, Mr. Macmillan made it clear that he was not interested in any of these as an alternative to Skybolt, but that he would be interested in the Polaris. Polaris, because it was carried by submarines, had the advantage of not being tied to a fixed base. After considerable discussion, the President agreed to provide the Polaris missiles to Britain.

When Mr. Macmillan described these discussions to me, he was obviously pleased with the outcome. Indeed, he appeared to me rather like the cat that had swallowed the canary. In a note I made at the time, I described his thinking:

Having submarines armed with Polaris with a range of 1000 miles makes it possible to have a moving launching-pad close enough to the USSR for Britain to be able to say that any time she was threatened she could launch an offensive against the USSR. Indeed, the communiqué as to the control of the Polaris missiles indicates that the British Government alone will decide their use. . . .

The British were also pleased by the fact that since the submarines returned to port only once every three months, they would form less of a political target for the anti-nuclear elements in Britain, represented by Lord Russell. They emphasized that in the final analysis control of the British Polaris Nuclear Submarine Force would remain in the hands of the British government. Although there was an obligation to move towards development of a multilateral NATO Nuclear Force, the Nassau Agreement between Britain and the United States made it clear that the final decision would rest with the British government when, in the words of the communiqué, "supreme national interests are at stake". In the course of dinner at the Governor's Residence that evening, Lord Home, the British Foreign Secretary, expressed the opinion that the multilateral agreement for a NATO nuclear deterrent would be "stillborn". However, from the British point of view, the agreement was eminently satisfactory: "It provides what we want," he said.

When I was asked in a press interview to interpret the passages in the joint United States–British defence statement concerning Polaris and development of a multilateral NATO Nuclear Force, I was careful in the expression of my viewpoint. I stated that what was involved was a bilateral agreement between the United States and Britain. Their intentions with respect to the development of a NATO Nuclear Force would be discussed with other NATO countries, but could not bind such countries. Thus, it would be for individual NATO countries, when consulted, to decide whether or not they wished to take part or make a contribution. When I was asked about the relationship of the agreement to questions of North American defence, I said that so far as nuclear weapons were concerned, Canada's general approach was to avoid extension of the "nuclear family". This was the stand which the Canadian government would take so long as there was any hope of making progress in disarmament. In the event, however, that the disarmament conversations failed and the situation required it, it would be my government's intention to arm Canadian forces in the most effective way possible.

As I considered the Nassau Agreement, however, it was increasingly obvious that the whole Western defence concept had been completely changed by what amounted to the announcement that the United States was now dependent upon Polaris weapons as their main deterrent.

The proposed multilateral NATO force was probably never intended to be practical in any sense other than providing a framework for the shift in United States broad strategy to reliance on Polaris-equipped, nuclear-powered submarines. If there was ever a reason to seriously re-examine every Canadian defence commitment, this was it. In my talks with members of the British government, they seemed very pleased with the wording of the Nassau communiqué concerning the importance of increasing the effectiveness of conventional forces. They emphasized the urgent need in the free world for elasticity in military arrangements.

For some time I had followed carefully developments in NATO thinking with regard to an increased conventional reliance. President Kennedy, when speaking in the Canadian House of Commons on 17 May 1961, said in part: "If we are to meet the defence requirements of the 1960s, the NATO countries must push forward simultaneously along two major lines: *First*, we must strengthen the conventional capability of our alliance as a matter of the highest priority. . . . " In essence, what the President seemed to be saying was that while the principal protection against nuclear attack by Russia would continue to be provided by the United States retaliatory forces, NATO forces in Europe must at the same time be prepared to defend themselves against attack by Soviet conventional forces without relying unduly on tactical nuclear weapons in the NATO shield. We considered at the time whether existing Canadian force goals and commitments ought not to be modified to attain increased mobility of Canadian conventionally trained forces by increasing their airlift capacity with Canadian-built planes (and thus using available Canadian defence-production resources more fully). At the NATO ministerial meeting in December 1961, references were made by some members to basic defence issues, including the question of NATO strategy. Although there was no real difference on defence questions, United States Secretary of Defense McNamara's statement clearly gave priority to improvement in NATO's conventional capabilities. Our policy in NATO was to encourage any development that on the one hand limited the tendency towards national nuclear forces and, on the other hand, emphasized the importance given to the build-up of non-nuclear weapons.

The day after Parliament reconvened on 20 January 1963, I summed up our considerations with this statement:

I think I should now make a statement with regard to the meetings with President Kennedy and Prime Minister Macmillan. At Nassau before Christmas I had discussions with the President of the United States and Prime Minister Macmillan on the grave policy questions facing the western alliance in the political and defence fields. I also had extensive discussions with Mr. Macmillan on the various problems of mutual interest to our two countries, and had the benefit of his views on the United States–British talks which had taken place prior to and for a short time after my arrival there.

The agreement reached by Britain and the United States at Nassau represents the first firm commitment to certain ideas concerning military policy in the western alliance which has been evolving for some time. I refer to problems mainly affecting the control of the nuclear deterrent forces of the west. The British and United States leaders agreed that in order to develop new and closer arrangements for the organization and control of the NATO defence effort, a start could be made by subscribing to NATO some of the nuclear forces already in existence, and in particular allocations from United States strategic forces, British bomber command and from tactical nuclear forces now held in Europe. This latter suggestion has relevance for Canada and in the NATO council is now the subject of intensive discussion in which Canada is fully participating. For the longer term the British prime minister and the president agreed to the furnishing of Polaris missiles to Britain to be made available for inclusion in an eventual NATO multilateral nuclear force, with a similar offer to France. . . .

It was also agreed at Nassau by the two leaders in question that in addition to having a nuclear shield it was important to have a non-nuclear sword and to increase the effectiveness of conventional forces available to the alliance. It has been the policy of the Canadian government to support the build-up of conventional forces in Europe. The house will recall that on the occasion of the Berlin crisis in the autumn of 1961, Canada increased the strength of its forces in Europe. The purpose of increasing the conventional strength is to ensure that if the western alliance is ever faced with aggression from its enemies it will have sufficient strength in non-nuclear forces to avoid the disastrous choice between surrender and all-out nuclear war.

These are the important questions of strategy which are now in the process of being exhaustively examined in the NATO council. Indeed, I believe that the whole future direction and shape of the military forces of NATO are now in process of review. The enormous costs of modern weapons systems and the speed with which they become obsolescent dictate the utmost care in reaching final decisions. It would be premature at this stage to say anything further about western defence policy until there is a clear indication as to whether or not some form of NATO multilateral nuclear force can be worked out. . . .

I suspect that had it not been for Mr. Pearson's *volte-face* on the nuclear question, we would have continued in government and that the entire question would have been resolved when the North Atlantic Council met in Ottawa in May. As it was, President Kennedy concluded that he could fix things so that he would no longer be obliged to deal with me or my government. It is interesting that on 11 January, the day before Mr. Pearson's Scarborough speech, the United States administration informed us that they regarded the "missing part" approach to arming the Bomarcs in Canada as impracticable! On 15 January, they made the ludicrous counter-proposal that the "missing part" be stored in Canada. The day following the defeat of my government in the House, United States Defense Secretary McNamara gave secret testimony before a Congressional subcommittee that the Bomarc was virtually useless, except to "cause the Soviets to target missiles against them, and thereby increase their missile requirements or draw missiles on to these Bomarc targets that would otherwise be available for other targets." I only discovered this when I read about it in the newspapers after the proceedings became public on 29 March, hardly more than a week before the 1963 election.

Yet, the morality of my government became a central election issue; could a government under my leadership ever again be counted upon as a good and true ally? Who, among those who voted in 1963, will ever forget the Kennedy-conceived message conveyed to the Canadian electors by the cover and contents of the 18 February issue of *Newsweek*; its editor was President Kennedy's close friend.

During September 1963, Olive and I visited the Middle East. During a tour of the Aswan Dam in Egypt, an American, a Mr. Loughman from Kansas City, came over to me and said: "I want to shake hands with the only Prime Minister of Canada who has ever been defeated by a President of the United States. I am a Democrat but I am not going to vote for Kennedy any more."

CHAPTER FIVE

✳

IT IS OBVIOUSLY TRUE that had we not been a minority government in 1963, President Kennedy would never have dared to intervene in Canadian politics. There is another story to be told before I complete the prime-ministerial side of my memoirs, and it begins with my decision to go to the people in 1962.

By mid-1961, the back of Canada's Liberal-bequeathed recession was finally broken. The expansionist policies of my government had begun to yield dividends obvious to all in greater trade, higher employment, and increased revenues to each level of government. Canada's economy was entering a boom period that would last a decade.

Fiscal policies such as public works, loans for new homes construction, loans to farmers and small businessmen, increased aid to provincial governments, etc., were deliberately expansionist and designed to increase the money in circulation and thereby create more jobs. My government had no interest in turning back the hands of time: we saw automation not as something to be stopped but as something to be used to provide more jobs and a better life for all Canadians. With all our resources and energy, with hundreds of millions of people in the world demanding a better standard of living, and with the good-will Canada had already established in the newly developing nations, we saw a tremendous opportunity to foster world trade in general and Canadian trade in particular. Thus, to meet a serious balance-of-payments problem in international trade, we rejected the path of restriction to balance our merchandise trading account. Such things as the trade promotion drives, tremendously expanded credit for exports, and legislative amendments to allow all companies to combine legally for export purposes are examples of our program to expand trade in a positive way. As the *Financial Times* noted on 27 October 1961: "The government is doing a great deal to improve the character of exports. We're beginning to move into markets we never bothered to try before."

Further, when the restrictive monetary policies of the Bank of Canada were eliminated through a change in the governorship of the Bank, we were able to proceed with a planned program whereby the Canadian dollar would be at a level commensurate with reality. To quote the *Financial Post* of 23 December 1961:

It is plain that many of the good things of 1961 were the free gifts of time and circumstance. But it would be nonsense to pretend that the federal government hasn't pushed the process to the advantage of all Canadians by a number of commendable actions. First, Ottawa brought to an abrupt end the disadvantageous and enervating premium on the Canadian dollar. As the effects of the discount dollar penetrate the current structure of prices and costs, this bold — if overdue — experiment in devaluation will be of increasing benefit to Canadians who must meet foreign competition in the national market. For many of our big exporters of resource material, the lower value of the dollar will continue to make for better sales, better profits. Second, Ottawa has made an important start in creating a climate in which Canada's exporters can better compete for foreign markets. The discount dollar is part of this, but we refer to Trade Minister Hees' vigorous and imaginative efforts to promote exports and the very practical beginning that has been made in supplying more adequate export financing. Finally, the government has openly admitted responsibility for monetary management and the interregnum of outward and inward conflict between monetary policy and government policy that was demoralizing for business confidence and debilitating for investment decision is now over.

Without doubt, we would have enjoyed an impressive electoral success had we gone to the people in the fall of 1961. Even *Maclean's* Magazine found itself compelled to recognize on 23 September 1961 that "Out of 62 specific pledges made by the Prime Minister during the 1957 and 1958 campaigns, 50 have already been kept, or are in the process of being discharged. Many Canadians are better off as a result of the past 51 months of Conservative rule." In our first five years, my government increased over-all social justice benefits by 79 per cent. Federal payments to provinces in 1961-62 were 603 per cent higher than they had been in 1956-57. Total health and welfare payments to individuals in 1961-62 were 72 per cent higher than they had been in the last year under the Liberals. In every category of social justice—old age security, old age assistance, blind and disability allowances, unemployment assistance, hospital insurance, health grants—increases had been made. When in August of 1961 I announced a five-million-dollar annual grant for amateur athletics designed to encourage amateur sport and, in general, to improve the physical fitness of the nation, the reaction of the Kingston *Whig Standard* for 28 August was typical: "Canadian sports leaders have joined in unanimous praise for the plan."

"Social justice", to me, meant dedication on a continuing and practical basis to the concept of fairness to each and fairness to all. It meant that government had a responsibility to encourage the development of every part of Canada. It meant that government had to provide the climate for expansion and growth. It meant as well that government had a responsibility to bring about a higher standard of welfare for all Canadians, and in particular for those who because of age, disability, unemployment, or other causes would not normally enjoy a reasonable share of the good life. I felt that we had made tremendous progress, as a government, in righting the balance for both individuals and provinces. This was just the beginning. Our aim, in short, was a strong economy and responsible citizenship, a nation in which Canadians regardless of racial origin would be equals.

With the benefit of hindsight one can say I was in error in not going to the people in the fall of 1961. Nevertheless, I did not feel then, and I do not feel now, that it would have been right or proper to do so before the fourth year of our mandate had been completed; and this despite almost assured prospects of success. I did expect, however, that the factors that made an election favourable in 1961 would remain constant into 1962. Further, the government looked forward to introducing measures that would extend and to a certain extent round out the social justice program, while at the same time providing opportunity to reduce the level of deficit financing in the 1962 estimates and budget. We knew that a balanced budget was in prospect. Unemployment levels, however, although well below those in the United States, would need further reduction before we would risk any sudden change in our fiscal approach. As a matter of fact, there would have been no federal deficit at all had we not undertaken to be of greater assistance to the provinces (and through them to the municipalities), so that they might fulfil their constitutional responsibilities in those areas which particularly affected the welfare of the people. The cumulative increase in federal contributions to the provinces over the period of my government was greater than the cumulative budgetary deficits for the same period. On a number of occasions, when the Leader of the Opposition was critical of our policy of deficit financing, I asked him to point out the items to which he objected. He never did so. I have wondered what he would say today with successive deficits nine and ten times greater than in 1962.

In the autumn of 1961, my good friend, the Honourable Leslie Frost, the Premier of Ontario, suggested that the time was right for an election. Frost was prepared to delay his retirement as Premier and Leader of the Ontario Progressive Conservative Party until after any 1961 federal election, and to delay the implementation of an Ontario provincial sales tax if I decided to go to the people that fall. A provincial sales tax was bound to be politically unpopular, and there is normally in Canada some measure of popular confusion over the various levels of constitutional responsibility. Thus, it was reasonable to expect that an unpopular action by a Progressive Conservative government at Queen's Park would rebound unfavourably against the electoral fortunes of a Progressive Conservative government in Ottawa; and this is exactly what happened. But for reasons indicated above, I declined Frost's offer. His successor as Premier, the Honourable John Robarts, was to reveal the full measure of Leslie Frost's value as a friend and political ally.

Initially, however, there was little to disturb me as I surveyed our political prospects for 1962. Political soundings at the year-end were encouraging. Of course, any election, no matter how propitious the climate, was bound to cost us seats—we could not expect to improve on our 1958 total of 208 seats. However, we could lose as many as forty or fifty seats and still be more than secure. I considered that our record as a government would speak for itself when an election came. I am not pretending that ours was a government without error. To err is human. But under my government, Parliament functioned as it should. There had been no pipeline debate. There had been no corruption or suggestion of it. There were no horses on our payroll. No one could accuse us of holding the people in contempt.

One had only to travel across the country to see the great undertakings we had begun. In 1957 and 1958 when I spoke of the need to develop our northern areas, this was ridiculed as being a policy of development from igloo to igloo. We could now point with pride to the achievements of the New Frontier Policy, to the development of the northern communities of Frobisher Bay and Inuvik, to the road program in the North, and to improved transportation and communication, allowing exploration of vast new mineral areas. For the provinces, there was assistance for our Roads to Resources program, forest access roads, and new railways designed to open up the country. There were tourist roads in the Maritimes. In Ontario, there was federal aid to the Upper Thames River Project. We had aided the provinces in power development. Under my government, the dream of the South Saskatchewan Dam became a reality. We had brought in the first legislation of its kind, as outlined in Volume Two, to end pollution of our vast fresh-water resources. We had brought on a national policy with regard to western gas. We provided subventions for Maritime coal. Freight-rates equalization received our attention. We had wrought a new concept in agriculture known as ARDA. We were building for the future.

Those who had expected the Speech from the Throne on 18 January 1962 and the budget speech of 10 April 1962 to be used as pieces of election campaign propaganda were sorely disappointed. Both were modest documents. Unlike the Liberal Party, it was not our intention to endeavour to buy the people with their own money. The Speech from the Throne served notice of the government's intention, among other things, to take action on implementation of the O'Leary Commission recommendations, on the Corporation and Trade Union Disclosure Bill, and on the establishment of a National Council of Welfare. There was included this important statement: "My government will ask you to take steps to ensure that the forthcoming redistribution of electoral districts is made in an equitable manner upon an objective basis. To this end you will be asked to approve for the first time in our history a measure to create an independent commission to recommend the changes required in the electoral districts as a result of the decennial census." Redistribution was to be taken out of politics once and for all. On the economic front, there was the long-hoped-for Matane–Ste. Anne des Monts railway in the Gaspé, the Manitoba floodway, the North Sydney–Argentia ferry service, increased university aid, and additional help for exporters and small businesses. Finally, there was a national power grid to be launched. As I said in the debate on the Speech from the Throne in the House of Commons on 22 January 1962:

The greatest need in the years ahead, as I see it, will be the assurance of power to all parts of Canada. It is for that reason that in the Speech from the Throne we make provision for the beginnings of action which we hope will bring about the establishment of a national power grid in all parts of Canada. Manitoba has already approached us in this regard; other provinces are interested. My hope is that we shall make progress, to the end that in this respect Canada will not fall behind but will be in the forefront in the maintenance of such necessary things as the provision of power to all parts of our country, assuring due equality of development in every part of our country.

I shared with the Minister of Finance, the Honourable Donald Fleming, the satisfaction he expressed in his 1962 budget address. He was able to report to the House that in 1961 Canada's Gross National Product had increased by $2.4 billion, a gain of seven per cent. (The Liberals, who by 1976 had reduced Canada to a no-growth rate, said it should be more!) The index of industrial output had risen from March to December 1961 by more than nine per cent, so that by the year end it was nearly five per cent higher than it had ever been before. Over the eight months from April to December 1961, labour income achieved an increase equal to that of the fifteen preceding months. Business profits also increased sharply, and by the fourth quarter of 1961 had reached a new peak of $3.8 billion, four per cent higher than ever before. Consumer spending rose by over $800 million during 1961. Yet, during the last nine months of 1961, the Consumer Price Index increased by only half of one per cent. Most encouraging was the fact that exports outran imports, with the result that we were able to achieve a sizable trading surplus on merchandise account totalling $179 million—the first favourable balance of trade of any consequence that Canada had achieved in a decade. This figure gains further significance when it is contrasted to the $728 million deficit on merchandise account in 1956, the last year of Liberal power. The total current-account deficit in the balance of payments had been reduced to $989 million in 1961, a nineteen-per-cent reduction from the deficit in 1960 and a twenty-eight-per-cent reduction from the deficit in 1956. A further measure of the health of the Canadian economy was to be found in the fact that from 1957 to the end of 1961 industrial production in the United States increased by fifteen per cent and in Britain by twelve per cent, whereas in Canada it grew by more than sixteen per cent. During this same period total British exports rose less than eight per cent and total United States exports less than six per cent, whereas Canadian exports in the same period surged forward by more than thirty per cent. Employment in both Britain and the United States increased by about three per cent, whereas employment in Canada grew by almost eight per cent. At the same time prices increased less in Canada than in either of our two major trading partners.

It may be argued that, given this economic upsurge, the first priorities should have been a balanced budget and an orderly retirement of the public debt. While we did not discount the importance of these objectives, to have based our 1962 budget thereon would have involved a degree of complacency about recent economic developments that we did not feel was warranted. Although the seasonally adjusted unemployment figure fell from 7.8 per cent in February 1961 to 6.0 per cent in February 1962, unemployment remained at a level higher than was consistent with our national objectives. Our balance-of-payments position needed to be still further improved. And although capital investment was picking up sharply, we still needed more. We saw it as important, therefore, not to apply any fiscal brakes by abruptly closing the gap between revenues and expenditures. Fiscal policy had to continue to provide stimulus to the economy and we sought through further specific measures to improve the quality and quantity of our industrial output, thereby stimulating employment and income.

As Mr. Fleming said in concluding his budget address: "This budget is designed to continue and to extend those policies which have contributed so much to dynamic growth in the Canadian economy and to the creation of two hundred thousand new jobs in Canada in the last year. It is also designed to stimulate Canadian enterprise to new effort and new peaks of achievement." We had reduced our borrowing requirements below the 1961-62 level. We considered that a balanced budget could wait until 1963. The *Montreal Star* on 11 April 1962 described the budget as "a highly responsible document". The Toronto *Globe and Mail* opined on 12 April that Mr. Fleming should be "commended for having, on the eve of a general election, resisted the temptation to present a vote-catching budget of indiscriminately distributed sops." The *Globe and Mail* further observed that the budget appeared "to have won wide support in the business community". Certainly there was nothing to indicate that a crisis of confidence in the Canadian dollar was looming on the horizon.

Canada's 24th Parliament was dissolved on Thursday, 19 April 1962. The election was to take place on Monday, 18 June. On 29 April, I was informed by Mr. Robert Bryce, Secretary to the Cabinet, that Canada was facing an exchange crisis of major proportions. This was the first time that I was made aware of any difficulties whatsoever in this regard. In January and February of 1962, the exchange fund sold $309 million of foreign reserves. This was explained by our officials as largely a reversal of purchases in the months of November and December 1961, done to promote orderly conditions in the exchange market. The published figures for March showed very little pressure against the Canadian dollar. It now appears that conditions began to worsen during the second week in April, but not to such an extent that anyone made me, as Prime Minister, aware of them, at least until the election day was set. On 30 April our exchange fund had had to sell a further $25,500,000, creating a net loss for the month of $124,804,000 in foreign reserves. This appeared to cause grave concern among the principal civil servants charged with advising the Minister of Finance on financial questions: the Deputy Minister of Finance, the Governor of the Bank of Canada, the Secretary to the Cabinet, the Under-Secretary of State for External Affairs, and the Deputy Minister of Trade and Commerce. They were afraid that the speculative pressure against the dollar would become a widespread "flight of capital". Despite the fact that our reserves of gold in U.S. dollars exceeded $1.5 billion, they considered that this was not sufficient to sustain the value of our dollar in the face of such a crisis. They contended that many owners of Canadian bank deposits and securities (stocks, bonds, treasury bills, etc.) and holders of other assets, whether these holders resided in Canada or abroad, might decide that the time had come to attempt to liquidate their holdings and to transfer the proceeds abroad. The amounts involved, they believed, could be staggering. In such a process, the destruction of capital values and the fall in the prices of securities and other Canadian assets could be serious. There would be widespread gains and even more widespread losses of a windfall character to many Canadians with business or investment interests. Widespread uncertainty and instability would result in the deterioration of production and employment. Moreover, serious instability in any important currency would be bound to set off repercussions around the world.

The government's senior advisors suggested that we had open to us four courses of action. One: we could support the Canadian dollar at the current rate of 95¢ in terms of United States currency. This, it was suggested, would involve a further depletion of the exchange reserves and might not produce a real solution. Two: we could support the Canadian dollar and announce our intention to hold it between 93¢ and 97¢ in United States currency. It was feared, however, that if the rate should fall to 93¢, the amounts of reserves required to prevent a further decline might prove substantial. Three: we could fix the par value of the Canadian dollar at 95¢ United States currency and seek the agreement of the International Monetary Fund to this arrangement. It was suggested that there was a considerable risk involved in defending this level. Four: we could fix the par value of the Canadian dollar at 90¢ United States currency. It was considered that the market would probably regard this valuation as reasonable, but that such a drop in the exchange rate would have a more severe effect upon domestic prices than the other options. Further, Canada might be accused of manipulating the exchange rate in order to obtain an advantage in international trade.

Mr. Fleming was convinced that fixing the par value of the Canadian dollar at 92½¢ United States currency offered the best solution, its advantages outweighing its disadvantages. The position of Canadian exporters would be improved, and any increase in exports would help to strengthen the position of the Canadian dollar in international exchange. Although complaints would be received from importers (it was to be expected that within a few months the price of imported goods such as automobiles and farm machinery might rise by an amount of up to five per cent), the proposed step would be generally popular in Canadian financial circles and the International Monetary Fund would welcome it as being in conformity with normal practice. Although the government might be criticized because of the reduced inflow of capital from abroad and on the ground that the lower value of the dollar reflected declining prestige, etc., such criticism, he argued, would not be very damaging because the Canadian public favoured a reduction in foreign influence upon the economy.

I was far from convinced. Although serious losses of confidence by investors at home and abroad in Canadian finances and in the Canadian currency have taken place since under Liberal governments, at the time there had been little experience with this sort of crisis. I demanded to know its causes. The best the economic advisors could come up with was that the run on the dollar was caused by a "crisis of confidence". Any economics undergraduate could have pointed out, as they did, that in recent years our imports of goods and services had been unduly large in relation to our exports of goods and services. Although progress towards a better balance was being made, the deficit remained large. In 1961 this deficit was slightly below $1 billion; some years earlier it had been nearer to $1.5 billion. Year by year, the current-account deficit had been covered by and interlinked with an inflow of capital from abroad in one form or another. Apart from the flexibility allowed by changes in the reserves, the only way that we, as a country, could buy more goods and services than we sold abroad was by capital inflow to cover the difference. Normally, the capital involved was readily forthcoming—indeed, from some points of view, at times too readily. I concurred that our international trade in goods and services ought to be brought into better balance. I agreed that we would be better off, at a time when the economy was less than fully employed, to borrow less and mortgage fewer of our assets abroad. Through most of 1960 and 1961 we were, in fact, attempting in various ways to lessen the inflow of capital that was outrunning our needs and maintaining the exchange rate at too high a level. The unanswered question was, why did the inflow quite suddenly first diminish and then actually reverse itself?

Finally, when it appeared that I would find no alternative, and with deepest reluctance, I agreed to sign the recommendation that the par value of the Canadian dollar be fixed at 92½¢ United States currency for the purposes of agreement with the International Monetary Fund. Implementation was to be dependent upon reports of the exchange market of 2 May. When considerable sums of United States dollars had again to be sold, it was therefore proposed that the government now obtain the concurrence of the International Monetary Fund, and that an Order-in-Council be passed that day to fix the par value as recommended. Under tremendous pressure to do so, I agreed to this course of action by telephone from Granby, Quebec. The speculative pressures against the Canadian dollar, however, did not ease until 9 May. We had in the meantime (from 1 May to 8 May) to deliver a further $130,700,000 of our exchange holdings to the market, $80,700,000 of it after we had taken action.

In retrospect, I can see no possibility of our having lost the 1962 election but for that so-called financial crisis, albeit an amateur thing when compared to those that have taken place since and are disregarded today. When I consider the exchange crises of 1968 and 1977 for example, I must wonder if official advice given me in 1962 was entirely free from partisan consideration. If I had stood my ground, we would have continued to buy Canadian dollars with our gold and foreign reserves, thereby maintaining the desired value of the Canadian dollar until after the election campaign. We could then have moved to a fixed rate of exchange in the first budget following the election. Quite probably, speculative pressure against the dollar would have diminished quickly in the face of a determined effort by the government to maintain its value. The international money market is the most sensitive, most skittish, most volatile of all markets. And once speculative pressures are brought to bear on any currency, a situation is created in which the speculators tend to bring about their own expectations. They had now won one gamble against our dollar and were soon pushing to win another. Contrary to the predictions of the officials, the pegging of the dollar did not bring an end to speculative pressures. Indeed, it provided but a three-week respite. By the middle of June the outflow of capital and the resulting drain on our exchange reserves were reaching critical proportions.

This situation provided those in the bureaucratic and financial communities with the opportunity to use the crisis to bring about a reversal of the declared fiscal policy of my government. On 28 May 1962, I received the following letter from Mr. Fleming:

I return to the urgent theme of my letters of May 3 and 21, namely, the necessity for an early statement as to the government's intention to seek an early balancing of the budget.

The announcement, on the night of May 2, that the value of the Canadian dollar was to be fixed forthwith at 92½¢ in terms of U.S. currency, and that Canada was thus, once again after nearly twelve years, in full conformity with the articles of agreement of the International Monetary Fund, has achieved its immediate objective. But the situation remains precarious and this carries implications regarding the nature of forthcoming policy pronouncements.

The most immediate objective of the announcement of May 2 was to staunch the outflow of our international reserves. By that date, the outflow had rapidly accelerated to such a high rate that it threatened our reserves, even though they still stood at more than $1.5 billion; moreover, it showed every sign of increasing rather than diminishing. The outflow has, indeed, been checked. Since May 3 up to the date of this memorandum, the loss of reserves to the market has been modest. While the movement has been checked, confidence has not been restored. Reports have come in from many quarters, both in Canada and abroad, of widespread nervousness that exists in business and financial circles. This is focused on the Canadian exchange rate. Thus, the foreign exchange situation remains precarious. The outflow could begin again in the weeks immediately ahead, and if it did it would undoubtedly feed on itself, gathering momentum. . . .

While the causes of nervousness and lack of confidence are explained and rationalized in many ways, the question most frequently asked is whether the Canadian government is really concerned about balancing its budget. People are, rightly or wrongly, wisely or unwisely, putting or keeping their funds abroad because they fear lest the basic value and integrity of the Canadian dollar may be continuously eroded by continuing massive government deficits in good times as well as bad. . . .

In this the Minister of Finance rejected his own budget to proclaim that government spending seemed somehow to have gotten out of hand; that the international value and integrity of Canada's currency could not ultimately stand up in the face of inadequate fiscal restraint, for which he was the Minister responsible; and that misgivings about the national finances had translated themselves into misgivings about the value of the Canadian dollar. No doubt, he was acting in good faith in accepting the advice of his senior officials. The fact remains that their advice was not only politically disastrous but continued to fly in the face of the basic facts of the Canadian economy.

The immediate political effect of pegging the Canadian dollar at 92½¢ United States currency was to provide the Liberal Party with an opportunity they would never have otherwise had. They were able to effectively foster and exploit the popular notion in the Canadian cities that bordered the United States that the Canadian dollar was now, in consequence of devaluation, somehow despoiled. The discounted dollar or "Diefendollar", as their election propaganda described it, was somehow seen as being worth far less than 92½¢ American. We had, prior to the election, used the exchange fund to force down the value of the Canadian dollar to a level of about 95¢ United States. Fixing the value at 92½¢ was hardly more than a formalization of government policy that had been in effect for over a year. But the Diefendollar caught the popular imagination as no other Liberal propaganda trick ever had or would, and it was associated in the public mind with gross mismanagement of the economy, which, as the preceding pages of this chapter indicate, was the furthest thing from the truth. The outcome, on 18 June, was that we lost almost every constituency that bordered the United States.

I do not raise objections to the utilization by a political

party of all available opportunities to increase its advantage in an election campaign. But the irresponsible charges by Mr. Pearson and his colleagues that the Conservative Party was somehow leading Canada into a rerun of the Great Depression could only add to market uneasiness and uncertainty. As I told the fifteen hundred people gathered in the Three Rivers Armouries on 6 June, I thought Mr. Pearson's misrepresentation of this matter "unworthy of any leader of a great party". The Pearson slogan in 1962 should have been "rule or ruin". Today, after fourteen years of Liberal financial wizardry, the purchasing power of the Canadian dollar is approximately half of what it was during my administration.

The only explanation of the 1962 financial crisis that makes any sense is that it was orchestrated for political reasons. Its object was to get rid of my government. Canada's point of economic vulnerability was the billions of dollars of foreign capital invested here. Thus, our "exposure" to the danger of outward movement of capital was enormous. The crisis began with a "spooking" of the New York money market. I believe that it is more than possible, indeed highly probable, that the administration of President Kennedy used its influence to bring this about. It is true that I have no direct proof of this, but given the relations of my government with the Kennedy administration as documented in Chapter Seven of Volume Two and in earlier chapters of this volume, and given the extent to which there is now public evidence proving the Kennedy administration's culpability in the most outrageous acts of direct interference in the domestic political affairs of other countries, and the extent to which the Kennedy administration is now known to have aided the Liberal Party in the 1962 election, I doubt that the average reader's credulity will be much strained by the suggestion that the financial difficulties in 1962 began with the help of the United States administration. The timing of the pressure against the Canadian dollar made the exchange-rate policy the major election issue. I have already described the utter ridicule that the Liberal Party heaped upon our decision to fix the rate of the Canadian dollar. Its leader stated categorically that this would be the first thing they would set aside if elected. They came into office in 1963. The exchange rate established by my government remained in effect for another six years!

Certainly the Liberals found allies enough on Bay Street. So accustomed were particular powerful interests to taking for granted their ownership of the Conservative Party that many have yet to recover from their shock at my returning it to the control of the people. These "fat cats" of finance discovered, to their horror, that mine was a government not prepared to bow to their whims and wishes. Their attacks on my government, as I recall it, began when I refused a request from the chartered banks to remove the six-per-cent ceiling on interest rates provided for under statute. These moguls of finance, who had now added James Coyne to their ranks, obviously found the Liberals somewhat more amenable. Indeed, after Mr. Pearson came into power, the interest ceiling was removed, and interest rates across Canada, along with bank profits, began to touch the heights. When it appeared in 1962 that there was going to be a move led by the oil companies and the major bakeries to exploit the pegging of the dollar for increased profits, I served notice on 7 June at Magog, Quebec, that I would not tolerate any group or corporation in this country, no matter how powerful, taking advantage of the situation. I promised them government action as "effective as it is drastic" if they tried. Shortly thereafter, representatives of both Imperial Oil and the George Weston Company announced that they would not be raising prices after all.

Not the least of the Liberal Party's allies was the Canadian Broadcasting Corporation. In its reporting of the

1962 election, it was guilty of rank partisanship. In a memorandum written immediately following the election, I noted of the CBC: "All we asked was that there should be no politics from without or any from within. There was none from without." What good are the facts if they are reported in such a way that no one believes them? My message, over and over again, during the campaign was that the economy was healthy. The record is there for anyone who would examine it. In 1962, Canada's Gross National Product increased by eight per cent; every quarter showed an increase over the preceding quarter. Manufacturing production rose by eight per cent. Mining output was up eight per cent. Corporation profits were up eleven per cent over the average in 1961. Labour income was up almost twelve per cent over 1961. Farm cash income was up about 4.3 per cent. For the second consecutive year Canada recorded a trade surplus. Total savings rose 21 per cent, to $6.9 billion. And Liberal predictions of doom and gloom to the contrary (Mr. Pearson actually predicted a 34-per-cent increase in unemployment in the next two years), total employment increased in 1962 by 168,000 persons, or about 2.8 per cent. At the same time, Canada, in 1962, had the best record of price stability of any industrialized nation. The above statistics can hardly be the picture of an economy being led to wreck and ruin through irresponsible fiscal policies. Yet my statements were treated with an air of disbelief. Conversely, three months after the election, Mr. Pearson was still being uncritically reported when he charged that during the campaign I had practised "gross and unpardonable deceit . . . in regard to the nation's financial position". On the evening of 14 June, Mr. Pearson stated in a major campaign address in Toronto that my government had had to spend over $300 million in foreign reserves in the last few weeks to maintain our dollar's value. This was false. It was not so reported. The

Leader of the Opposition was anticipating events by eight days and over $200 million.

Had we formed a majority government on 18 June, however, the run on the Canadian dollar would have abated without our borrowing a dime or changing one item in our fiscal approach. There was still a chance that we might succeed, and this despite a deliberately inspired and abetted dollar crisis. The Gallup Poll showed a Liberal decline of six per cent between 26 May and 13 June, as some of the Liberal tactics began to backfire. The Canadian public was beginning to appreciate the deception of the Liberal Party. Prices remained stable. Unemployment was decreasing. Exports were increasing; indeed, devaluation greatly assisted the balance of our merchandise account.

Our campaign promises, certainly, could not have led to public misgivings about future national finances. The program that I outlined at London, Ontario, on 5 May, which the Toronto *Telegram* called a "16-point prosperity blueprint", was a far cry from the ill-conceived, "pie in the sky" Liberal platform which some estimated might cost the taxpayer as much as a 45- to 50-per-cent increase in taxes. I called for the appointment of a Royal Commission on Taxation; updating measures of social justice to include portable pensions and a contributory health insurance plan; new government support for the modernization of secondary industries; production of foods now imported; construction within a reasonable time of an oil pipeline across Canada; a start on a second trans-Canada highway; action to underwrite economic growth in all its phases; steps to keep Canada's credit facilities in line with the advantages available for foreign competitors; research into northern natural gas and resource possibilities; more national-development projects, such as the causeway to Prince Edward Island and new harbours and wharves; an integrated national plan for land and water use; ample credit for agriculture and a revised policy for the movement of feed grains; an extension of vocational-training programs to retired people; and means to provide the small investor with a share in the development of Canada. As an outline of our intentions for the next four to five years, it was an extension of the national development program we had begun in 1957 and 1958. Certainly it was well within our means as a nation and did not, as did the Opposition parties' programs, hold forth the prospect of never-ending federal deficits. I might add that this platform encountered criticism from within our party ranks in Toronto and Montreal for being so restrained.

The entire Liberal campaign had been Kennedy-inspired. Leading Liberals have admitted that their political handbook for the 1962 election was Theodore White's *The Making of the President, 1960*; certainly they had enough Democratic Party personnel floating around the country to make their handbook redundant. Louis Harris, the pollster upon whose work President Kennedy had built a winning campaign, was "lent" to the Liberal Party. According to Professor Denis Smith's biography of Walter Gordon, *Gentle Patriot* (pp. 86-7), Harris's presence was kept a closely guarded secret, even within the ranks of the Liberal Party. It was Harris who directed Keith Davey, Walter Gordon, and Tom Kent in the organization of the Liberal campaign. Wisely, Mr. Pearson was counselled not to dwell on the specifics of the Liberal platform, which were as socialist as anything to be found in the New Democratic Party program. Hazen Argue, who was the left wing of the CCF's left wing before he joined the Liberals, was right at home with Lester Pearson, Walter Gordon, Tom Kent, Mitchell Sharp, and Maurice Lamontagne—the so-called Liberal brains trust. It was the one time in my life I expressed in public a sympathy for the plight of Jack Pickersgill; he had been left out of his party's "brains" group.

I was under no illusion in terms of the probable outcome of the campaign. The only time that I was more than three or four seats off in my personal prediction was in 1958. When the election was called on 19 April 1962, I predicted 178 Conservative seats. When we pegged the dollar on 2 May, I thought we might lose. As the campaign progressed, I began to revise my estimate upwards to the point where it seemed possible that we might squeak through. The turning point, as I saw it, was the Vancouver meeting on 30 May. When I stepped to the podium in the Forum that evening, I was not allowed to speak. Organized anarchy had brought together the voices of the young communists, socialists, and university Liberals under the direction of a Vancouver Liberal who was later distinguished for his services by the Pearson government. Ten thousand people had gathered together to learn my views. They were prevented from doing so. The protesters that evening had no interest in the meaning of democracy; they had no interest in the right of each and every person to express himself. I appealed to them. They would not listen. The Forum was filled with cries of "Ban — Ban — Ban the Bomb", "Jobs — Jobs — Jobs", rude jeers, ruder signs, fights, yells, screams. Had it not been for Colonel Cecil Merritt, v.c., who, in the spirit of his leadership at Dieppe, led a contingent of Young Conservatives into the centre aisle to form a human barrier, the platform would have been overrun by hooligans. The Liberal Party overreached itself that evening. By denying me the right to speak, by subjecting the Prime Minister of Canada to such harassment, they made us tens of thousands of friends in every part of Canada.

The following Saturday at a meeting at Chelmsford, adjacent to the city of Sudbury, there they were again. Not the same people but the same spirit and the same "Vote Pearson" banners. Again the reception was noisy, raucous, and rude. But a new dimension was added: Olive and I were threatened with physical violence. Indeed, it was the worst example of mobocracy that I have ever witnessed. The Conservative candidate, Mr. Don Gillis, was so shaken by a blow to the back of his neck as he entered the hall that he was unable to speak. Following my speech, to the accompaniment of rocks striking the walls and windows, our organizers wanted us to leave by the back door. I would have none of it. I suggested that Olive do so, but she refused and stayed, as always, by my side. She was superb. How much I now regret her being subjected to the brutal itineraries of five national election campaigns; during two of them she was on crutches. She insisted on being at my side. I could not have talked her into staying home. That day in Chelmsford, as the threatening crowd closed in and a placard swung by a Goliath struck me on the head, she gave that assailant an experience to remember: her sharp elbow in his solar plexus and did he double up! Finally we got to our automobile. The mob tried to tip our car on its side. Although I had an egg-sized swelling on my head for a couple of days, this scene was another black eye for the Opposition. When the Vancouver and Chelmsford meetings were taken together with Donald Fleming's non-meeting in St. John's, Newfoundland, on 7 June, the public caught a view of a conspiracy to prevent the truth from being heard, a side of the Liberal Party that their Madison Avenue strategy tried to hide.

Mr. Fleming had been invited to address the Rotary Club of St. John's to explain the Conservative policy on devaluation. Premier Smallwood intervened to prevent this meeting by threatening to withdraw provincial sponsorship of a Rotary convention if the St. John's branch let Mr. Fleming speak. Public reaction to these events was so strong that a letter was sent from Liberal headquarters to its candidates everywhere saying that nothing further must be done against me because it was hurting the Liberal cause.

One intervention that I did not expect was that of the Minister of Agriculture. On 8 June, Mr. Hamilton announced in Vancouver that the 92½¢ exchange rate was a compromise between those in the Cabinet who favoured a 90¢ rate and those who supported a 95¢ rate. He went on to indicate that he favoured the 90¢ rate as "defensible with Canada's negative trade balance". His statement did the government a great deal of harm. His views were interpreted to mean that there might be some immediate change in the exchange rate. Because he was an important Minister, was from Saskatchewan, and was a close personal friend of mine, he was believed. Thus, despite the strongest statements to the contrary by Mr. Fleming, the confidence that remained in the dollar was for the moment shattered. On Tuesday, 12 June, four days after Mr. Hamilton's statement, we had to deliver $35.3 million of our foreign exchange holdings to the market. On 13 June, sales totalled $17.4 million; on 14 June, $17 million; and on 15 June, $30 million. On Monday, 18 June, election day, the selling activity in Canadian dollars in New York began what has been called "a frantic week". On Monday, sales were $41,250,000; on Tuesday, $65,400,000; on Wednesday, $46,300,000; on Thursday, $44,050,000; and on Friday, $43 million. The consequence was that we not only had to seek international financial assistance to shore up the Canadian dollar, but had to introduce a program of emergency financial measures. In the midst of all this, Mr. Hamilton appeared on television on 21 June to state that there was no crisis! Had the Minister involved been anyone other than Alvin Hamilton, who had retrieved the farm vote after the disastrous period of Douglas Harkness in the Agriculture portfolio, I would have fired him on the spot, as some of our colleages demanded.

Election day 1962 brought the following results:

Conservatives	116
Liberals	100
NDP	19
Social Credit	30

We had lost seventeen per cent of the popular vote. The Liberals had gained four per cent. The urban centres had in large measure fallen for the Liberal Diefendollar tactics. Significantly, twenty-six Quebec constituencies had chosen to believe neither Liberal lies nor Conservative truth: in confusion, they fell victim to the simplistic economics of Réal Caouette's Créditistes. On 8 July 1962, Daniel Johnson, then Leader of Quebec's Union Nationale Party, wrote me:

> You deserved better and more from Quebec and Ontario. I am sorry that the people did not get the message—not easy to beat the C.B.C.
>
> Knowing your exceptional ability as a parliamentarian, I am sure you will pull the party through this crisis.
>
> Mr. Théo Ricard scored beautifully against a big gun—it could have been alike in many other constituencies.
>
> I hope your health is holding up. Very best regards to Mrs. D.
>
> Daniel J.
>
> My full cooperation is yours.

Having failed to win a majority, we had now to stop the run on the dollar by other means. We were a minority government with a national crisis on our hands. I had little choice but to accept the advice of the senior officials as to a program of emergency measures. Our exchange reserves had now fallen below the $1,000 million level, which these officials contended was the minimum we could safely hold. There was a danger that they could vanish entirely within a month or two, leaving us at the mercy of the market from day to day. The essence of the problem was to regain the confidence of foreign and Canadian investors in the Canadian dollar. The fact that they were wrong in feeling that we were not paying enough attention to "sound" financial policies was no longer the point. They were the ones whose opinion was important now, and if we were to regain confidence we would have to demonstrate convincingly our intention to balance the budget within a reasonable time, and to improve the balance of our international income and expenditure so that there would be less dependence on imports of capital. The circumstances required that I act promptly, decisively, and without compromise. I was the Prime Minister. I was where the buck stopped. I expected to be vilified for this abrupt change of course made necessary by the election outcome. It was up to me to be strong enough to take a position that transcended normal priorities and policies. Thus on Sunday, 24 June, I called upon "all Canadians to support, in a spirit of national purpose, these measures which are required to assure and conserve the strength of the national economy."

The program I outlined included four major elements. One: temporary tariff surcharges were imposed on approximately one-half of Canada's imports. The surcharges applied to imports from all countries except the few subject to general tariff rates. A temporary graduated surcharge was imposed on all imports except for an exempt category of highly essential goods which entered directly into the stream of Canadian production and costs. A five-per-cent surcharge was placed on $2,300,000 in imports where Canadian substitutes were available or where surplus capacity existed in Canada. Imports valued at $650 million bore a surcharge of ten per cent, and on another $150 million, mainly luxury items, a fifteen-per-cent surcharge was imposed. It was estimated that this measure would produce revenues upward of $200 million in a full year. Two: duty exemptions for tourists returning from the United States were reduced to $25 worth of goods three times a year, and from overseas countries to $100 once a year. It was estimated that this action would greatly reduce the upwards of $100 million of foreign exchange per annum consumed by the Canadian public in this way. Three: I indicated that revised estimates would be placed before Parliament providing for a $250 million reduction in government expenditures, which, combined with the increased revenues from surcharges, would reduce the budget deficit by approximately $450 million. Further, I gave assurance that cash balances increased by purchases of Canadian dollars would be used to finance increases in reserves and not to meet ordinary expenditures. Since 1 January 1962, accretions to cash through this source had amounted to approximately $1,000 million. Finally, I announced that the government had arranged for a drawing of $300 million from the International Monetary Fund, that reciprocal currency arrangements had been made with the United States Federal Reserve system and the Bank of England for credits of $250 million and $100 million respectively, and that a line of credit of $400 million from the Export-Import Bank of Washington had been opened.

The surcharges were effected by Order-in-Council. The power under Section 4(1) of the Customs Tariff Act was used to withdraw the benefits of preferential and most-favoured-nation rates. Then, under Section 22 of the Financial Administration Act, all tariff increases were remitted in excess of five, ten, and fifteen per cent. Tourist exemptions were reduced under the Export and Import Permits Act and the Bretton Woods Agreement Act. In addition, there was the Liberal precedent of 1947 when the three steps taken to conserve foreign exchange involved, one, the reduction of tourist exemptions; two, the prohibition of imports of certain goods; and three, the imposition of special excise taxes on certain goods. The difference between our actions and those of the King government in 1947 was that their actions were clearly illegal; ours were not. The Opposition suggestion that we had taken an unconstitutional course was in keeping with their conduct during the election campaign. As the Deputy Minister of Justice noted in a memorandum to his Minister on 7 October 1962: "There is no principle, law or custom to the effect that the complete text of a taxation measure must be found only in Acts of Parliament. It is surely so elementary that it does not require demonstration that Parliament can confer on subordinate agencies authority to impose taxes."

The economy and the country needed a cooling-off period after the heat of the election. I therefore rejected the advice of those who felt Parliament should be immediately called. I said in speaking to the nation on 24 June that this was necessary "so that time will be given for political passions to subside and be followed by calm reason which, I have always found, is the basis of effective discussion and consideration."

To round out the story, the run on the Canadian dollar completely abated by the beginning of July. The figures for that month showed a gain of $310,751,000 in our foreign reserves; for August, $248,350,000. The economy proved as healthy as I said it was, and the Opposition charges a sham and a fraud, so much so that I was able to announce on 30 March 1963 that all import surcharges were being eliminated, effective Sunday midnight, 31 March. Major relaxations of the surcharges had already taken place on 16 October 1962, 15 November 1962, and 19 February 1963. Canada's foreign-exchange reserves stood at $2.59 billion at the end of February 1963.

As I said in making the announcement: "The final abolition of the temporary import surcharges only nine months after their imposition reflects the strength and resilience of the Canadian economy and the firm confidence of people at home and abroad in the stability of the Canadian dollar."

CHAPTER SIX

ALTHOUGH THE PROBLEMS TO BE FACED following the election of 18 June 1962 were very serious indeed, it is true that there were consolations. Support for the One Canada policies of my government had not been seriously eroded in the Maritime and Western provinces. And I could not blame our failure to attain a majority on Quebec; there was only a four-seat difference between the number of Conservatives defeated in Quebec and those defeated in Ontario. We were still the government, albeit a minority one.

In retrospect, the party did a poor job during the election campaign in capitalizing on the benefits that would (and did) accrue from devaluation. We entered the electoral fray full of confidence; I recall no one in Cabinet who did not agree, when the decision to go to the people was made, that the political climate was favourable. Their attitude, apparently, was that no one had to worry, the leader would carry the load, and things would turn out as they had before. We stood on our record and did not adapt sufficiently to meet the challenge of the Liberal attack. The final phase of the exchange crisis had come upon us so suddenly that there was no opportunity to fully consult the entire Cabinet before its first post-election meeting on 23 June. The emergency program had to be announced to the nation on 24 June. Events had crowded in upon us. There was to be little respite in the months that followed.

The Liberals immediately served notice that they had thrown scruple to the winds in a naked pursuit of power. In his public statements of 24 and 26 June on our program to end the exchange crisis, Mr. Pearson allowed partisan considerations to govern his response to a serious situation; and this despite the fact that the Governor of the Bank of Canada, on my instruction, had provided him with the fullest information before the emergency measures were announced. Further, he and his colleagues rejected my appeal for a political cooling-off period. Their public attacks were unrelenting. When the session opened on 27 September, they threatened to plunge the country into a constitutional crisis by using the Liberal majority in the Senate to defeat any bills that passed the House with which they disagreed. As the session entered its second month, the Liberal Party completely abandoned its heritage and suffered the ignominy of failing to defeat us even when sinking to the unprecedented depths of supporting the Social Credit myth of debt-free money in an effort to do so. Although I could never have predicted this particular event, the writing was on the wall from the beginning that the Liberal Party would do anything to regain what they had lost in 1957.

The CCF–New Democratic Party, with nineteen seats under Tommy Douglas (after he entered the House in a by-election), was a party in which principles had some meaning. Social Credit, despite all the absurd posturings by Robert Thompson and all the contradictory statements by Réal Caouette, could be expected to behave more responsibly than the Liberals. Though they held thirty seats (twenty-six from Quebec), it was possible that the next election might prove the Socreds something of a twelve-day wonder; I believed Mr. Caouette to be a responsible man and enough of a practical politician to know this.

As to my own options, my first decision was to reject the idea, supported by some, of an immediate dissolution. The country and the dollar needed a chance to recover from the election just past. This meant that I would carry on as Prime Minister, at least temporarily. I needed time to weigh carefully my responsibilities. What concerned me most about the election was that part of the electorate seemed to have been convinced by Liberal propaganda and the willing media that I was to be distrusted in every public utterance. This was the Liberal strategy—to destroy me personally and thereby defeat my government.

The position of Prime Minister is at all times a lonely one. A Prime Minister must guard every word, except with those few people who over the years have proved themselves completely trustworthy and politically wise. My two closest friends and political supporters, both with me since the Leadership Convention of 1942, at this critical moment were lost to me. The Honourable David J. Walker, having been defeated by a few hundred votes in Toronto's Rosedale riding, returned to his law practice in Toronto. Then, on 7 July, Senator William R. Brunt was killed in an automobile accident. Senator Brunt was to me as Colonel House had been to President Woodrow Wilson of the United States. He was my confidant in every political matter. A tower of strength, he was possessed of an abundant common sense, a philosopher with a practical knowledge of politics.

In the circumstances of the financial crisis, Leslie Frost thought it would be beneficial to give the Canadian business community a visible sign that we were sensitive to their needs and aspirations. This might be achieved by the appointment of Wallace McCutcheon, a Bay Street giant, to the Senate and to the government. I regard my agreement to this idea as the most serious mistake I could have made. I believe, however, that had Bill Brunt lived, I would never have had cause to make this judgment, for he would have found out what McCutcheon was up to in time to offset it.

Bill had served as Deputy Government Leader in the Senate. I wanted to honour him with the Speakership of the Senate when Parliament was convoked. He replied, "Under no circumstances. I can't do any political work in that." I urged him to stay in Ottawa over the weekend to study the Speaker's position and to review some of the past Speakers' rulings. I looked forward to discussing further my offer to him when I returned the following Monday. On Saturday, 7 July, Olive and I flew out to Winnipeg. That same day, Bill Brunt decided to drive home to Hanover, Ontario. He never reached his destination.

In Winnipeg, I was to attend a never-to-be-forgotten gathering of Canadians of Ukrainian descent, which is distinguished in my memory by the address of Harry Hays, then Mayor of Calgary, who ventured into the fields of poetry and philosophy, recommending a study of the Renaissance as a solution to national and international problems. It was during the course of my after-dinner remarks that Olive received word of Senator Brunt's death. Knowing the effect that this news would have on me, she did not tell me until the last of our official duties for the evening had been fulfilled. I was shattered.

Two weeks later, I sustained a painful fracture of my right ankle. At the time, Olive and I were at Harrington Lake, the Prime Minister's summer residence in the Gatineau hills. I might mention that when we came into office in 1957, the summer house at Harrington was scheduled for demolition. We looked it over and thought that, with a bit of fixing up, it would serve our needs as a place to relax during the hot and humid Ottawa summer. I decided that a small expenditure would make it livable. Olive bought material and made curtains and slip-covers. It would never have occurred to either of us to require more. In any event, it was there that my ankle fell victim to a groundhog hole.

My physicians decided not to put a walking cast on my fractured ankle and prescribed a bed-rest cure. Their advice was medically sound, but politically disastrous. An invalid's bedroom is neither an ideal place for Cabinet meetings nor a location suited to keeping track of the political manoeuvrings about one. But flat on my back I remained. As to my own future, I accepted the advice of the Honourable Gordon Churchill to stand fast.

"Stand fast, Craigellachie!" The battle cry of the Clan Grant, these words symbolize in Canadian history the determination of Sir John Macdonald, George Stephen, and Donald Smith to defy near-overwhelming adversity in bringing to completion the Canadian Pacific Railway. When, on 7 November 1885, the last spike to bind Canada together was driven, it was at Craigellachie, British Columbia. In the months following the 1962 election, I took courage from Donald Creighton's magnificent volumes on Sir John A. Macdonald, especially his victory over that "malignant host" of enemies who tried to thwart his nation-building work.

It was in the circumstances described above that I decided on the composition of my new Cabinet. Five Ministers had gone down to defeat on 18 June, including three from Quebec—the Honourable William Hamilton, the Honourable Noël Dorion, and the Honourable Jacques Flynn. Several other portfolios were also open to change. Those that I did not intend to alter were: the Honourable Howard Green in External Affairs; the Honourable Douglas Harkness in Defence; the Honourable Alvin Hamilton in Agriculture; the Honourable George Hees in Trade and Commerce; the Honourable Angus MacLean in Fisheries; the Honourable Michael Starr in Labour; and the Honourable Léon Balcer in Transport.

The changes that attracted the most attention were the shift of the Honourable Donald Fleming from Finance to Justice, the Honourable Davie Fulton's move from Justice to Public Works, and the Honourable George Nowlan's from National Revenue to Finance. It had become obvious that, as Minister of Finance, Donald Fleming unfortunately had lost the confidence of the business community. Many expressed the view that the basic fault of devaluation was that it was five years too late. They felt that the origins of the exchange-rate problem went back to the days when the Honourable Douglas Abbott had been Minister of Finance under Mr. St. Laurent. There is some justification for this view: one of our first items of business as a government in 1957 had been to review the purchase in the last days of the St. Laurent government of $6,250,000 of United States exchange in an endeavour to create an artificial demand for United States dollars so that the Canadian dollar would be held down to a premium of less than five per cent. Also, the Department of Finance came under increasingly heavy criticism, not for often doing the wrong thing, but for often doing the right thing in the wrong way. As Revenue was a proper training-ground for the Finance portfolio, Mr. Nowlan's move from the one to the other was logical.

I informed Mr. Fleming of my decision to change his portfolio to Justice on 2 August, following a Cabinet meeting held in my bedroom. This he accepted without argument, although he did call me on the evening of 7 August to inform me that he would like me to consider appointing him President of the Council as well. I said this could not be done because it would create divisions among our colleagues, who would consider it an act of preferment. Mr. Fleming immediately withdrew his request; no one could have been more considerate throughout these discussions than he.

Davie Fulton was less agreeable. When I advised him on 7 August that a change had to be made, I told him that I was reluctant to speak frankly and fully because, if the future was anything like the past, our conversation might find its way into the papers. He said there was no basis for my attitude. I then referred him to what had taken place in 1957 when, following the election, I attempted to secure his agreement to be Speaker of the House of Commons. He had refused. No one knew about our conversation. I kept no minute nor did I tell anyone, but an account of it later appeared in the Montreal *Gazette*. I also reminded him that in December 1961, prior to our Cabinet meeting in Quebec City, I had a lengthy chat with him at 24 Sussex. There he had argued strongly against the Cabinet changes I proposed. Again, no one knew about our conversation. Yet, shortly thereafter, it was referred to in the press, in Arthur Blakely's column, with Mr. Fulton receiving an undeserved credit for convincing me not to make those changes. I had no quarrel with Mr. Blakely in this regard; I considered him a worthy representative of his profession.

When I told him that I planned to move him to National Revenue, Mr. Fulton told me that he could not accept this. When I pointed out that three weeks before, he and five of our colleagues had called on me and each agreed that they would accept whatever portfolio was given them, he claimed that he had made his acceptance conditional with the words "within reasonable limits". If he had to move from Justice he wanted either External Affairs or Finance. I told him that I had no intention of moving Howard Green and that I knew of no one who thought him qualified for Finance. He considered a transfer to National Revenue demeaning; I believe he rather alienated Mr. Nowlan when he presented his views on the relative unimportance of this portfolio the next day.

On 8 August, Mr. Fulton informed me that he would be

agreeable to accepting Public Works. I had earlier considered having the Honourable Hugh John Flemming move from Forestry to Public Works in view of the fact that he had held a similar portfolio in New Brunswick for six years. This question was settled when my colleagues arrived at 24 Sussex for an informal meeting on the morning of 9 August. Mr. Fulton was absent when I outlined the problem, and Mr. Flemming volunteered to make way for him. I said that I had no objection if our other colleagues agreed. They did. Mr. Fulton arrived and was so informed. He did not respond immediately and it was only after he had received a telephone call that he had been waiting for that he handed me this note: "I will take Public Works."

Immigration policy had proved a serious problem during the election campaign. The Honourable Ellen Fairclough had done well in this portfolio, but the ethnic communities had never fully accepted her, despite the fact that our 1962 immigration legislation, for the first time in Canadian history, eliminated racial discrimination from our immigration laws. Further, because of action taken against illegal Chinese immigrants, one of our Members had been defeated: Parliament's first Member of Chinese descent, Douglas Jung of Vancouver Centre, an able parliamentarian with an outstanding record of war service in the Far East. In November 1961, following a meeting in Winnipeg with representatives of the Chinese community of that city, it was decided that prosecutions under way should be proceeded with, but, as there was no hope of making much progress otherwise, that there should be an immediate acceleration in granting entry certificates to those Chinese who had entered Canada illegally but had co-operated with the authorities by admitting their wrongdoing. It was further directed that the Hong Kong police should no longer be employed by the RCMP to screen prospective immigrants to Canada. Mrs.

Fairclough had done her best to follow through on this, but Mr. Fulton apparently continued to use the Hong Kong police, whose conduct was reprehensible and tyrannical.

After some discussion, all in good spirit, Mrs. Fairclough agreed to transfer to the Post Office. Had we had a majority, she might have gone to the Senate. When I mentioned this, she said that she would have considered it a happy conclusion to her political career.

After much thought, I decided to leave the Honourable Raymond O'Hurley in Defence Production and the Honourable Pierre Sévigny as Associate Minister of National Defence. Mr. O'Hurley raised no complaint. Pierre Sévigny, however, was very disgruntled when he did not receive a new portfolio. Unfortunately, he had a higher opinion of his own talents, and a lower opinion of his Quebec colleagues' talents, than did anyone else. I came very close to moving Sévigny to Veterans Affairs, although I doubt now that this move would have pleased him as important enough. It is sufficient to note that the Minister of Veterans Affairs since October 1960, the Honourable Gordon Churchill, gave lie to the notion that in the practice of my government one portfolio was regarded as senior to another. Sévigny could not see this, and his immediate reaction was to threaten to resign when he discovered that his position had not been "advanced" in the new Cabinet. When I saw Sévigny again, he had changed his mind; he would not break ranks and let down the other members, he said.

With regard to a fourth Minister from Quebec, my choice came down to either Paul Martineau or Théo Ricard. Both had claims to promotion. Ricard had won a handsome victory in St. Hyacinthe–Bagot, Martineau a narrow one in Pontiac–Témiscamingue (although not as narrow as his 1963 victory in which his one-vote margin was decided by the Returning Officer's flip of a coin).

Paul Martineau, a Royal Canadian Air Force veteran, had served as my Parliamentary Secretary from 19 November 1959 until his appointment as Deputy Speaker on 18 January 1962. He became the Minister of Mines and Technical Surveys. Ricard became my Parliamentary Secretary and remained so until I made him Minister without Portfolio on 18 March 1963.

The Honourable J. Waldo Monteith had served as Minister of Health and Welfare since August 1957. He was a good and trusted friend and an excellent Minister, who was never the puppet of his senior officials and would have served well in any number of portfolios had I decided to make more extensive changes.

The Honourable Ernest Halpenny had become Minister without Portfolio on 11 October 1960; he now became Secretary of State. From London, Ontario, he had been in the pharmaceutical manufacturing business. Although he had come highly recommended by Wallace McCutcheon, his presence in the Cabinet can only be justified if one considers it imperative to provide the city of London with Cabinet representation.

Finally, I come to that error to end all errors: the appointment of Malcolm Wallace McCutcheon as Senator and Minister without Portfolio. He was Canadian big business's Mr. Big, one of Canada's leading industrialists and financiers. Wealthy, charming in a blustering sort of way, with a big, rough, gravelly voice, he was possessed of Machiavellian cunning. He pretended to be my friend and convinced me that he was.

Initially I hoped McCutcheon would be my answer to Kennedy's McNamara. I appointed him to the powerful six-man Treasury Board. When the Glassco Commission Report was brought down, I put him in charge of its implementation. It does not take long to gain the measure of a Cabinet colleague's capabilities. It was obvious after three or four weeks that he was not going to make a successful transition from business to government, at least not in the short term. Given his general lack of aptitude for things governmental, I would never have imagined that he seriously entertained political ambitions. Had anyone told me at the time that during the period of my convalescence he was at the centre of meetings designed to develop and encourage dissent within the Cabinet, I would not have believed it. Of course, no one did tell me until it was too late; not a word, not a boo. It was, I suspect, McCutcheon's wealth that drew to him certain types of hangers-on, be they Cabinet Ministers or whatever, much in the way a magnet attracts paper clips.

After the new Cabinet was sworn in, on 9 August 1962, in my bedroom at 24 Sussex, it was a question of getting on with the business of the nation. I was to attend the Commonwealth Prime Ministers' Meeting that September in London (see Volume Two, Chapter Seven). More important, the Cabinet had to prepare for the opening of the new Parliament. In the circumstances of a minority government where there were no guarantees as to how long we would retain Parliament's support, the course of wisdom was to consider the Speech from the Throne an Election Manifesto. I held the view that something out of the ordinary must be forecast in the Speech from the Throne, and carried out. This would be difficult, however, because the emergency program of 24 June had provided for a reduction of the government's role in Canada's economic growth. In only one area had we permitted an increase in expenditures, and that was in maintaining the development of the vocational training program. We might state our commitment to development, expansion, growth, the production of jobs, the acceleration of industry, and the maintenance of agriculture, giving to the people of Canada a degree of assurance such as no other government ever had, but how were we to achieve this on a housekeeping budget? Before I left for London, I gave Donald Fleming, who would be Acting Prime Minister in my absence, the following memorandum:

I am somewhat concerned that when I get back everything will not be ready for the Opening of the Session and would therefore appreciate it if you would fully explore the possibility of the legislative programme additional to that already prepared, for as in my opinion the enactment of the uncompleted portion of the last budget will be insufficient.

1) There must be something of a nature that will bring about new hope for the people as a whole. . . .

2) The Speech from the Throne should be drafted at once. This may be considered to be an election manifesto and as such should set forth not only the general plan for development in the next five years for national expansion in development, trade, etc., it should emphasize the fact that the economy is rising very considerably and has been in the last year, and to meet the Opposition argument that the international exchange situation did not come about suddenly might very well contain references to the exchange trials that Canada passed through in 1947. . . .

Parliament opened on 27 September 1962. The Speech from the Throne, read by Governor General Georges Vanier, and televised nationally, was a progressive, forward-looking document. It read in part:

My government will ask you, as a significant step in rounding out the concept of confederation, to consider a resolution to provide for the "repatriation" of the constitution of Canada and to invite the concurrence of the provinces to this end.

As another means of making manifest the Canadian identity, my government will invite the provinces to a conference for consultation regarding the choice of a national flag and other national symbols.

Measures will be placed before you to provide for the division of the Northwest Territories into two territories, and to provide more self government for the residents of that area as a step toward the ultimate creation of new provinces in Canada's great north. . . .

A measure will be placed before you to establish an Indian claims commission to investigate claims on the part of various tribes and bands that certain of their rights have been restricted or abrogated, and to make recommendations for the equitable and final settlement of such claims. . . .

As one of my government's measures to develop the Canadian economy, maintain a high level of employment and strengthen the balance of payments, you will be asked to approve legislation establishing a national economic development board. This board would be broadly representative and would review and report upon the state of the economy and upon economic policies. It would also have the duty of recommending to the government particular projects or measures which it considers would be in the interest of national development, including projects which may require direct governmental participation by way of financial aid or otherwise. . . .

A royal commission has been established to review the whole field of federal taxation and its impact on the Canadian economy, and to recommend reforms and improvements. . . .

Legislation will be proposed to enlarge the funds of the Farm Credit Corporation, and allow greater flexibility in their use. . . .

In order to permit the introduction of a national system of contributory old age pensions with disability and survivor benefits, an amendment to the British North America Act is required. The governments of all provinces except Quebec and Newfoundland have concurred in such an amendment. My government is prepared to recommend to you the approval of an address to Her Majesty requesting the amendment when the concurrence of these remaining provinces has been received.

As pension plans have become ever more widely extended in Canadian business, it has been increasingly recognized that measures are essential to protect the interests of those affected and in particular to ensure that the benefits earned are portable when workers move from job to job. Provincial legislation would be required for this purpose in most cases, and several provinces are considering proposals of this nature. My government will be prepared to place before you complementary legislation to deal with industries under federal jurisdiction when adequate progress has been made by provinces. . . .

The Session, from my point of view, started out better than I had anticipated. When I wrote to Leslie Frost on 7 October that: "On the basis of what has taken place so far there is reason to hope that the Government will secure a vote of confidence, a necessary step before the legislative programme can be put before the House," I had in mind the vote on 11 October. We had already survived three non-confidence motions, and would survive a fourth before that crucial vote. And we did, by a margin of 136 to 108. It was not until after the Cuban crisis that the Liberal Party moved from sullen opposition to active obstruction.

The business of Canada's Twenty-fifth Parliament should have been to deal with the implementation of the Glassco Commission Report, measures to create new jobs, the establishment of a national power grid, the repatriation of the Canadian constitution, the division of the Northwest Territories, or the establishment of an Indian Claims Commission. But no! Following the passing of the Supply Motion on 6 November, the Liberals dug in their heels and simply refused to do the business of the country.

On 14 November, the first item of the Department of Agriculture estimates was debated; it was debated again on 23 November and again on 30 November. This item was not passed. On 24 January 1963, the first item of the Department of External Affairs estimates was considered by the House. On 25 January, the same item was again considered by the House. Again, the item was not passed.

11. In February 1963 Prime Minister Diefenbaker received the Freedom of the City of London. A Pikeman in ancient armour looks on as the Prime Minister arrives at Mansion House, the official residence of the Lord Mayor of London.

12 & 13. With daughter Carolyn Weir and grandchildren at Stornoway, August 1963. (*Below*) With Happy II.

14 & 15. (*Right*) A visit to the Hebrew University of Jerusalem, September 1963. A delighted fisherman with his "limit" of salmon caught in Georgia Strait, January 1964.

18. (*Left*) Elmer Diefenbaker, Mr. Diefenbaker's younger brother, who died in June 1971.

19. (*Below*) A meeting at the Kremlin in Moscow, 15 October 1969. From left to right: Ivan Spiridinov, Chairman of the Supreme Soviet of the USSR; Howard Morgan, First Secretary at the Canadian Embassy; Joel Aldred; R. A. D. Ford, the Canadian Ambassador; and Mr. Diefenbaker.

20. Mr. and Mrs. Diefenbaker were received in audience at the Vatican by Pope Paul VI, September 1967.

On 30 January and on 1 February, the first item of the Department of Labour estimates was considered by the House for approximately seven hours. Nor was this item passed. Not one of the 492 items ready for consideration was passed, despite the fact that the complete book of estimates (the proposed spending program for the fiscal year 1962-63) had been in the hands of all Members for several months. From December 12 to 20, the full seven days available for consideration of the estimates were taken in discussing interim supply, which usually takes thirteen minutes. Only one piece of major legislation was passed: the creation of the Atlantic Development Board. The Liberals were as good as their "rule or ruin" word. Indeed, two of their front bench boasted that the Opposition would block every estimate. We survived one major or minor crisis after another. The Liberals were confident that I would be true to my word and never follow the course of the St. Laurent government in 1956, when closure was invoked to cut off the Pipeline Debate. We made no deals with the other parties and we were not defeated on the floor of the House until the United States State Department issued its infamous press release.

If the Cuban affair served to energize the Liberals in their attempt to harass us out of office, it also served as a rallying point for the gathering forces of rebellion within the Conservative Party. On 8 November 1962, George Hogan, a National Vice-President of the Progressive Conservative Association of Canada, in an address prepared for the press, but delivered to a Conservative study group in Toronto, advocated taking all possible steps to ingratiate ourselves with the United States government. In point, he argued that we should break off diplomatic relations and suspend all trade relations with Cuba; that we should give the senior Canadian officer at NORAD *carte blanche* to place Canadian air defence forces on maximum alert; and that we should move quickly to acquire defensive nuclear weapons. His analysis was simplistic and impracticable, but guaranteed to make headlines. Although I did not know it at the time, he was a close friend and under the influence of Dalton Camp. Retrospectively, Hogan's speech was the beginning of a concerted attack on my leadership that was to continue until the Convention of 1967. What McCutcheon, Hogan, *et al.*, did was to take advantage of the very real fear that had been injected into our people during the Cuban crisis. These Toronto Tories purported to see in the stance of the government an immoral anti-Americanism abhorrent to them all. The rather macabre joke was that they assumed they were attacking me when, in fact, they were simply undermining their own party to the ultimate benefit of the Liberals.

Apparently, this was part of a deliberate effort to stir up the Young Progressive Conservatives (YPC) and the University Conservatives against my leadership. They succeeded early in Manitoba, where the YPC took a public stand critical of the government on 26 October 1962. On 1 November, I wrote to the President of the Manitoba YPC, Mr. D. W. Leatherdale (son-in-law of G. W. Baldwin, M.P., who was most annoyed that he had not been made a Minister), to apprise him of my view of his actions:

While I am at all times most appreciative of ideas, to give the views of your association publicity would have been understandable if sending of the message had been a publicity stunt but I am sure that was not the case. Your telegram brought about a series of similar telegrams, one of which was from the Young Liberal Federation of Canada in which they associated themselves with the remarks directed to the government by your organization.

I went on to say that the harm done by his decision to release his views to the press might be "unrepairable". By early December, there were reports that the young Tories would demand my resignation at the party's forthcoming Annual Meeting.

Finally, I had to tell my colleagues that I would not tolerate any more of this foolishness. At our informal meeting on 8 December, I stated that if it continued, there would be only one course for me to follow. Howard Green took the view that if I resigned, the party would never come back into power. Other Ministers supported him. When I spoke with Senator Grosart that evening, I mentioned that I had in mind that the meeting in January might be a nominating convention. He said he would have no objection, providing my name was on the ballot, because this would sweep all opposition out of existence. I said that, of course, this could not be. The McCutcheonites, for the moment, pulled in their horns.

When the Annual Meeting took place in Ottawa in January 1963, my leadership was enthusiastically endorsed. What is more, the resolution on defence policy was not debated but was merely "referred to the government for its consideration and decision". The press thus was denied the spectacle of a divided Conservative Party. I was entirely satisfied with their defence resolution, which read:

WHEREAS the Progressive Conservative Government of Canada has, with courage and vigour, made an important contribution to the international deliberations on disarmament;

AND WHEREAS this meeting recognizes that the survival of mankind may well depend on reaching a proper solution to the problems of disarmament;

AND WHEREAS the Government of Canada has by its defence policy recognized its full responsibility in the field of North American defence and defence of the Free World by assuming an important integrated defence role in NATO and NORAD;

AND WHEREAS it appears to this assembly that while a sound defence policy must take into consideration the problems of disarmament such a policy need not be incompatible with a constant striving for peace;

THEREFORE BE IT RESOLVED THAT:

1) This meeting commends the Government of Canada for its part in international disarmament conferences and urges the Government to continue its constant efforts to achieve a proper and satisfactory disarmament agreement;

2) This meeting commends the Government for the role it has accepted in NATO and NORAD and for recognizing its obligations for the defence of North America and the Free World; This meeting recognizes, however, the Government's need to constantly re-assess its policy in view of technical and political changes, and nothing in this resolution shall be construed as not recognizing the need for a flexible and changing policy to promote disarmament and to protect the national security.

3) This meeting recommends to the Government of Canada that such steps as are necessary be taken, and that such negotiations with the United States as are required be concluded that recognize fully and completely Canada's sovereignty so as to make readily available for the Canadian installations and equipment that form part of the NATO and NORAD forces such nuclear warheads as are required for the defence installations, provided that the use of NORAD armaments be under the joint control of Canada and the United States, in the event that a system of nuclear disarmament with proper inspection controls is not adopted by the major powers by December 1963.

I agreed with Mr. E. A. Goodman, Q.C., who had written me in his capacity as Chairman of the Resolutions Committee on 15 January: "I strongly feel that the policy outlined in the resolution is in keeping with the feeling of the country, that it takes advantage of the great weakness in Pearson's [Scarborough] statement [on nuclear arms], and is in the best interests of Canada's future." It is of significance that Goodman was John Bassett's lawyer and George Hees's principal backer, a powerful man within the Toronto Tory hierarchy with a considerable influence over Ontario's Premier, John Robarts.

The fundamental problem affecting Conservative Party unity was, of course, the 1962 election result. To many, it seemed that the privilege of five years in office was in danger of disappearing. To the disenchanted, I was the goat. Ambitions or expectations had been endangered or thwarted.

Davie Fulton was one of those whose ambition would not let him be. I noted earlier his disenchantment with his shift from the Justice portfolio in August. He had won his Kamloops riding by over four thousand votes, so he was not in personal political danger. However, he now broached the suggestion that he move to provincial politics. When he first brought this to my attention in October 1962, I was maladroit enough to tell him that I did not believe him capable of beating the old master, W. A. C. Bennett. Fulton replied that his roots were in B.C. politics. His place, he said, was provincial. My last conversation with him before he yielded to the "draft", as he described it, was on 23 November. My notes of that meeting read as follows:

I asked him if he had made any decision as yet to go to British Columbia. He said he had not but that he was giving serious consideration to it and while he would indicate his views to a private group over the weekend at the Coast he would not make a final declaration until his return to Ottawa. . . .

He said he was surprised at the degree of support that he has and I asked him where he would run and he said he thought he would be a candidate in Salmon Arm or possibly Victoria. I asked him who would be the federal candidate in Kamloops and he said he had not come to a conclusion on that. . . .

He then asked me whether I would tell him what I would do

after the next election. I said that of course was something I
was not dealing with or even considering now although in July
I had given an indication as to what I would have done then.
This seemed to be the major reason for his calling on me.

Fulton announced his decision to accept the B.C. draft on
29 November. Yet, contrary to the stories of my vindic-
tiveness towards him that appear in some published
works, I kept him on as Minister of Public Works until
our defeat in the federal election of 8 April 1963.

There were many others who suffered a loss of their
political courage with the results of the '62 campaign.
One of these was the former Speaker of the House of
Commons, Roland Michener, who did not exactly help us
when he announced immediately after the election that
he would never run again. His argument that anyone who
had served as Speaker could not take part thereafter in
"partisan politics" was a view that has not found consen-
sus among former Speakers. When he came to see me on
14 August to present me with his credentials for appointment to the Senate, I told him it was important that he
run again. It was his understandable inattention to party
politics during his Speakership that had cost us his constituency. I had informed him many times that he was being undermined by the ideas of his Liberal "friends", but
he had never seen fit to agree. I considered that if he ran
again, he would win easily. I made it clear that I would
not award him a Senate appointment at that time. There
was nothing antagonistic in my action. I was prepared to
recognize his contribution as Speaker (even though his
rulings had often left much to be desired). It was, after all,
on my recommendation that he was subsequently made a
Privy Councillor.

Among those I did appoint to the Senate on 25 September were Grattan O'Leary, long-time Conservative and
editor of the *Ottawa Journal*. O'Leary had never been

one of my supporters, indeed he had fought me openly through the years, but he had served the party over a long period and I hoped that this recognition would contribute to the unity of the party. Appointment to the Senate, however, seemed to lessen his sense of party responsibility. Indeed, in a speech in the Senate on the evening of 7 December 1962, he devoted himself to building up the Opposition.

Another whom I appointed to the Senate was Allister Grosart, who had indicated a desire to retire from his position as the Conservative Party's National Director. This I could understand; his health demanded it. For six years, he had given unstintingly of his ability and had made personal sacrifices in the interests of the party, all at my request. Unwittingly, I contributed to my own difficulties by the appointment of Dalton Camp as his successor. At the time, I was unaware that he was the anointed of the McCutcheon group. In a memorandum of a conversation with McCutcheon, dated 12 January 1963, McCutcheon reported that party reaction to the news of Dalton Camp's proposed appointment had been excellent. "It couldn't be better," he said. I'm certain, from his point of view, this was absolutely true.

CHAPTER SEVEN

O N WEDNESDAY, 6 February 1963, the morning after defeat in the House of Commons, I called a meeting of caucus for nine-thirty a.m. This action foiled the plans of the cabal in Cabinet who, after months of clandestine meetings, had finally come up with an agreed plan to force me out.

Cabinet had been scheduled to meet that morning before caucus. At Cabinet, I was to be overwhelmed. Wallace McCutcheon, George Nowlan, George Hees, Léon Balcer, Richard Bell, Pierre Sévigny, Ernest Halpenny, and one or two others planned that each would throw down his resignation with the challenge: "It's either you or us." Davie Fulton, even though he had already accepted the Conservative leadership in British Columbia, would hand in his resignation for good measure. In the face of this mass of resignations, I would agree to their appointment of me as Chief Justice of the Supreme Court of Canada. George Nowlan would be interim Prime Minister. Caucus could do no other than acquiesce to this *fait accompli*. As I would no longer be Prime Minister, I would not be in a position to advise the Governor General of Tuesday's non-confidence vote and of the necessity for an election. The House of Commons would give the Nowlan government the confidence they had denied me. Thus, there would be no election.

A National Leadership Convention would be scheduled in the months ahead, where McCutcheon, Hees, Fulton (who would renounce provincial ambitions for this greater call), Balcer, and one or two outsiders would be the principals vying to be Leader and Prime Minister. Following the Convention, George Nowlan would retire to be Chief Justice of a newly created Nova Scotia Court of Appeals (thus satisfying his lifelong ambition to gain pre-eminence over his arch political rival, the Right Honourable James Ilsley, who was Chief Justice of the Supreme Court of Nova Scotia and who would then be Nowlan's inferior).

It was all very neat, except for one detail: it was completely dependent upon my co-operation. The fly in their ointment was their basic incompetence. They had not considered that I might change the scheduling of the Cabinet or caucus meetings. Also, they appeared not to know that the appointment of the Chief Justice of the Supreme Court of Canada, the position that was to be my "reward", is a prerogative power of the Prime Minister; they were in fact offering me what only I could give. What is more, they completely misjudged me. In a memorandum, dated 14 Feburary 1963, I wrote: "If I had chosen the easy way I would have fallen in line with them. I chose to fight. I chose to believe that the people could not be deceived and would understand."

I should have been aware of these machinations long before I actually was. I had heard rumours, as early as November 1962, that certain of my colleagues were skulking around with the message that, "for the good of the Party", I must be pushed out. I asked McCutcheon and Nowlan if they had any knowledge concerning these rumours. Nowlan, whom I had questioned on more than one occasion, expressed shock at the very thought of it. Both he and McCutcheon were most vociferous in their claims of devotion to me. No one was prepared to indicate where he stood until Harkness put in his resignation as Minister of National Defence.

It was Sunday, 3 February, and Cabinet was scheduled to meet informally at 24 Sussex from nine a.m. until two p.m. As I noted in Chapter One, I had been forewarned that Harkness was going to resign. I did not know whether this actually would happen or, if it did happen, whether he would be acting alone. I did know that my leadership had just endured a week-long editorial barrage from the pages of John Bassett's Toronto *Telegram*, and that this thundering might prelude some action by Hees or McCutcheon. At any rate, I was ready, or as ready as I could be in these circumstances.

Douglas Harkness took the opportunity provided by our discussion of whether we should immediately go to the people on the issue of United States interference in Canadian affairs (see Chapter One) to begin an assault, boldly claiming that I lacked the confidence of everyone: the Cabinet, the caucus, the party, and the country as a whole; if I refused to resign, he would! I have always felt that his use of the defence policy issue was in this instance a ruse. To make the point, and for the record, his letter of resignation and my reply are reprinted below.

My dear Prime Minister:

For over two years you have been aware that I believe nuclear warheads should be supplied to the four weapons systems we have acquired which are adapted to their use. Throughout this period I believed that they would be authorized at the appropriate time.

During the past two weeks particularly, I have made absolutely clear what I considered the minimum position I could accept, and several times have offered to resign unless it was agreed to. It has become quite obvious during the last few days that your views and mine as to the course we should pursue for the acquisition of nuclear weapons for our armed forces are not capable of reconciliation, thus it is with a great deal of regret that I now find I must tender my resignation as Minister of National Defence.

Until the last few weeks I enjoyed my five and a half years as a member of your Government and trust I have made some contribution to it and to Canada.

Yours regretfully,
Douglas Harkness

My dear Mr. Harkness:

I am naturally very much disappointed that you have taken the course of action set out in your letter of the 3rd instant and frankly I find it difficult to understand your decision.

Following lengthy discussions with our colleagues, in which you participated fully, a decision was reached which is embodied in the statement on policy I made, as reported at page 3136 of Hansard for January 25, 1963.

When I concluded my speech, you shook my hand and expressed your approval. From the position I took in the House of Commons on that day, I have not deviated. Since you approved it then, and since you later made it clear in your speech of January 31st, as reported in Hansard at page 3322 and following pages, that you supported my stand, I am at a loss to understand your suggestion now that your views and mine are not in agreement. We were on January 25th and January 31st. My views have not changed. Between then and Sunday you must have changed yours.

Much as I regret your decision, I can do no other than accept your resignation. At the same time, I wish to thank you for your service in the Cabinet, which was at all times most cooperative. I wish you well in the days ahead.

I am,
Yours sincerely,
John G. Diefenbaker

In Cabinet, I took the Harkness challenge for what it was, an attempt to unseat me. As it was obvious that he expected others to follow his lead, I seized the initiative and demanded that those of our colleagues who supported me stand up and be counted. Of those already named, all remained seated. With that I left the meeting to continue its deliberations without me.

There are many versions of what transpired between my colleagues during the hour and a half that followed. As Olive and I were having lunch together in the library, I cannot attest to the truth of any of these. What I do know is that Harkness was the only one to resign. The rest agreed to the following document:

The Cabinet expresses its loyalty to the Prime Minister and its willingness to continue to give him full support.

Without in any way imposing any condition in respect of the foregoing resolution, Cabinet is of the opinion that immediate dissolution is most undesirable and that we should meet the House of Commons tomorrow and seek by every means to avoid defeat.

Feb. 3/63

Of course, I agreed that we should stand together. I also agreed that we should attempt to continue as the government and carry on with our legislative program, if possible. The Harkness resignation was unfortunate, but it had turned out to be no more than the resignation of a single Minister. It is interesting, given the heavy play his action was to receive in the press, that resignations from successive Liberal governments since 1963 have not been portrayed as evidence of Cabinet disintegration. It was Douglas Harkness's right to resign if he disagreed with his colleagues. I have never questioned that right. Indeed, I publicly endorsed his Conservative Party candidature in the election that followed. Although he was not present when I spoke on his behalf, his wife was on the platform.

Later that Sunday afternoon, Senator McCutcheon had made the startling proposal that I become Chief Justice of the Supreme Court; he had checked it out with the other Judges, he told me, and they were agreeable. Indeed, he said to Olive, "Well, day after tomorrow your husband will be the first man who has occupied both positions in this country, and only one other person in a democracy will have done the same. Taft was President of the United States and also Chief Justice of the United States." He proposed that Nowlan be interim Prime Minister.

Then George Hees telephoned to say that he wanted to come over. When I asked where he was, he replied that he was with Davie Fulton and their wives. My initial reaction was that they should come over in the morning, but finally I agreed that they should come right over. "By yourselves," I told Hees; "leave your wives wherever they are; this is no time for the social amenities."

They arrived at nine o'clock, both in a state of some excitement. Fulton sat in the big chair in the northeast corner of the library, Hees on the other end of the davenport from me. "We're just friends meeting together," Davie said. He was not going to call me Prime Minister, but John; we were going to talk personally. Looking at Hees, he began a eulogy that put Pericles in the shade. "George is a wonderful man, they don't make them any better." At one point, Hees interjected, "Now don't, don't, don't, now Davie really, you're making it embarrassing." But despite the danger of embarrassment, Fulton continued to outline the tremendous personality and capability of this remarkable man. It was an amazing performance. Fulton said that I should give up the prime-ministership. "It is for the good of the party. We will make you Chief Justice of Canada." After about ten minutes of this, George finally said: "You have said enough now, Davie, don't say any more," and he put his hand on Fulton's right arm to quiet him. In short, my reaction to both the McCutcheon and the Fulton/Hees proposals was that I would not agree to anything of the kind, under any circumstances.

About half an hour after he left, Davie Fulton telephoned me: "I'm coming over to see you." I said, "Not now." He insisted: "I want to come, I have something very important." He came. We talked in the hallway, he at the top of his voice. "You didn't pay any attention to what I had to say about Hees. Surely you saw through what I was doing." "Well," I replied, "that's strange, after all the praise you gave him. What suggestion have you now?" "Well, surely you know there is only one person to hold the party together. Only I can do so." "Davie," I answered, "you're out. You put yourself out weeks ago. I told you not to take on the leadership of the party in B.C." He said, "I've arranged all that. I phoned today, and they're prepared, in the interests of the country, to release me." I said, "You'd better phone them back and tell them not to subject the province to that. You've got your place in B.C."

It appears the cabal became fearful that their plans would be frustrated, as it was rumoured that I might go to Government House to secure the immediate dissolution of Parliament. This is indicated by the following handwritten note from Senator McCutcheon, dated nine a.m., 4 February:

Mr. Prime Minister

I had hoped to see you before Cabinet this morning but this note will have to do.

My firm conviction is that for the good of the party we should not dissolve without being defeated—and we should endeavour to avoid defeat—which I think we can do.

For what it's worth the taxi driver this morning told me he hoped you were feeling good—because he wants you to stay in and not give way to Pearson.

To dissolve before meeting the house or before making an

honest effort to survive leaves us with only one issue as to which there is to my mind no issue as all Canadians are agreed about the U.S. action.

No one knows better than I that one does not lay down conditions to the Prime Minister—and I am not doing so.

In fairness however I must repeat that if dissolution occurs before the House meets today or before we make a determined effort to carry on the government of the country I shall be forced—with the greatest reluctance—to resign as a member of the Cabinet.

That Monday morning, I called Dave Walker, in Toronto, to advise him that an Order-in-Council was going through appointing him to the Senate. I asked him to come to Ottawa to discuss the situation that was developing. His diary for that day shows I told him that I was being asked to resign by Hees and McCutcheon.

At two-thirty p.m., the House met. On the motion to proceed into Committee of Supply, the Leader of the Opposition, Mr. Pearson, moved the non-confidence amendment. As I indicated in Chapter One, I was entirely unimpressed. At twenty minutes to six, Robert Thompson rose to state that the thirty Social Credit–Créditiste Members would not support the Pearson motion. This ensured that the non-confidence motion would be defeated. He was still speaking when the House adjourned at six p.m.

Accompanied by Dave Walker, I returned to 24 Sussex, where we had dinner. I decided that I would not return to the House that evening; instead, I would retire early for a good night's rest. As I told the new Senator, "There will be nothing there tonight, Thompson is voting with us." I was unaware that while we dined, the course of Canadian history was changing. Réal Caouette had gone to Montreal for a meeting, leaving Mr. Thompson on his own. Thompson apparently was not able to resist the pressures that were brought to bear upon him. He decided at some point between six and eight o'clock to vote with the Liberals. Réal Caouette told me some four years later, in the presence of seven other Conservative Members of Parliament, that had he been in the House after dinner that night, the twenty-six Créditistes would have voted for us. There would have been no defeat.

As to an explanation of Mr. Thompson's actions, he has alleged that he was waiting for a message from me agreeing to the four conditions he had released to the press that morning as a basis for his continuing support. There was, however, no message to send. He knew what the policies of the government were. He had agreed to support the government in the vote.

It is certainly a fact that Mr. Thompson was actively lobbied by the McCutcheon-Hees combination. Their conduit was Ottawa columnist Patrick Nicholson. It had become more important for the Conservative cabal to stop Thompson from voting with the government than it was even for the Liberals. The Liberals would be given another chance, the cabal would not.

First, however, Mr. Nicholson had to be persuaded to act as go-between. His ambition was to be a Senator. I knew this, and I was sufficiently sympathetic that he would have received this elevation in due course. I told him he would have to wait his turn. One of the cabal told him that I had blocked his appointment on every occasion and would never allow it to happen. It was made clear to him that if he co-operated now, one of the first acts of the Nowlan government would be to ensure his entry into the Red Chamber.

The second part of the cabal's task was to assure and convince Mr. Thompson that an election would not follow if the government was defeated, and that he could reverse himself without looking absurd. They further had to convince him (and this was the critical part) of the necessity to move an amendment to the Liberal amendment, one that the Liberals could vote for, thus committing his party to the defeat of the government. All this had to be achieved in the less than two hours before the House resumed at eight p.m.

I could not believe my ears when I first heard the news of the Monday night Social Credit turn-about. The pieces began to fall into place only the next morning when, at eight o'clock, George Hees appeared at the door of the Prime Minister's residence to once more demand my resignation. I told him where he could go. Shortly thereafter, Alvin Hamilton telephoned to say that the members of the cabal were gathering at Hees's Centre Block office. It was then that I realized the complete picture for the first time.

Mr. Hamilton, with the able assistance of M.P.s Jack Horner, Dr. Hugh Horner, Robert Muir, Deane Gundlock, Terry Nugent, and Senator Orville Phillips, did a fine morning's work in apprising our Members of what was going on. It is a simple fact that unless a leader has the support of his party's caucus, he has nothing. Caucus is the body and soul of any government. With the exception of a handful, the Members had been ignored by the plotters, and with good reason. Few and far between were the Conservative Members of Parliament who were prepared to see their party regress to its pre-1957 days of Toronto Establishment control. They saw immediately what this clique was up to. The result: when I arrived at the House of Commons shortly before two-thirty that afternoon, I was met in the government lobby by a cheering Conservative caucus. The private explanations offered by the cabal members that they were trying only to "save" the government fell on unbelieving ears.

When at last it was my turn to speak, I told the House, and in particular I told those Créditiste Members whom Mr. Thompson had so successfully boxed in:

. . . If our hands are tied, they are tied not by the other two parties but by the official opposition. They bear the responsibility. . . . We place before you our views on defence. . . . We will bring in new estimates—they are available—within a period of . . . one week. . . . We will bring down a budget . . . by the end of February. . . .

I told them that they had the chance to permit the rest of our legislative program to be placed before the House and that this, in addition to what we already had on the order paper, was a program needed in every part of our country. I continued:

. . . I do not come before you to ask for your support. I simply say this. If you vote against us . . . you are actually playing into the hands of the official opposition.

I made it clear to the Social Credit Members that "no part of our policy is determined elsewhere than by ourselves." But I did remind them that where I had given their legitimate aspirations every appropriate consideration, the Liberals had seen them only as the butt of every Grit joke; I epitomized their attitude in these words: "he loves thee, but he loved thee not until yesterday."

Pearson had spoken in his amendment about confusion and lack of leadership. I asked the Leader of the Opposition:

Is it leadership that he is showing in preventing parliament from dealing with these matters?

"Confusion"—who used that word?

First he said, "I don't believe in nuclear weapons." Then he went to New York and came back and said, "yes." Then he went to his constituency and said, "I did not say 'yes, I was in favour of nuclear weapons,' I would only have them until I am able to get an agreement not to have them."

I concluded my speech with these words:

Mr. Speaker, I ask this house for a vote of confidence, for the opportunity to do the things we want to do and have been denied the opportunity of doing. . . . The other day I saw the benefits of calling an election, thinking only of the political consequences in our favour. But I asked, "What will its effects be on a rising economy in the years ahead and the months ahead, unless we get those things on the statute books that would continue the upsurge of the economy of Canada?" I now ask for a vote of confidence from all hon. members in the house.

The die, however, had been cast. The "fix" was in and I knew it. The two votes of 142 to 111 that defeated my government were anticlimax. At 9.05 p.m., 5 February 1963, the Twenty-fifth Parliament adjourned. It would not meet again, although I suspect that even at this late hour, there were those who still believed the cabal would deliver up my head on a silver platter, and that the election that they with such prescience feared would be avoided.

I cannot say that I was not deeply concerned by the defeat in the House, or at least by its circumstances. I knew that defeat comes to everyone in politics, and to some sooner than later. The turn of events, the swing of the pendulum, are essential to the preservation of democratic principles in parliamentary life. The British adhere to this belief and concept. I presume because I am saturated by a study of the British parliamentary system from Shaftsbury to Churchill that I share it. In Canada, we have been greatly influenced, however, by the American concept that nothing else matters in politics except victory, and that whatever one's political opponents may do must be placed in such a light as to destroy them and their reputations. This philosophy ultimately bore its poisonous fruit in Watergate.

The Victoria *Daily Colonist* for 7 February 1963 carried this editorial:

A voice worth listening to among the partisan views aired in the crowded lobby of Parliament on Tuesday night was that of Dr. Eugene Forsey, former research director of the CLC and a recognized authority on constitutional matters.

It is a pity Mr. Pearson was not within hearing range.

Dr. Forsey poured scorn on the idea that voters are supposed to elect only a majority government. This was a constitutional absurdity. They elect a Parliament and it is Parliament's duty to carry on the nation's business, not to invoke a series of non-confidence motions designed to upset a government simply because it is a minority government. Nor is there justification for the assumption that repeated elections should be held for lack of a majority administration.

Once having been sustained in the customary vote of confidence following the Throne Speech, he made it clear, a minority government should be enabled to carry on through the earnest attention of all party groups to national welfare.

That is the constitutional position, and it is one that is bound to strike many people as an eminently sensible one. It recalls also Burke's famous dictum that as an MP he was the independent representative of his constituents.

This is not the course followed nowadays by parliamentarians, as has been amply evident in the deliberate Liberal attempts to bring the Diefenbaker government down ever since it was elected last June. Just as though the rules of the game did not matter; election rules that bestow office on the party winning most seats.

Unfortunately the constitutional views of Dr. Forsey have not won much favor on Parliament Hill. Canadian politics are bedevilled by excessive partisanship which puts party ahead of the national interest. . . .

I told those who were with me at the Prime Minister's residence on the morning after our defeat—dear Olive, Senators Grosart and Walker, and an old friend, Nick Berry, Q.C.—that I had decided to go to Government

House to tender my resignation. The only thing left to decide was whether to resign before or after caucus at nine-thirty. En route to my East Block office, Dave Walker counselled me not to decide anything until I had heard caucus. Howard Green, who came in shortly after we arrived, was incensed when I told him I was resigning: "Like hell you are," he cried; "you can't give in to those bird-brained b——s." Gordon Churchill echoed his sentiments. Finally, I decided that the least I could do would be to go to caucus to expose the cabal, their plots, and their deal with the Social Credit.

The voice of Oakley Dalgleish, editor of the Toronto *Globe and Mail*, had been added to the rebels' chorus that morning. In a front-page editorial he demanded my resignation, "for the good of the party", of course. Further, I had received from Mr. Goodman his resignation, dated 5 February, from the Ontario Committee on the party's federal organization, but not his resignation as Vice-President for Ontario of the Progressive Conservative Association of Canada. I considered the reason offered for his action self-serving: "our strong disagreement on what is the proper defence policy for Canada". Everyone was posing as an expert on defence policy. It was an effective cover for some, but as I considered Goodman's letter, I could not but recall that, following Pearson's Scarborough speech on 12 January, his advice to me (in a letter dated 15 January) had been based on a survey of the opinions of garage and washroom attendants.

At caucus, George Hees, who had been designated chairman, began to read a prepared text outlining the reasons why I had to go. Apparently he had been assigned the task of pulling the plug on me. He wanted this and he wanted that. Caucus was up in arms. There were boos and catcalls; "Judas" was one of the kinder expressions hurled at him. He presented in detail Cabinet deliberations on the nuclear-weapons question, something that his oath as a Privy Councillor forbade him to do. Finally—he was reading on and on—I interrupted him to demand he explain to caucus what he had been doing at 24 Sussex the morning before, and about the subsequent meeting of the cabal in his office. Protesting all the while that he was an honest man, Hees started to cry. And the tears ran down his face like rain in an Asiatic monsoon. Pandemonium best describes caucus at that point. I will never forget some of the spontaneous speeches. Alf Brooks and Angus MacLean achieved an oratorical splendour as inspiring as it was amazing, quite beyond anything they had ever done before. Others rose to the spirit and challenge of the occasion with pleas for party unity. Everyone was cheering and yelling. Each of the cabal forswore his past activities against me or swore that he had never taken part at all. Each answered: "Yes, we are with you." George Hees ceased demanding my resignation and, in Toronto Argonaut pep-rally style, withdrew his threat to resign and volunteered with eloquence and fervour to campaign for any Member who wanted him. A united party went out to meet the nation's press. "We're going to knock the hell out of the Grits," Hees proclaimed to the whirling cameras, as he stood with his arm around my shoulders. "Unity" was the word on every Member's lips.

I still believe that we would have won that election had it not been for Hees's decision to resign a few days later. The one question in the 1963 campaign I could not answer was: "Why did George Hees resign?" This failure on my part appeared to lend substance to the charges which began with the Harkness resignation that the government had disintegrated. The facts were: Harkness had resigned on principle; Fulton had launched himself provincially; Halpenny had decided to retire from politics (he would not have been in my next Cabinet anyway); and Donald

Fleming had decided not to be a candidate for very personal and even tragic family reasons. None of these resignations was related one to the other.

Mr. Fleming wrote me of his decision on 18 February:

My dear Prime Minister:

I enclose herewith a copy of the press release which I issued following our talk this morning announcing my retirement from public life.

The decision has been, as you know, a very painful one for me, and I thank you for your sympathetic understanding of the reasons which made it necessary.

I concluded the statement to the press with the following paragraph:

The precise date of my retirement from the Government will, of course, be a matter for decision by the Prime Minister. I shall leave him and my other colleagues in the Government with deep regret and with the most cordial and friendly feelings. I thank the Prime Minister for the privilege of serving Canada and the Crown as a Member of the Government for the past six years and for his personal friendship and confidence.

These eighteen years in Parliament and the last six as a Minister have involved sacrifice, but I shall always be grateful for the honour of being a member of your Government. I shall always treasure your generous recognition of my loyalty to you as the Leader of the Progressive Conservative Party, as Prime Minister of Canada, and as a personal friend.

What I said of Donald Fleming in reply still stands:

Canada and its Parliament will be the poorer for his decision. The Conservative Party will lose a stout-hearted member of the first rank who has made a hard and difficult decision, because of personal reasons which are fully understandable and understood by me.

Over the years, I had found him a devoted and effective

colleague. Totally frank, he made the strongest possible case for his views, accepted whatever decisions were made, closed the book and gave his all to the defence of whatever the Cabinet decided to do.

As to George Hees, there was nothing to indicate any second thoughts on his part when Cabinet met on the afternoon of 6 February following my call on the Governor General. Parliament was dissolved, the election set for 8 April, and we had many things to tidy up before we took to the hustings. Cabinet met again the next day, and on Friday as well. Indeed, Hees made arrangements with various candidates to speak in over twenty ridings across the country during the campaign. The only incident of note occurred at our Friday meeting and did not involve Hees at all. Following Harkness's resignation, I had given the Associate Minister of National Defence, Pierre Sévigny, acting responsibility for the Defence portfolio, pending the appointment of a new Minister. Mr. Sévigny was well aware that there was no possibility that I would permit him, however much he may have wanted it, to become Defence Minister. Despite this, he commenced signing documents as Minister of National Defence. When I asked him about this, he explained that he had run out of stationery as Associate Minister. I told him, "Then you'll have to use plain paper, because you're not going to be Minister."

Saturday morning I was up very early, at about four a.m., trying to clear away a large amount of detail that had to be dealt with before the campaign started. I had been working for some hours when Olive told me that Mr. Hees and Mr. Sévigny were downstairs. I asked, "Was there an appointment?" "Not that I know of," she replied. I said I would go right down, but she suggested that I not go down in my dressing-gown. I dressed and went downstairs, into the library where they were standing. Mr. Hees, in an abashed way, said: "Here's my resignation." I said, "Your what?" And Mr. Sévigny said:

"Mine too. My honour won't allow me to stay." I said: "Your what? What did you say your honour won't allow you to do?" Caught completely off guard, I asked for time so that each of us might consider the matter. I said, "We're going to have a Cabinet meeting on Tuesday; why not wait until then and we'll talk this over. I can't understand what you are trying to do." They refused to wait. Mrs. Sévigny gave the story of the resignations to the media in Montreal before any of our colleagues or sober second thoughts could intervene.

What had happened? Why did those two come to see me? There was no question of a policy disagreement, although Mr. Hees later stated he could not stand my anti-Americanism. His letter of resignation read:

Dear Mr. Prime Minister:

As you know, I have been extremely concerned for some time about our defence policy and our relations with the United States.

I have outlined to you, to my colleagues, and to the caucus of the Conservative party why I consider that our present defence policy does not either fulfil our international commitments or provide for the security of our country. I have also stated clearly that I consider the present attitude of the government cannot but lead to a deterioration of our relations with the United States.

I had hoped that the views which I expressed would lead to changes in policy which would permit me to remain a member of the government. However, since that time there has been no indication of such change. I feel these matters to be of vital importance to the welfare and security of our country, and therefore I have no alternative but to tender my resignation as a member of your cabinet.

I do not propose to be a candidate in the forthcoming election.

Yours sincerely,
George Hees

One has only to read some of his speeches since to realize that the reasons he gave were specious. In recent years, he has gone far beyond any stand I took at any time on Canadian policy being determined in Canada.

A thousand times I have asked myself about their motivations: what had provided their common ground? Why did they suddenly become so close to each other? Hees and Sévigny were not dear friends, nor did their ministerial duties bring them into contact that did not involve every other of our colleagues. Both men had been condemned by the Conservative press for their lack of moral courage in not resigning on 6 February, but so had their co-conspirators. Sévigny may have been piqued because I refused to make him Minister of National Defence or because I had taken him to task concerning his self-promotion. This was not the first time I had had to tell him home truths. In any event, it would not have proved earth-shaking had Mr. Sévigny resigned alone. He had talents and an admirable war record, but he had proved a troublesome colleague. Early on in his political career, I had warned him against his connections with figures like Willie Obrunt and John Doyle; I have since discovered that my warnings did not have the effect I was led to believe they had. I knew that Hees had experienced the immediate displeasure of both Bassett and Goodman for his failure to resign on the Wednesday. I know that both Hees and Sévigny tried to encourage others to resign. Only Léon Balcer responded to their call and agreed to meet with them. (I know of Balcer's involvement only through a report of his wife's comments.) It appears that Hees and Sévigny expected Balcer to resign the following Monday, thus maximizing the media impact of the event. This, they were confident, finally would drive me from public life. Balcer, or his wife, obviously had second thoughts, as his resignation was not forthcoming. This brings us back to the question of why Hees and Sévigny resigned.

Following his resignation, Mr. Hees went abroad for the duration of the 1963 election campaign, a skiing holiday, if I recall. When he returned, he immediately telephoned Prime Minister Pearson to offer him his congratulations and his services, if there was any way he could help. Pearson subsequently appointed him a Director of Expo 67. It is now rumoured that Mr. Hees will soon receive appointment to the Senate.

During the 1963 campaign, I was asked over and over again: "Why did George Hees resign?" "What happened between the Wednesday, when he came out of the caucus and announced to the press, 'We're all together,' and Saturday morning, when he resigned?" I could have told the Canadian people, and possibly I should have. I have said it was an error, not of the head but of the heart. Had I revealed what I knew, this would have brought harm to the innocent members of families. Prime Ministers, according to the late Earl Attlee, have to be butchers; I never reached the point where I could do anything intentionally that might bring harm or hurt to the innocent. Sir John Macdonald once said: "Be to our faults a little blind, and to our virtues always kind."

CHAPTER EIGHT

✳

WHEREAS THE REVERSE easily might have been true, the 1963 election campaign was one of the more uplifting experiences of my life. Defeat was in the air. As I took to the hustings, the road ahead seemed unbelievably long. My itinerary was awesome; I could ignore no riding in which the party had so much as a fighting chance. This was particularly so in Ontario, and I was reminded of Sir John Macdonald's comments on the 1872 election: "I had to fight a stern uphill battle in Ontario. Had I not taken regularly to the stump, we would have been completely routed."

In the last chapter, I wrote about the desertions and the insurrections inspired by the Bay Street and St. James Street Tories which led to the defeat of the government. They continued their bedevilment of the party during the election campaign. Traditional sources of election financing were reduced, although I was informed that there was any amount of money available for my retirement. Despite Premier Robarts' declared commitment to party unity, Ontario's "big blue machine" was never put in gear. Those with past election experience stayed away from our provincial office and constituency committee rooms in droves. Although we had some fine candidates (such as Joel Aldred, D.F.C., in Toronto St. Paul's), many good prospective candidates were discouraged from seeking nomination, and there seemed little I could do to convince them of their duty. To take a case in point, had Arthur Maloney agreed to run again in Toronto Parkdale, where, in 1962, the Liberal candidate had beaten him by less than two thousand votes, I would have appointed him to the Cabinet. As it was, I added Frank McGee to the Cabinet as Minister without Portfolio on 18 March to maintain traditional balances and to prevent a situation where we would be without so much as one Minister standing for re-election in Toronto.

Earlier, on 11 February, I had shifted Senator McCutcheon to the Trade and Commerce portfolio, following George Hees's resignation. My obligation was to hold the party together, and I hoped that McCutcheon, given his acceptance of this important responsibility, might help to still some of the storms surrounding us. Instead, he spent the entire election threatening to resign, with appropriate media fanfare, if I treated forthrightly the major issues of the campaign. I recall that when he was a candidate in the 1967 leadership race, he took the opportunity to express his hope that I bore him no grudge. I told him I thought him the biggest political double-crosser I had ever known. During the 1963 campaign, our circumstances had not allowed me the luxury of firing him.

In Quebec, the National Union party, despite the election of Daniel Johnson as Leader in October 1961, had yet to recover from its 1960 decimation at the hands of the Liberals under Jean Lesage. Old, rich, and spoiled, the Union Nationale had simply fallen apart after the untimely death of my good friend, Premier Paul Sauvé. The impetus to internal reforms, new personnel, and modern programs that would have revivified the party and government he had inherited from Maurice Duplessis was lost under Sauvé's successor, Premier Antonio Barrette. The 1960 Lesage campaign (something of a dry run for the federal Liberals in 1962 and 1963) was preceded by extensive motivational research to discover those policies that would attract the Quebec vote. Given the Liberal definition of leadership, the results of this research became Lesage's platform; "*Il faut que ça change*" was indeed a slogan to usher in a new age in Quebec politics! When the inevitable happened and the Lesage government was not able to deliver on its promises to end unemployment or to solve the problems of Eastern agriculture, they blamed my government. Premier Lesage lent his full support to Mr. Pearson during the 1963 campaign; from the floor of the legislature, he used the provincial budget as a propaganda vehicle to dispute the economic benefits that had come to Quebec, as to the other provinces, under my government. A Liberal government in Ottawa, he proclaimed, would solve all Quebec's problems! The Lesage administration even went to the lengths of using the Quebec Provincial Police to harass our candidates; the Honourable Raymond O'Hurley's chances in Lotbinière were hardly improved by the well-publicized QPP raid on one of his meetings in search of illegal alcohol. It was the Liberal Party's unscrupulous play on traditional racial antipathies, however, that took the situation in Quebec beyond the realm of what might pass for acceptable politics in any of the other provinces. The Liberals had attempted always to portray me as the enemy of French Canada. This was false, but in 1963, such purely partisan charges were ineffectively challenged.

Daniel Johnson was unable to lend his usual assistance. The Conservative Party's Quebec wing was still reeling from the shocks of the 1962 election. Further, when I appointed Jacques Flynn to the Senate in November 1962, so that he might concentrate on organizational work, the Honourable Noël Dorion, former Secretary of State, who had been defeated in the '62 election and coveted Flynn's appointment, publicly attacked me as a racialist who would assimilate French Canada. Quebec's Young Conservatives, both English and French, often proved unsuited for any activity that might result in winning seats. Pierre Sévigny kept his resignation from my government before the public by running as an Independent, aided in this by a substantial campaign contribution from John Doyle. Social Credit, under Réal Caouette, appeared to be far from spent, and was competing for votes that might well have been ours. The press gave us no help; the Montreal *Gazette* switched to the Liberals, and certain elements of the French-language press, such as Gérard Pelletier's *La Presse*, were particularly vicious.

I found it difficult to get our Quebec Ministers to campaign beyond their own constituencies. In the trips that I took into the province (to, among other places, Quebec, Montreal, St. Eustache, Matane, Cap-de-la-Madeleine, Vaudreuil, Cowansville) my reception was not unencouraging. Gerald Morin, who has an exceptional relationship with the press and the public, worked hard, as he always had, to make this so. When the vote was counted, we held eight seats. We would hold them again in 1965. Those who would assess the record in Quebec would do well to look at the number of Conservative Members elected from Quebec in the elections both before 1957 and since 1965.

In Newfoundland, Premier Smallwood and his Ottawa echo, Jack Pickersgill, ran the constituencies outside St. John's as if they were the rotten boroughs. In Nova Scotia, New Brunswick, and Prince Edward Island, I considered that we had more than a fighting chance. Our policies had served the Atlantic region well. On election day, we won exactly fifty per cent of those twenty-six constituencies. On the Pacific coast, we had been weakened by Davie Fulton's decision to quit federal politics. Only in the three Prairie Provinces did our fortunes remain virtually unchanged. We held forty-two seats going into the election; we would hold forty-one when it was over. No one could convince the Western farmer that the prosperity he saw around him was a mirage. He had heard twenty-two years of Liberal promises before we came into office, and he knew what they were worth.

It has been said that no Prime Minister in the history of Canada ever went into political battle in circumstances less fortuitous than were mine in 1963. Of the country's major newspapers, only the Fredericton *Gleaner*, the *Ottawa Journal*, the Winnipeg *Tribune* and the Victoria *Colonist* supported the return of my government. Every United States periodical with a Canadian circulation lined up against me: *Time, Newsweek, Look, Saturday Evening Post*. As to the Canadian Broadcasting Corporation, I quote Brigadier Michael Wardell, editor of the Fredericton *Gleaner* (16 November 1963):

I would say, from my own observations, that the C.B.C. commentators were one-sided Liberal propagandists, giving tongue to the most prejudiced, tendentious utterances on every phase of the campaign, invariably referring to Pearson with the tone of pride, Diefenbaker with disgust.

There was no question that everyone was against me but the people, and that unless I could find a way to get the message across, I would be lost. I have detailed some of the difficulties I faced. But, at least, I knew how great those difficulties were, and I have never been one to run away. I don't think anyone who saw me during that campaign was ever convinced from my appearance that I realized the closeness of defeat. As I fought on, I drew my strength from contact with people at every level. Campaigning by train was an important part of this. Whistle-stopping is an extension of Main Streeting, part and parcel of establishing a personal relationship with the individual citizen. I like people. We form an understanding, they with me and I with them. When they come away from our meetings, they require no one to tell them their conclusions. I have an unwavering conviction that if given a chance the people are not easily misled. And I remembered the philosophy of the immortal Abe Lincoln:

If I were to read, much less answer, all the attacks made on me, this shop might as well be closed for any other business. I do the very best I know how—the very best I can; and I mean to keep doing so until the end. If the end brings me out all right, what is said against me won't amount to anything. If the end brings me out wrong, ten angels swearing I was right would make no difference.

Thus, I decided to return, so far as possible, to campaigning by train. This was something no political leader had done for many years. In the United States, Harry Truman had been the last to master this technique. I once told President Truman that I felt his most effective contribution to the art of modern electioneering was his reinstatement of the train campaign. (He thought so too.) The story of his 1948 election had always been an inspiration to me. In background, I had been present in Philadelphia in June 1948 when Thomas E. Dewey received the Republican nomination for the Presidency. I had been silently cheering for Harold Stassen. I thought that Governor Dewey was above the people, removed from the average American; a New Yorker, who saw things only from the vantage-point of being Governor of that great state. Nevertheless, everyone conceded his election; Harry Truman, it was agreed, had no chance at all. The Gallup Polls confirmed this view. Yet Harry Truman unrelentingly pounded on, from meeting to meeting and at every whistle-stop in between. A couple of weeks or so before election day, the Dewey-ites began to suspect things were not as the Gallup Polls said. They endeavoured to offset the Truman campaign by following him into the various centres where he was speaking. It was Truman one night,

Dewey the next. Then, Truman produced the story that stopped them dead. He told his audience: "I haven't been feeling very well. I've been unsettled. I went to see my doctor. I told him that I was beginning to feel that someone was following me wherever I went. My doctor said, 'Don't worry about that Mr. President, there's one place he's not going to follow you, and that's into the White House.'" That story spread across the United States and got Harry Truman hundreds of thousands of votes. Campaigning from the back of his train, he got to know the people and they got to know him. They admired his courage, appreciated his wit, and found truth in his down-to-earth relationships. More importantly, President Truman, in this way, was able to counter the falsehoods being spread by influential newspaper interests opposed to his election.

When I first suggested to my advisors that I travel by train during the '63 campaign, their answer was: "That's out of date!" I knew otherwise. I had listened to their advice in 1962, with the result that some election post-mortems criticized me for not being sufficiently prime-ministerial, while others contended that I was not sufficiently combative. The contradiction aside, the basic point was that so far as the leader is the medium, I had not got my message through to where it counted. For one thing, I met very few people at twenty-five thousand feet. Aircraft are excellent if your meetings are separated by half a day and half a continent. But limiting a campaign to flying from one major meeting to the next causes one to miss all the people in between who would like to see the leader, to exchange or hear a word.

To take an example from my itinerary, apart from Winnipeg or Saskatoon, how else would I have been able to visit, even for a moment, the people in any of the towns en route?

Thursday, February 28

12:20 a.m.	Leave Ottawa—CNR Continental
8:25 a.m.	Arrive Capreol—30-minute station stop
9:05 a.m.	Leave Capreol
1:05 p.m.	Arrive Foleyet—10-minute station stop
1:15 p.m.	Leave Foleyet
4:45 p.m.	Arrive Hornepayne—20-minute station stop
5:05 p.m.	Leave Hornepayne
7:22 p.m.	Arrive Longlac—10-minute station stop
7:32 p.m.	Leave Longlac
8:30 p.m.	Arrive Nakina—15-minute station stop
8:45 p.m.	Leave Nakina

Friday, March 1

8:25 a.m.	Arrive Winnipeg—1½-hour station stop
10:05 a.m.	Leave Winnipeg
1:30 p.m.	Arrive Rivers—10-minute station stop
1:40 p.m.	Leave Rivers
5:10 p.m.	Arrive Melville—20-minute station stop
5:30 p.m.	Leave Melville
9:35 p.m.	Arrive Watrous—10-minute station stop
9:45 p.m.	Leave Watrous
11:30 p.m.	Arrive Saskatoon
	Stay overnight on railway car

My message throughout was consistently pro-Canadian; charges that I was on an anti-American rampage were patently false. Indeed, for reasons earlier explained, I did not give the weight it deserved to United States interference in our affairs. As to our platform, most of it had been set out before: in the January 1962 Speech from the Throne, the 1962 Budget, our 1962 election platform, the September 1962 Speech from the Throne, my final address in the House of Commons on 5 February 1963. All the documented facts that belied Opposition charges of our ruination of the Canadian economy. I also had the record of the irresponsible Opposition in Canada's Twenty-fifth Parliament.

Basically, my speech in Toronto on 19 February 1963 contained the message I would take to every city, town, village, and hamlet across our country:

... I see where the Leader of the Opposition said we didn't pass much legislation. Well, we had 31 matters on the Order Paper when they defeated us.

I think of the occasion in December which was so represent-ative of the attitude of the Liberal Opposition in the House. Never before in Canadian history when a Prime Minister rose to speak was he howled down by the Opposition and denied that right. ... I couldn't believe that those [Liberals] of 1956 had not changed in the interval. The greed for the opportunity for power was there. Obstruction was the order of the day. Re-sponsible government was the victim of irresponsible oppo-sition. ...

What were the Bills? ... They asked what we were going to do about amending the Unemployment Insurance Act, follow-ing the Gill Commission Report. They wouldn't let us bring it in because they wouldn't pass anything. What about the Royal Commission on Publications, in order to assure that Canada shall have preserved in Canada the right to determine through the press the destiny of Canada? What about the Manpower Consultation Services to handle labour problems? What about the National Economic Development Board to which I have al-ready made allusion? What about a fodder policy on behalf of the farmers of Eastern Canada so that they may secure their fodder at fair and reasonable prices? What about a policy on behalf of the urban municipalities of Canada?

We had all this legislation ready. It would all have been available, once the 61 Bills (of which only 21 were passed) had received the attention of Parliament.

In Social Security they refused us the opportunity to bring into effect a system ... in connection with portable pensions.

They denied us the right to bring about, through Parliament, an increase in the Old Age Pensions by the adoption of contributory pensions. . . .

Well, what is the position today? In the December issue of the London *Economist*, in the year-end edition, it says: "Canada in 1962 outstripped every nation in the world in the rate of economic growth." By their sins ye shall know them. They deceived in 1962 in April, May and June. Now they are looking for another issue to divide us. They want to get the eyes of the Canadian people off the facts. . . .

There's the picture. Do you wonder why they wanted Parliament closed down? Because if they came in—and there were some who advised me last June and July that it might be better to resign and make way for the Opposition—they would have come in and said, "See what we did." I made sure that we were the ones who would be able to tell the Canadian people the facts. . . .

As a point of interest for students of constitutional history, not only had I to wage a one-man, whirlwind campaign in defence of the government, I had also to see to the day-to-day administration of the country. Fortunately, I had Donald Fleming in Ottawa to attend to purely housekeeping matters. Fortunately, also, the Governor General was appropriately appreciative of the constitutional rights of a minority government, defeated in Parliament and facing the people's verdict, to make appointments. I made note of a conversation that I had with Governor General Vanier on 27 February:

I dealt at length with the question of appointments and advised him that I would be making some recommendations Saturday week back in Ottawa.

He said he had read the two legal opinions that he had before I departed for London last week and had come to the conclusion that while my recommendations would be constitutional there might be political considerations. However, we came to full agreement on what course I would follow.

I rather jocularly referred again, as I had in my last discussion with him, that if he failed to take my recommendations he would have to get another Prime Minister who would be able to give him the kind of advice he wished to have.

We also discussed the Chief Justiceship of Canada. . . . [Donald Fleming had expressed a desire to be appointed Chief Justice, but I declined to recommend him for anything more than a puisne Judge of the Supreme Court. The Governor General agreed with my view. Mr. Fleming, however, would not accept this appointment.]

I pointed out that there had been two Catholic Chief Justices in succession, and he said if it was becoming a question of religion without regard to race it seemed to suggest that a French Canadian should be appointed.

I told him I would make some other recommendations although I did not specifically refer to Senate appointments.

However, I did inform him that even after defeat in 1896 the Tupper Government made appointments. I said I did not agree with that. His answer was, that even after defeat, until the change of government, the Prime Minister is still the Prime Minister.

One can never calculate in advance what will happen in an election campaign. Heaven knows I was immeasurably helped in 1963 by the political ineptness of the Liberal high command; they seemed to mistake our country for the United States. And their Madison Avenue techniques came a cropper with their colouring books, white pigeons that flew off never to be seen again, and that never-to-be-forgotten "truth squad". Poor Judy LaMarsh! I had much fun with her in Moncton and Halifax. She had a specially designated table right down at the front of the hall so she could hear everything. Although the people thought she was a great joke, they also were offended by the impudence of those who had sent her to challenge the truth of my every statement. The Liberals quickly got the message and ended the Truth Squad in two days. Had they kept her on, however, we might well have picked up several extra constituencies. The Liberal Party "brain trust" seemed to experience great difficulty in relating to the average Canadian: in 1963, they thought laughable my decision to return to the train; in 1965, when I used the train even more extensively, they reacted in exactly the same way; in the 1974 election, when they sent Prime Minister Trudeau on his train campaign, they showed that, finally, they were beginning to understand what those who have spent their political lives in "safe" constituencies seldom understand.

With the perspective of the intervening years, while it is clear that everyone makes mistakes and that no one with the responsibility of a Prime Minister can do other, I declare that there was nothing in the 1963 campaign that, in the light of events then so regarded, I would now change. Of course, the media's cognoscenti, who never had anything to do with campaigns other than to report them, felt that I was on a disaster course; the most generous considered that we would return with a maximum of sixty seats. There were even some leading Conservatives who, with assurance, predicted our return to a 1935-like rump of less than forty Members.

As always, I was in Prince Albert when the vote was counted on Monday, 8 April. Those who so confidently had expected my total annihilation must have been shocked. We had lost but eight seats, not enough to give the Liberals a majority. The standing, when the civilian votes were counted, gave us ninety-eight seats (with the final standing after the service vote and recounts at ninety-five). In a television interview that election evening, I noted that the situation was much the same as in 1925, when Prime Minister King had decided, as was his right, to meet Parliament on the basis that no party had a majority.

My message, unprepared and spontaneous, to the Canadian people was neither one of victory nor one of defeat:

As of this moment it is apparent that no Party has a majority of seats in the next Parliament.

The decision is the democratic right of the voters of each constituency.

Naturally I regret that the Conservative Party did not secure a majority. That is natural.

As to the course to be followed, this is not an appropriate time for any statement, nor will it be until the vote of the Armed Forces will have been counted.

I have never exulted in victory nor been craven when things went against me. That's the spirit in which I have tried to serve this country over the years.

I thank all who gave their support to the Conservative Party and trust that they will not feel that I have failed them.

I gave the best that was in me and I followed the course that I believed right. That course was based on my conscience and my faith in the future of Canada.

Speaking as one of the candidates who had the good fortune to be elected, I offer my congratulations to the Leader of the Opposition and to the Leaders of the other parties, and the candidates of all parties who won election.

At the same time I think of those who were defeated. My sympathies are with them for I know from experience what it means to lose. I hope they will find consolation in the knowledge that as candidates they have performed a worthy public service—service that all too many are reluctant to give.

It has been a hard fought election.

My wife is here with me, as she has been throughout the campaign.

My prayer is that Canada will be God-guided during the days ahead.

I hope that any bitterness that developed in the campaign is past, and in the democratic tradition all of us will do our part in solving the difficulties that face the nation.

·The next morning, I had telephone conversations with Gordon Churchill, Alvin Hamilton, and Senator McCutcheon, discussed the election result at length with Senator Grosart, and visited with those local friends and supporters who came to call on me at my railway car. Although I kept my own counsel, the more I talked to people and the more I considered the situation, the more I realized that I was out. This is reflected in the following note of my telephone conversation with Jack Urton of Duck Lake, just before I returned to Ottawa on Wednesday, 10 April:

I think this will be the last call you get from me as Prime Minister. It looks as if the C.C.F. [NDP] will support the Liberals and if they do I am out. I am so grateful to the people of Prince Albert and I am so grateful to you. Your father and I used to go out to Garthland and Duck Lake. . . . I think we have to do something in this province. No more of the nonsense of supporting the Liberals in this province. If we could get a man like Hamilton to lead [the party in] this province . . . It would weaken us in Ottawa and I would lose a friend. I am going to speak to him at once. If you think it sound you wire me.

I went down there to see what I could do for the common people and the big people finished me—the most powerful interests. . . .

I told reporters on my return to the nation's capital that my plans were to meet with Cabinet and to watch eventualities. One reporter asked me to define "eventualities". I replied: "Eventualities are matters that arise and you have to wait till they arise before you realize that they have." At the time, I did not know how particularly apt my reply was.

I had been calculating on the basis of an expected NDP (CCF)–Liberal arrangement. It appears, however, that certain important Liberals took my election-night comments literally and were afraid that I might decide not to resign, but to wait until I had met Parliament and had suffered a want of confidence before relinquishing office. They thus determined to force my hand by securing by any means the support they were short in their quest for a majority in the House of Commons. Pierre Sévigny has stated that he was approached by John Doyle on election night (Sévigny had been defeated as an Independent in his Montreal riding) for the names of any Conservative Members who, for an appropriate consideration, might switch to the Liberals. Sévigny, to his credit, refused to be a party to this plan. Thus, Doyle and his associates turned elsewhere.

The facts did not become public until the middle of the 1965 election campaign. On 13 October 1965, at a press conference in Quebec City, Dr. Guy Marcoux, Social Credit Member for Quebec-Montmorency in the last Parliament, said that Liberal front-bencher J. W. Pickersgill and mining promoter John Doyle took part in negotiations which led six Social Credit Members of Parliament to pledge their support to the Liberal Party after the 1963 federal election. He had released that day a twenty-four-page pamphlet entitled *Dans le Même Sac*, in which he described "the affair of the six" as the shadiest usurpation of political power in Canada's history.

At his press conference, Dr. Marcoux said he had been under pressure not to publish his pamphlet. As to the bribes, Dr. Marcoux stated that a twenty-five-thousand-dollar bribe offer was floating around for anyone who would finger M.P.s who were ready to "sell themselves" by signing an affidavit pledging their support to the Liberals. This declaration was signed by the necessary six Créditistes (M.P.s Perron, Boutin, Langlois, Rondeau, Plourde, and Beaulé), and was sworn before Moise Darabaner, a Commissioner of the Superior Court of Quebec District. It was delivered to Governor General Vanier on 12 April 1963 (with a copy to Mr. Pearson). It read:

. . . Nous annonçons publiquement être prêts à donner notre appui à un gouvernement libéral dirigé par monsieur Pearson, non parce que nous sommes libéraux, mais parce que nous croyons que le plus grand intérêt du peuple canadien consiste à maintenir un gouvernement stable, capable d'agir avec assurance pour régler les graves problèmes intérieurs et extérieurs auxquels notre pays fait face.

Nous donnons cette assurance d'un appui parce que nous espérons que monsieur Pearson est sincère dans sa détermination de faire tout en son pouvoir pour réaliser un Canada dans lequel les Canadiens français et les Canadiens anglais seront les Canadiens partenaires égaux dans la Confédération.

Nous comptons que monsieur Pearson réalisera le biculturalisme au Canada, donnera au pays un drapeau distinctif, reconnaîtra "O Canada" comme hymne national et augmentera les allocations familiales proportionellement au coût de la vie tel que promis par le parti libéral lors de la dernière élection et ce, dans le plus bref délai réalisable. . . .

Cette offre est faite volontairement et librement.

Nous n'espérons aucune faveur en retour sinon la satisfaction du devoir accompli. . . .

Si toutefois il se présente devant la Chambre une motion concernant les armes nucléaires, nous nous réservons le droit d'un vote selon notre conscience.

The switch of the Social Credit six had the effect that the planners desired. With Mr. Pearson guaranteed majority support in the House, there were no further eventualities for me to wait upon.

I telephoned Mr. Pearson at 11.10 a.m. on Saturday, 13 April. I extended my congratulations. There was no reaction on his part. I said I had been trying to get him on the phone but had been unable to do so and had therefore wired him. I told him we could meet at his convenience on Monday to discuss the change-over of government. He replied that three o'clock would be agreeable to him, at my office in the East Block.

Accordingly, we met. Mr. Pearson was agreeable to the change-over from my government to his on the Monday next. We would exchange our residences a few days later. We discussed in general the coming session, and he indicated that he expected to call Parliament on 23 May, to sit until 1 July, then to adjourn until September. (In fact, he called it on 16 May, it continued until 2 August, and then adjourned until 30 September.) There had been some speculation that a Member of one of the third parties would be offered the Speakership but he indicated that a Speaker would be appointed from his own party. As to the Estimates, he advised me that an opportunity would be given the House to deal with Governor General's warrants, at which time there could be a wide range of discussion; when approved, the result would be that the Estimates for 1962-63 would be wiped out; he had not yet determined what he would do with regard to the Estimates for 1963-64.

As a courtesy, I asked him whether he wanted the office I had in the Centre Block and he said he did. (The office in question had been intended originally as the Prime Minister's office, but Mackenzie King, during his long tenure as Prime Minister, had declined to move into it, breaking the tradition.) I told him I wanted to have my staff's positions agreed upon and would send him a list later in the day or on the following morning. I told him that Mr. St. Laurent had asked me to retain the services of Gordon McCartney, his chauffeur, and Mr. Pearson replied that he would keep him as well, and he did.

At 12.05 p.m., Wednesday, 17 April, I went by car from 24 Sussex Street to Rideau Hall. There I tendered my resignation, to take effect at twelve o'clock noon on Monday, 22 April, as Prime Minister of Canada to Her Majesty's representative, Governor General Georges Vanier.

The atmosphere natural to this occasion, however, was lightened by a touch of humour. General Vanier told me that he had been particularly tickled by Howard Green's answer to the press men who asked the reason for his defeat: "I have given the matter the fullest consideration and having examined the problem from all its angles reached the conclusion that it was because I didn't get enough votes!" In turn, I told the Governor General a story that Arthur Meighen used to tell of his early days in Portage La Prairie, Manitoba. Not long after he had opened his law office in 1906, Mr. Meighen ventured into Portage's only book store. While he was there, a lady came in and said to the clerk: "Have you a 'Life' of Saint Paul?" The clerk replied: "I haven't the life of a dog and I'm getting the hell out of here on Monday next!"

After five years, nine months, and one day in the life of the Thirteenth Prime Minister of Canada, I had to wonder whether continuing as leader was worth all the calumnies that it brought. The Liberals had hailed my election at the 1956 Convention because they felt I couldn't stand up to them. Four elections later, I considered that I hadn't done so badly: three victories (including the largest in Canadian history) and a near victory. With ninety-five Members, the Conservative Party was still a force to reckon with, providing it could stop its lemming-like tendency, established over the years, of rushing into the seas of dissension and defeat.

I did not have a great deal in the way of past experience as Leader of the Opposition: only from 8 January 1957 to 21 June 1957, for much of which time I was campaigning. I decided to take things on a day-to-day basis, to see what fortunes time brought along, and to keep my options open.

My letters to my brother over the months that followed the 1963 election reflect my thoughts about the new role I had assumed, as well as many of the personal and party considerations involved.

May 13th.

Dear Elmer,

Olive and I had a very good time in Saskatoon thanks to you. . . .

While we were away the staff at the house [Stornoway, the home of the Leader of the Opposition] worked very hard and got everything in readiness. As soon as some of the furnishings that we had shipped from Prince Albert arrive here it will become very homelike. . . .

I have so much to do to get ready for the session and have done very little, but the staff in the office have gathered together a lot of material for me which I will have to carefully collate and have ready for one week from today.

May 16th.

The first hurdle is over. Mr. Pearson and Mr. Chevrier proposed the name of Mr. Macnaughton as Speaker and I spoke in support of the Motion, as did the leaders of the other parties.

This afternoon the Speech from the Throne will be revealed and I am sure will contain nothing beyond what has already been referred to in detail by Pickersgill. . . .

Tomorrow there will be a short session and then on Monday the debate will begin. I will send you Hansard daily so that you won't have to wait for your regular copy.

May 23rd.

The Nato Conference is on. We invited them [the NATO Ministers] but the new Government does the entertaining and is receiving the applause. Lord Home went out of his way yesterday to build up Mr. Pearson by saying, in effect, that he became Prime Minister because he wanted Canada to be a good ally. Several of my colleagues are most annoyed at this because I refrained at all times from making political speeches in London that would in any way criticize the Government or assist the Opposition. . . .

Olive is still working on the house. Some of the furniture came from Prince Albert although the cost was very high. . . .

I have to attend a luncheon at Government House for the Nato people and am not looking forward to it. Tonight there will be another vote in the House and I will have to be back here for the evening.

May 24th.

I do not intend to go anywhere over the weekend except possibly for a couple of hours' drive to look over the Pioneer Village near Morrisburg, in which one can relive the early days of the United Empire Loyalists.

It is far less work being Leader of the Opposition than Prime Minister and I am getting a great deal of rest and also more reading done than has been possible [in the last few years]. . . .

Olive bought a chesterfield yesterday and this evening she intends to go to a sale of antiques. She made an examination of the offerings yesterday and there are two or three pieces of furniture in which she is interested. When she gets in some of the furnishings, including what was shipped from Prince Albert, the house will begin to look like a home.

May 27th.

The House is going along quietly. I am quite pleased with the progress made. . . .

The sugar situation is one in which a few wholesalers will make tremendous profits. . . . The price has gone up about 10 cents a pound since [31 March] which means that someone will make $40 million on what is in storage.

I didn't phone you yesterday although I had lots of leisure

time as I put in the laziest two days for years. I read a bit and puttered around in the garden.

May 30th.

Olive is in Toronto today getting drapes, etc., for the house. I shall be there on Monday to speak to the Cleaners and Launderers Association. . . .

May 31st.

. . . The "Globe & Mail" and "Telegram", and to a lesser extent until today, the "Gazette", are spending their time in personal criticism, as certain of the big interests have determined that there must be a change of leadership of the Conservative Party. . . .

It is more than a coincidence that Davie Fulton was here on Monday and this is the third time that such a visit has been followed by an article by Arthur Blakely. However, I have got no intention whatsoever of falling in line with their plans and schemes. They should have learned that many years ago.

Olive was in Toronto yesterday and bought some furniture for the house. It is now approaching an end in this regard and she has made it most liveable and attractive.

June 4th.

Time flies, as father used to say. It is 44 years ago today that I was called to the Bar and the very thought of it is frightening. . . .

I intend to speak in the House tomorrow on the subject of defence. . . .

I had Senator Pearson in today accompanied by Dr. Leishman and Jack Sangster. They are most anxious to get Alvin Hamilton to take over the leadership [of the Saskatchewan Conservative Party] although they realize that his health being what it is he may not accept. They are strongly of the opinion that his acceptance of the leadership would ensure his being Premier whenever the election takes place. I agree with them, but naturally do not want to hurt a very loyal supporter, Martin Pederson, but certainly their view is that excellent as he is they would not expect him to do the job that Alvin would do. . . .

At the rate we are proceeding in the House it will not be before the 15th of July that I come West.

June 7th.

We have had quite an interesting time this week. The "60 Days of Decision" is rapidly approaching an end, although the Globe and Mail and the Telegram still kick us around. However, I think the Opposition Members have done very well.

Dave Walker gave a dinner on Wednesday night for the Conservative Members of the Senate and the House of Commons and he made a typically frank speech in which he told them they would not have been there if it had not been for me, much to my embarrassment. However, when speaking, I pointed out that I had no intention of falling in line with the desires of the Liberal Party to get me out of the leadership with an assist from a few of my former colleagues.

Mr. Pearson will be speaking today on the defence question and of course will endeavour to show that everything they [his government] have done to provide nuclear arms is being done because of the commitments of the former government. He knows that is not so, but it is the Liberal excuse for their complete change of front.

Olive has her driving license now having passed her examination so we will be able to get around a lot easier than we have since moving into "Stornoway". Furthermore, most of the furniture and flatwear, etc., arrived yesterday so we will soon be very comfortable. . . .

June 12th.

. . . Pearson is in very bad humour these days which indicates that he has lots of trouble. Besides Lesage's ultimatums and a host of other problems, the 60 Days have been anything but a harvest for him and have become a famine in legislative enactment. . . .

As yet there is no indication when the Government intends to adjourn the House. Certainly there is nothing to indicate today that it will be before the 15th of July. A summer break will not be unwelcome as last summer I had no vacation at all because of my ankle injury. . . .

Last night I went to the High Mass in memory of Pope John XXIII. It was an impressive service with the Apostolic Delegate in charge.

June 25th.

While the Opposition did not have a very large vote last evening [our non-confidence amendment was defeated 113-73] the Pearson Government has been badly shaken. How the N.D.P. can justify refusing to vote in condemnation of the Government's policies in applying the sales tax on building materials and production machinery I do not know. They said they were against that and other portions of the Budget. The Social Credit spoke against the Budget and then voted for it.

I don't know when I am going to speak. I am ready to do so at any time but don't want to interfere with the plans of our Members. Mr. Ed. Nasserden will be speaking this afternoon.

The weather has been very warm the last couple of days. Today it is 90 degrees but both my office and the Chamber are air-conditioned and the heat does not have the same effect it used to have when I first came here and when the summer heat came over Ottawa we knew adjournment was not far off. There is no indication to date that the summer adjournment will take place earlier than the 1st of August. . . .

June 28th.

. . . As you know Mr. Pearson has gone into hospital. It is not expected to be serious in any way. He has had this condition for some weeks. It is being generally remarked that he is not able to stand up to the pressure. I know what it is and sometimes wonder how anyone stands up to it at all.

The Government will have to retreat on its budget taxation measures. The whole country is aroused and the Liberal Members are scared out of their wits and another retreat is to be expected. . . .

July 9th.

. . . Yesterday Olive and I decided to visit Israel. . . . It is now almost ten years since I was there and it will be of interest to learn at first hand the changes that have taken place in the intervening years.

I would like as well to visit Egypt and Syria but may not be able to arrange it. . . . This prospective trip will not deny me having a couple of weeks in Prince Albert. I hope that you will feel like taking your holidays at the same time.

July 12th.

Your letter written from Watrous came today and as always it tells me of encouraging things and events. Of this I am certain, that there has been a great alteration in viewpoint across the country and with every day that passes this shows clearly on the faces of Mr. Pearson and those associated with him. They are worried and perplexed. . . .

July 15th.

. . . The Opposition has been going ahead effectively and Mr. Pearson made another about-turn today.

I expect that there will be further changes in the budget which I think I will describe as "the vanishing budget". . . .

July 19th.

. . . The Government is tied up in knots. . . . They go from one crisis to another. President Kennedy certainly gave them a shocker yesterday [when he announced a fifteen-per-cent tax on purchases by American nationals of common stock issued in a list of twenty-two countries, including Canada]. The fall in prices on the Stock Exchange was the most pronounced in two years. You will recall how the Liberals ridiculed Canada's handling of the financial situation when we received assistance from the International Monetary Fund. The United States, although the richest country in the world, had to do the same yesterday....

The ridicule they heaped on me in May of 1962 could, if I were to follow their course, be used now against them....

July 26th.

It begins to look now that the House will adjourn towards the end of next week and immediately thereafter I will be going West....

The Government is going to bring in a measure to increase the indemnity by $8000 of which $4000 will be non-taxable. I think it is a serious matter that Parliament should vote an increase for itself. What should be done is to increase the amount and make it applicable to the next Parliament. However, it will go through. I intend to make it very clear that it is a Government measure and that at no time was I consulted, directly or indirectly....

August 1st.

... Olive had the Members of Parliament and Senate and staff at home last evening for a little get-together. The weather could not have been more beautiful and the only disgruntlement was shown by Happy because he was tied up! ...

August 2nd.

You will be hearing the news about Olive being bitten by Happy. It was an accident but she received a severe bite from him. There wasn't one word of complaint and she was, as always, completely calm. She had an anti-tetanus shot and while she has much pain she brushes the incident aside as of no importance.

I think we will finish the session tonight and I will be calling you early on Sunday morning to let you know when we will be going West. . . .

August 27th.

. . . Yesterday Olive and I had lunch with the Attaché of the Israeli Embassy and tomorrow will have lunch with your friend, the Ambassador of Egypt. . . .

August 28th.

I had lunch today with the Ambassador of the U.A.R. and told him that you had informed me that he was a propagandist! We stayed there for 2½ hours. I do not know where the time went but it was far and beyond the time we should have stayed, but he covered a lot of ground and argued with me that in everything the Israelis were wrong.

He was very pleased that you enjoyed your visit and said that we would as well. I told him that you had given me a list of people to whom you were indebted for kindnesses shown which naturally interested him. He is sorry that we are not going to stay the extra day as we found it necessary to delete one day's arrangements. I hope that doesn't exclude Luxor and Aswan Dam. . . .

August 29th.

Following our phone conversation this afternoon my birthday present arrived but I haven't opened it yet. I am just filled with expectation but feel that it would be quite unjustifiable to open it now. However, you never can tell how long I will be able to withstand the ravages of desire.

Olive has the camera that you gave her ready and as you told us that it is fool-proof we feel that it is in good hands. . . .

I have just had handed to me a copy of our itinerary for Egypt and am enclosing a copy.

August 30th.

I decided last night that I could not wait until my birthday to open up the package and when I did I was very pleased by what I found. . . . The card is one that will be preserved for the Archives with the wording "To the Old Chief from the Young Brave". Pearson might object to this because of his association with the Indians, as he was recently made "Chief of the Birds"—no connection, I understand, with John Bird of the Toronto "Star"! . . .

September 20th.

Wherever we travelled in Egypt and in Israel where you had been we had warm greetings extended to you. When we were in the Valley of the Kings Olive got a sphinx made of alabaster which she will be sending you, as well as a dozen or so slides. She is having extra copies made of these so that a set may be sent to Dr. Rynard so it may be some time before you receive them. We hoped to be able to get a set taken from the roof of the Cairo Tower to take the place of the pictures which you had taken there and which did not turn out well, but were unable to do so. . . .

The return trip from Israel occupied my birthday [18 September] from morning till night, as we left Tel Aviv at 8.00 A.M. and arrived at Ottawa at 10.00 P.M., with stopovers at Athens, Zurich and Paris. We were met by Ambassador Barrette at Athens and had a pleasant visit with him. Olive has always spoken of the beauties of Switzerland and I know now how right she was. I have never seen anything more beautiful anywhere.

The next two weeks will be busy ones but I have decided that I am going West for two or three days. . . .

September 24th.

I am in the midst of clearing up the backlog of work that piled up during my absence. . . .

I heard a little story today which you might enjoy. The President of the United States was shocked one morning when outside his office he heard little Caroline singing: "I'm going to marry a Negro, I'm going to marry a Negro"—she sang as she marched up and down. As always in time of trial and difficulty the President called his brother, the Attorney-General. The latter was shocked and turning to the President said: "This is a very serious situation, an unbelievable situation. Do you realize," said he, "that nearly all Negroes are Baptists?"

September 26th.

The election in Ontario yesterday was a tremendous rebuff for the Pearson Government. Tens of thousands of people voted against the provincial Liberals (who had the active support of Chevrier, Hellyer and LaMarsh, and I imagine that they are holding their heads today!)

Of course the outcome having been so unfavourable to the N.D.P. will act as a brake on their desire to vote the Government out.

This election convinces me that letters I have been receiving, which indicate a disillusionment with the Pearson Government, were not just solitary viewpoints but represent a widely felt antagonism to the federal government.

I am going to start to take appointments now to speak at various places across the country, and two I have will be in Alberta on the 12th and 13th of October at Red Deer and Edmonton, and on the 26th of October in Winnipeg for a Conservative dinner. There is also another in New Brunswick. The National Executive meeting will take place here in Ottawa on the 26th and 27th of October, and the Annual Meeting in Ottawa in January. These several events will tend to test the atmosphere. . . .

Olive has presented me with a blue-blood Golden Retriever now of the age of eight weeks. He will be delivered on Saturday. His name will be Happy II, although Olive spells the second part of his name "too"!

October 2nd.

Your letter written from Swift Current arrived in the office this morning. We have had a busy few days in the House. The Liberals have been in difficulty. Miss LaMarsh is now the "centre of political attraction" and her statement (while denied by her), that if the Government of Quebec goes ahead with its [own pension] plan it will have powers which might lead to national socialism such as was the case under the Nazis has made her very popular in reverse. . . .

Happy II is full of life. He is a beautiful golden retriever with an aristocratic genealogical tree. He is wonderfully alert and is going to give me a lot of pleasure. At the moment, however, he is causing lots of work around the house. If he were in the dry areas of Egypt or on the Israeli desert their irrigation problems would be solved.

The Conservatives in British Columbia sustained an overwhelming defeat. I am very sorry about Fulton's personal defeat. I warned him not to go to B.C. as there was no hope and particularly suggested that he should not run in Kamloops. . . .

Olive has received the transparencies of the pictures she took and I will be sending some on to you later. They were very good. While she disclaims any additional pleasure in taking pictures it was noticeable towards the end of this trip that she was more enthusiastic in this regard than at the beginning. . . .

October 3rd.

. . . We have had a very interesting week in the House and our

Party has done well, but yesterday due to the absence of so many of our Members the Government was not defeated. It is true that the Liberal Party Members were also absent but that did not help us. They had more absentees than we had. However, whatever happens the Toronto papers are still very critical.

I am now making arrangements to go West. I will be in Red Deer next Saturday and will arrive in Saskatoon at 2.25 P.M. on Sunday. If you are available we could drive to Prince Albert then. I think this will be the course I will follow but I will have to let you know when I talk to you on the phone. It might be better for you to call me as I may miss you.

We had Lord Amory for breakfast this morning but Happy II did not take kindly to him and let out a little growl! . . .

It seems that the Pearsons imitate everything Olive and I do. Mr. Pearson had no interest in fishing in his life and he decided to imitate me. Now they have a dog—a poodle.

We expect to get delivery of our car at Oshawa tomorrow and the chauffeur will be picking it up. It is a Buick 5-passenger bearing the name of "Wildcat". It is a Canadian-made car and while we would have preferred a better Buick felt that we must not purchase a car manufactured outside Canada. . . .

October 11th.

. . . As soon as we get to Saskatoon on Sunday we will go on to Prince Albert unless you have other plans. I naturally do not want it known that I am going shooting on Monday, otherwise much might be made of it. . . . I will be back on Tuesday afternoon for the vote, which is important. . . .

October 16th.

I had a fast trip down yesterday and was back in the House last evening and voted on the two motions of non-confidence.

The goose and ducks have been photographed and also drawn and quartered.

I had an enjoyable visit even if short. The Alberta Annual Meeting was an excellent one although by the time I got back here last night Harkness had told everyone that it was the poorest meeting in years and that there were only 85 present. It was quite natural that he was annoyed at the success of the meeting but annoyances should never be allowed to influence one not to tell the truth.

Last night's Telegram and Toronto Star attacked me bitterly and stated I must go but although they have a great influence they have not yet regained the position that one of them once held of being a "King Maker"....

October 18th.

... The Toronto papers are still conducting their vendetta against me—even more bitter than previously.

The outcome of the mayoralty elections in Alberta will be surprising to many people but not to me. I predicted that Hawrelak would win in Edmonton. In Calgary, Art Smith was alleged to have made an arrangement with Harry Hays whereby he would not run again in Calgary South and in return, Hays would support him for mayor. I can't believe the arrangement was made but certainly Smith lost a lot of votes by saying that the reason he didn't continue in Ottawa was because I was continuing as Leader of the Party....

There is much being said today regarding the Conservative Executive Meeting the end of this month and the Annual Meeting the end of January. The Toronto Star says the one "Who has the guts to face" me is Davie Fulton. I do not think that after his recent experience in his own province that there is any foundation for the statements being made in this regard....

October 25th.

... I am going to meet with the Executive tomorrow morning and then go on to Winnipeg, arriving there at 8.45 tomorrow evening, and will be at the Marlborough Hotel Saturday night and will leave there Sunday morning. I will be calling you on Sunday morning.

The conspirators are still working hard. . . . I am more definitely set than ever before against resigning no matter what they may do. It is going to be a big fight and when these great and powerful financial interests determine on a course of action they exert a tremendous influence. I beat them before and intend to do so again.

The summer weather continues here. It is 75 degrees today. There has been no rain for six weeks and the local dairy farmers are finding a pronounced reduction in milk production.

November 5th.

Newman's book is being widely advertised by the Liberal Party. . . . I heard him as he appeared on TV last evening being interviewed by a young woman. (I don't have the name at the moment.) He said the reason he called me a "Renegade" was that I was a "Robin Hood" who robbed the rich provinces to help the poor. That of course is not true. What I tried to achieve was to equalize opportunities for all Canadians wherever they lived. What the effect of the book will be I don't know but the last couple of days have indicated that a reaction is setting in. The Toronto Telegram spreads it out in detail and accompanies the articles with frightful pictures of me. . . .

Olive is going to make a speech today to the Conservative Members' wives on her trip to Israel. I wish I could get the notes but there is no encouragement in this regard! I would like very much to hear what she has to say but that is out.

November 14th.

. . . Olive has finished reading the Newman book . . . it is written with such obvious venom it may well react. It does reveal one thing—that President Kennedy sent a public-opinion analyst (one Harris) who was closely connected with him in Washington, to work with the Liberals prior to and during the 1962 and 1963 election campaigns....

November 15th.

... Olive was on television yesterday afternoon for half an hour. I am told she did exceptionally well. The programme was arranged for the wives of various leaders in Parliament. Mrs. Pearson was on a week ago....

November 19th.

Olive and I returned from the Maritimes yesterday after a most enjoyable trip. In fact, the Newman book has done me good. On every hand several who had not been very enthusiastic have now announced that we will win every seat in that province....

December 3rd.

Olive is most anxious for you to come for Christmas. She feels that you will be very lonesome and that it would do you good to have a break. If it is possible to do so I think it would be a good idea. Arrangements can be made later about your attending the Annual Meeting if you so desire....

Olive and I celebrate our Tenth Anniversary on Sunday and I haven't the faintest idea what I should get her. The Tenth Anniversary is an aluminum one and that is out.

December 6th.

Olive and I returned this morning from our two days' stay in Western Ontario. We left Chatham before six this morning and drove some 45 miles into Windsor where we caught the morning flight. There I learned of an incident that I never heard of before but which is entirely confirmed.

When the Airport was being opened, a prominent Liberal politician was shaking hands with everybody and making himself generally agreeable. There were two ladies standing by themselves. He went over and shook hands benignly and at length, and when he left Harold Danforth, our Member from Kent, and Mr. Campbell, a Conservative M.P. from Lambton-Kent, came along. Danforth said to him: "Who are those ladies, and do you know them?" He said, "Well, I do not know their names but one is my agent at one of my polls, and the other looks after two or three polls." Danforth said: "Isn't that interesting. One is my wife and the other is Mrs. Campbell."

I am going to stay around home for the weekend and see what I can do about getting a back-log of work brought up-to-date. The last two weekends I have been away and it is hard on one to burn the candle at both ends.

The reception in Western Ontario, at Wallaceburg, Ridgetown, Chatham etc., was as warm as anything Olive and I had received in 1958, but the Anvil Chorus against me in the Toronto papers still continues with undimmed fury....

As 1963 ended, I was becoming inured to the attacks of my opponents, within and without the Conservative Party. Their fury had long since reached the point of overkill, and, as I told the press, I was not losing any sleep over it. Indeed, some of this caused me to be reminded of the experience of old Senator Clay in the United States in 1834. He had been attacked most bitterly. When a previously unheard voice was added to his detractors, he replied: "I can't understand it. I don't remember ever doing anything for him."

CHAPTER NINE

※

M Y HEARING IS NOT THE BEST, but I have always had more than sufficient to assure my knowledge of what was going on about me. I often wondered if the would-be power brokers within the Conservative Party, who so assiduously devoted themselves to my removal from office, had any appreciation of the fact that, for the most part, they had no secrets. In the days and months that followed the defeat of the government in 1963, I was reminded of a story told about Sir Winston Churchill before his return to office in 1951. One day at Westminster, having wearied of the House, he retired to one of the Members' lounges to partake of some refreshment. He was sitting alone, engulfed by his thoughts, when several of the younger Tory M.P.s came along, engrossed in conversation and oblivious to Churchill's presence in the same room. One said: "It's too bad the old man's stayed so long." Another added: "You know, they say his mind is going." A third remarked: "They say he really doesn't understand Parliament any more." Finally, Sir Winston leaned forward, turned to his critics, and wryly observed: "They also shay he can't hear."

I wondered also if the self-styled power brokers understood the damage they were bringing on the Conservative Party, to which they gave vocal support, or if they cared what bitter harvest the party might reap. It was said that I had no "guiding right" to the Leadership of the Conservative Party. This was true. But those who took up this cry missed the point that I had not received my mandate from the party's great and powerful, but from the average Canadian. I knew to whom I was accountable and it was not to those who, for their own ends, decided to subvert the institution of democratic free will and unfettered Canadianism that the Conservative Party had become during my leadership.

From being an Ontario-based, Toronto- and Montreal-dominated, racially exclusive party, appealing mainly to those of British ancestry, except for the old *bleus* of Quebec, the Conservative Party had opened its doors to encompass most if not all the races that comprised modern Canada. There were men of thirteen different national descents, other than Canada's founding ones, represented among Conservative Members of Parliament under my leadership. My election as leader in 1956 could only have taken place in a democratized party, in which those other than the chosen of Bay and St. James streets found opportunity to give effective voice to their aspirations. When the Toronto clique talked about taking the party back to its "good, old days", I knew what they had in mind. I remembered my own experiences as a candidate in 1925 and 1926.

I want to make this perfectly clear: I did not declare war on any person or group within the Conservative Party. Although I beat back challenge after challenge, there was never a point when I was not prepared to agree to let bygones be bygones. For example, when I addressed the meeting of the National Executive of the Conservative Party at Ottawa's Château Laurier Hotel on 26 October 1963, I stated sincerely that I was not going to resurrect what took place within the party in February 1963. I summed up my views with these words: "I want to see the spirit of this Party directed to fighting Grits, not fighting Tories from within."

At the time, there seemed little point in commenting on the activities of the former Conservative Member for York West, who was attempting to organize all of Toronto's unsuccessful Tory candidates in the '62 and '63 elections for the purpose of a public declaration that no Conservative ever again could be elected in Metropolitan Toronto so long as I continued as leader. I knew this to be part of the clique's campaign to undermine me at the party's 1964 Annual Meeting, scheduled for early in the new year. They were trying to muster support for the proposition that there should be a secret (they lacked the courage to fight in the open) ballot on my leadership. If they were successful, I would be out directly. If they failed but came close, they hoped to advertise the split between the party's pro- and anti-Diefenbaker elements so as to render my continued leadership ineffective. Naturally, they were encouraged at every turn by new-found friends in the Liberal Party, because with either result, Prime Minister Pearson would be able to bail his government out of its morass by calling a snap election, in the expectation that the Conservative Party would be decimated in its outcome.

As I noted in Chapter Eight, the Pearson government, fumbling and stumbling, was doing an effective job of defeating itself. Mr. Pearson's "Sixty Days of Decision" became "Sixty Days of Derision". His "co-operative federalism" became an excuse to surrender at every turn to the demands of a government in Quebec which regarded every submission as a reason for still greater demands. His Hyannisport honeymoon with the Kennedy administration, announced on 10 May 1963, to herald a new age of active and productive co-operation between Canada and the United States failed before it began. The 28 October edition of *U.S. News and World Report* observed: "Washington's relations with the new Liberal Government of Canada are more strained than ever before in history." Mr. Pearson, of course, denied this. He said he could just pick up the telephone and call President Kennedy any time he wanted to. But would President Kennedy answer? The Liberals had won many votes with their contention that I was anti-American. I was not, and never was. It was not my government but the Pearson government that introduced a thirty-per-cent tax on foreign investment. Liberal Finance Minister Walter Gordon said that the tax would save the nation. Yet, they cowered at the storm of protest it aroused and, in their retreat, left uncertainty, confusion, and resentment throughout the investment community. And where were the measures Pearson had promised to restore the pegged Canadian dollar to par value with the United States dollar? What had been heresy in 1962 became dogma in 1963, and was continued to 1970. The Prime Minister boasted that his government would prove that my government had broken its commitments on nuclear weapons. I demanded that he produce the relevant documents. The files were searched and he decided that it was not appropriate to make anything public. The reason was obvious: there was nothing to make public.

In the 1963 campaign, the Liberals boasted that they would usher in a new era in labour relations. Epitomizing their approach to this problem was the case of Hal Banks and the labour war on the Great Lakes. Who was this pampered pet of the Liberal Party? Harold Chamberlain Banks was a United States citizen who had been welcomed into Canada by the St. Laurent government, despite his career in crime. Over the years he had been variously charged with offences that ran from bad cheques and burglary to murder, and in 1930 he had been sentenced to a maximum of fourteen years in San Quentin Penitentiary.

Yet this man was welcomed into Canada, where, at every critical step in his career, he was assisted by a cloak of Liberal government protection. Normally, an ex-convict would not be allowed into our country, or, once in, would be liable to deportation. At the time of Banks's initial entry, however, he was not required to answer any embarrassing questions about his criminal record (see Hansard, page 3978, 12 April 1954).

In 1948, Canadian shipowners and prominent Canadian trade union officials, with the approval of the Liberal government, had approached the United States-based Seafarers' International Union of North America for help in breaking the Canadian Seamen's Union, which was causing major labour strife and was charged with being Communist-dominated. The man who came to Canada as International Representative of the SIU and, subsequently, President of the Seafarers' International Union of Canada was Hal Banks. If ever the alleged cure was as wretched as the disease!

The immigration laws and procedures were twisted, altered, and reshaped to bring in one who by any reading of the law was undesirable. In succession, Liberal Labour Minister Milton Gregg, Secretary of State and later Citizenship and Immigration Minister J. W. Pickersgill, and Citizenship and Immigration Minister and later Finance Minister Walter Harris supported Banks with their "personal judgment". Their cry was that Banks was not nearly as bad as he had been painted, that he had been more sinned against then sinning, and that, good or bad, he was necessary and fulfilled a public service in ridding Canadian maritime unions of the Communist menace.

So bad was Banks's record in Canada that when he applied for landed-immigrant status in June 1954, the Inquiry Officer designated by the Minister of Citizenship and Immigration, under Section 11 of the Immigration Act, recommended that Banks be deported on the basis of crime involving moral turpitude. Banks appealed to the Minister against his deportation order. The Liberals allowed his appeal. On 6 July 1954, an Order-in-Council pursuant to Section 5(d) of the Immigration Act, as amended June 1954, authorized his status as a landed immigrant. Citizenship Minister Harris, in explaining the government's decision, referred to Banks's "successful rehabilitation" — Banks was a valued source of Liberal campaign funds and election "muscle". Given this status and his established Canadian domicile, the possibility was eliminated of Banks's ever being deported from Canada, even though his application for Canadian citizenship was later rejected on the grounds that his "whole career and conduct" showed he had not behaved as "the average Canadian citizen would, should or does".

From 1957 to 1963, my government made every effort to deal with Banks. But at every turn we were frustrated by developments, legislative and otherwise, initiated during the previous administration. From his invulnerable position as a landed immigrant, he feared no legal move against him. When the Canadian Maritime Union challenged the SIU's supremacy on the Great Lakes, and open violence erupted in 1961, we took the only step possible to open the door to effective prosecution: we appointed an Industrial Disputes Inquiry Commissioner, Mr. Justice T. G. Norris, to investigate the matter. It was the heat generated by the evidence brought before the Norris Commission that started to melt the seams of Banks's tight empire of tyranny. For the first time, witnesses were emboldened to testify, officials previously silent spoke out, light was shed, facts emerged.

The Norris Report was brought down on 15 July 1963, by which time the Liberals had taken office. Banks told an international convention of his SIU in the United States shortly after the 1963 Canadian election that his friends were back in power. What he had not calculated on was the weight of public indignation forcing his "friends" to act. The Judge's findings turned the erstwhile amiable and eligible friend of Liberalism into an odious and dangerous associate. The Pearson government found itself obliged to implement, albeit cautiously, the recommendations of the Norris Report. The SIU and four other maritime unions were placed in trusteeship.

From the number of possibilities available, Banks was charged with conspiracy to commit assault, an offence that was one of the few that provides no ground for extradition proceedings. He was convicted on 5 May 1964 and sentenced to five years. He gave notice of appeal. Significantly, when bail was set, Banks was not required to remain within the jurisdiction of the court that had convicted him. Any law student would know that this was tantamount to giving Banks immunity from arrest should he leave Canada. He disappeared. His twenty-five-thousand-dollar bail was forfeited. When asked, the government repeatedly stated it had no knowledge of his whereabouts. He could not be found. Yet, it took an enterprising newspaper reporter only two hours to find him: on an SIU yacht in Brooklyn harbour, his white Cadillac convertible parked alongside.

When, much later, the Attorney General of Ontario initiated proceedings to have Banks extradited from the United States to face a perjury charge, the United States Secretary of State, Dean Rusk, personally intervened to protect Banks. The Banks affair, of course, was just a foretaste of disclosures yet to come, revealing a moral rot that astounded even the government's supporters. The Liberal Party's only hope was a critically divided Conservative Party in Opposition. We were, of course, still in the midst of this Banks business when the Annual Meeting of the Conservative Party took place in Ottawa from 1 to 5 February 1964.

I approached the Annual Meeting with confidence.

Caucus was overwhelmingly behind me. Our record in Opposition was generally admitted to be effective. What was more, the revelations and events since 8 April 1963 had resulted in a positive reassessment of our record as a government. As to dissident voices within the party, if they wanted a showdown I was prepared to meet them. At stake was something fundamental, and more important than my leadership.

The organizational structure of a national political party, from the poll worker to the national president, and at every level in between, must complement its parliamentary caucus. The men and women elected to the House of Commons carry the load and bear the ultimate democratic responsibility. The national executive (where caucus representation is minimal) has an advisory and consultative role.

Over the years, I had watched the would-be kingmakers, the Warwicks of the Conservative Party. I have written in Volume One about the fates that in turn befell the Right Honourable R. B. Bennett, the Honourable "Fighting Bob" Manion, and the Honourable John Bracken. It cannot be denied that whenever the effective management of the party fell into the hands of non-parliamentary pashas, electoral disaster had followed. After my election as leader, I attempted to balance the influence of the National Executive by initiating the practice of National Annual Meetings in non-election years. These would be large gatherings, with as many as fifteen hundred or more delegates, broadly representative of the party's popular base. They would serve to keep the leader in regular association with the rank and file of his party. Equally important, they would help to maintain the commitment and sense of purpose of those who supported the party where it counted most: at the constituency level, and particularly in those ridings where we did not have a sitting Member. Thus, I found it difficult to take seriously reports I received in January 1964 that those who opposed me were engaged in attempting to convince the rank and file that I had stifled both freedom of expression and the forward march of our party. This from people the majority of whom could not get themselves elected to any public office.

I placed the question squarely before the Annual Meeting on the afternoon of 4 February:

I come before you knowing that you are about to decide a question of leadership which I want decided. No leader, no man whatever his dedication to his country and his party may be, can ever march forward facing the foe if he is afraid that there is somebody behind him who is interfering directly or indirectly. . . . I now come to a question that is on the minds of many. I have never given my opinion on the question of a secret ballot on the motion of confidence, except to say that the annual meeting would decide. The constitution of the party says that the regular course shall be followed. In the wisdom of the years, the vote has always been an open one. I know there are many as conscientious as I am, who feel there should be a secret vote. I will not say to you what that will mean in the years ahead. On the other hand, I do not want to leave here and say that if we had had a secret vote, the results might have been otherwise. I want you the delegates, to decide, and if you decide on the secret vote that is fine with me. I want to know where I stand with you. *I want to know where you stand too.*

A thousand and more delegates jammed the hall. The diehards were at the centre: J. M. Macdonnell, Douglas Harkness, Art Smith, Jr., Heath Macquarrie, Richard Holden, and Egan Chambers of Montreal, the same old group. I watched them as I spoke. I saw the Fulton supporters break ranks, led on by the enthusiasm of Gerald Coultas, a young lawyer from Vancouver; their organized hostility turned to cheers. The Prairie and Maritime delegates, with few exceptions, were solid in their support. The Ontario group was splintered: Bassett had broken with Goodman to support me. The motion on the secret ballot was defeated by three to one; the resolution of confidence in my leadership carried overwhelmingly by some ninety-eight per cent. I considered that, finally, the issue of my leadership had been put to rest.

As to the Toronto *Telegram*'s puzzling complaint the next day that I had failed to grasp the necessity of conciliatory gestures: this was not true. Despite past differences, I had gone the extra mile in designating the Honourable Léon Balcer as first lieutenant in Quebec. I had made him my seat-mate in the House of Commons. Although this was not formally announced until the day after the leadership vote, every delegate from Quebec was aware of what was happening. Mr. Balcer had made an impressive "One Canada" speech in the House in October, and I hoped to encourage him in the practical business of re-establishing Conservative constituency organizations throughout his province.

I soon realized, however, that I was not going to succeed in attempting to turn Léon Balcer into a modern George-Etienne Cartier. He began to insist that he had become Deputy Leader. The party had never had a Deputy Leader, and if it had, he would have been elected in a regular way by a National Convention. Mr. Balcer must have had something else in mind. His attacks on my leadership must be regarded in the light of his later public conversion to the Liberal Party. This did not take place, however, until he had played out his role in the 1964 flag debate and had initiated yet another assault on my leadership. The Liberals were openly pleased with the services Balcer rendered in keeping up the image of a divided Conservative Party.

I am not going to dwell on the flag question. We have had the maple leaf flag since 1964. There are, however, certain things that need to be put down on paper, for the record.

First of all, I disagreed completely with Prime Minister

Pearson's approach to the flag question. On Sunday, 17 May 1964, he announced to a Royal Canadian Legion Convention in Winnipeg that Canada was going to have a new flag. Although he made much of the fact that he brought the flag resolution before Parliament on 5 June, he forgot to mention that he had no choice in the matter because the Order-in-Council which made the red ensign the official flag of Canada provided that it was subject to change only by Parliament. Before the flag resolution was brought in, the Prime Minister should have consulted with the other parties, and particularly with Her Majesty's Loyal Opposition. Instead, he committed his government and his party on the issue and boxed in the minor parties, who were afraid of an election.

This was not a piece of proposed legislation like any other. We could not let it pass in expectation that when we came into office we then could follow the Pearson course and change it to our heart's desire. The flag of the nation cannot be changed with the political seasons. Thus, we had to oppose it or forever hold our peace. The Conservative Party took a reasonable stand. To stand fast was the only weapon we had.

In Cabinet, on Monday, 23 April 1962, I had asked my colleagues to support a Dominion-Provincial meeting on the subject of the flag so that if a design were there agreed upon it could be recommended to Parliament. I canvassed them again in November 1962, with the result that this important issue would have been laid before the Constitutional Conference, which was aborted by the 1963 election result. Mr. Pearson took Canada another step down the road to disunity by forcing his flag on Parliament. He refused in every way to allow the Canadian people to decide whether they wanted to change their flag, or, if they did, what they would like to have in its stead.

Canada had a flag. It flew over the Headquarters of the Canadian Corps in France in 1918. A meeting of the Mackenzie King Cabinet on 27 October 1943 decided that our army should fly the Canadian red ensign wherever Canadian forces were serving with the forces of other nations. It was officially recognized as Canada's flag by Order-in-Council in 1945. On 21 November 1951 Mr. St. Laurent in reply to the question: "What steps are being taken by the government with respect to the adopting of a distinctive national flag?" answered: "See Order-in-Council P.C. 5888 of September 5, 1945." Canada had a flag, a flag ennobled by heroes' blood. Mr. Pearson believed that a distinctive flag was one in which there should be no relationship with the past, nothing to indicate our heritage: the greatness of the French régime or the contribution of Great Britain.

One Canada, I believed, should be symbolized by a flag containing both the Union Jack and the fleur-de-lis. This new flag would take the red ensign, remove the Canadian coat of arms from the flag, and replace it with a fleur-de-lis approximately the same size as the Union Jack. I realized that such a flag would be objected to by some on the grounds that it had the Union Jack thereon, and by others who would object to it because it had the fleur-de-lis thereon, but I believed the Canadian people would realize that such a flag would be most acceptable in the interests of Canadian unity. Neither the Union Jack nor the fleur-de-lis was a sign of subservience to a colonial past. There was no colonialism in honouring our history.

The stand of Her Majesty's Loyal Opposition was neither frivolous nor captious. We were charged with a filibuster. We held up no legislation brought before us; the fact that the government had no legislative program ready was not our responsibility. Indeed, at a meeting of the various party leaders in the House of Commons at eleven-thirty a.m. on Friday, 21 August 1964, I stated that I was most anxious to come to some compromise on the flag question. I again offered (this was our third meeting) to agree that the flag debate be closed after a day or so, and that a committee of the House be set up to make a recommendation on the flag. This would have given Members an opportunity to go back to their ridings and secure the opinions of their constituents. I suggested that the committee report at the end of two months. Mr. Pearson said it should be able to report in three weeks. I remarked that I had heard that he was anxious to have the flag flying by the time the Queen visited Canada in October. Mr. Thompson interjected that he thought nothing would give her greater pleasure. I rejoined that no matter how she felt she would not be able to reveal her feelings, given the constitutional limitations of the Crown. We found that we could not agree on either the committee's time limit or a limitation of debate in the House following the committee's report. Eventually, a compromise was reached and the flag question was sent to a committee made up of seven Liberals, one of whom was to serve as a non-voting chairman, five Conservatives, and one each from the NDP, Social Credit, and Créditistes, with a report to be made within six weeks.

On the afternoon of 21 August, in something of a "double think" stratagem, Mr. Pearson announced that the government would allow its Members a "free" vote on the flag. This meant absolutely nothing. The Honourable Yvon Dupuis, Minister without Portfolio, and soon to be summarily dismissed from the Pearson Cabinet for alleged involvement in a race-track scandal in Quebec, kept close watch over the debate from the government side. (Until now, Mr. Dupuis has not been given proper credit for his contribution in this connection.) By the time the flag was referred to committee on 10 September, no one who had any feeling at all about the flag had not publicly committed himself to a position. This was why I refused to agree to a short time limit for debate on the committee's recommendations.

Because of a secret prior arrangement between the Liberals and the third parties, the Conservative Members of the flag committee were badly out-manoeuvred. Thus, we could not accept the committee's report, brought down on 29 October. Again I had to refuse the Prime Minister's demand for a time limit. There were still some thirty Conservative Members who wanted to speak. Knowing that the battle was lost, the overwhelming will of caucus was that each Member be given a final opportunity to stand for what he believed in.

Our eight colleagues from Quebec, however, under Balcer's leadership refused any accommodation with the rest of caucus. Any flag containing the Union Jack was anathema to them. We could find no common ground. The fleur-de-lis was of no importance whatsoever in Quebec, they claimed. They argued that the consequence of the Conservative position would be that all Conservative candidates would be wiped out in Quebec in the next election. Early on in the debate, Balcer told the House that closure would be necessary, and on 9 December, he asked the Prime Minister to invoke it. This Mr. Pearson did on 17 December. These facts speak for themselves.

On 21 December 1964 I expressed the following views in a letter to a concerned Canadian:

The Progressive Conservative party, Her Majesty's Loyal Opposition, stood alone in the House of Commons against the removal of the Union Jack from Canada's national flag. The Liberals, with one exception; the N.D.P. party, and the Social Credit party, with only four to the contrary, and the Créditistes party joined in a united stand that the Union Jack should have no place on that flag.

We fought for what we believed was right. We have lost. We

could take no other stand than that Canada's flag should have thereon symbols of Canada's heritage.

The Liberal government was able to have closure imposed on debate in the House. However, it will not be able to impose closure on the minds and souls of millions of Canadians.

Earlier, on 17 November, I had written to another worried citizen:

We have a government that is determined to bring down all our traditions. Their first consideration is to remove the Union Jack from any Canadian flag; their next has been to bring about the right of provinces to set up "associate states" within the nation, and while only one Liberal has been openly advocating a republic, the latest action of the government in removing The Queen's portrait from Canadian Citizenship Courts accentuates the trend.

If Mr. Pearson hoped to set in motion a nationalistic crusade, marching under his new flag, he failed. What Canada had was a flag by closure. Yet, he and the Liberals proclaimed to all who would listen: "Now all the difficulties in Quebec have been ended." Ended? This was just the beginning.

Of course, Canadians generally found it difficult to accept that the Pearson government, so highly recommended by virtually every media report, could have such feet of clay. Every imaginable excuse, every charitable view, has been presented in aid of the Pearson government. Was it my responsibility that under that administration scandal followed scandal? Was I their inspiration? The government that I had had the privilege to lead from 1957 to 1963 was an honest government. In Opposition, we were able to bring to the attention of the Canadian people only those things that the colossal ineptness of the Pearson government made possible. Hal Banks gave way to Lucien Rivard.

The details of the Rivard or Denis scandal are available in a variety of published books, beginning with the *Report* of Mr. Justice Dorion, who investigated the affair. Briefly, Lucien Rivard, a Montreal underworld figure, was arrested on 19 June 1964 on a United States warrant, and charged with smuggling heroin. He was held in Montreal's Bordeaux Jail while awaiting completion of the proceedings for his extradition. He and his associates were desperate that he must avoid trial. Consequently, the lawyer retained by the United States government in this case, Mr. Pierre Lamontagne, was offered a twenty-thousand-dollar bribe if he would co-operate and not oppose bail for Rivard. Had the bribe been offered by some thug, it would have been one thing. But it took on an entirely different aspect when made by Raymond Denis, Executive Assistant to Canada's Minister of Immigration, the Honourable René Tremblay. And intensifying our concern was the fact that when Lamontagne proved uncooperative, others associated with the Pearson government brought pressure to bear on him. These men were Guy Lord and André Letendre, assistants to Justice Minister Guy Favreau, and Guy Rouleau, M.P. for Dollard and Prime Minister Pearson's Parliamentary Secretary. Mr. Lamontagne reported all this, and more, to the RCMP. The Commissioner of the RCMP informed Mr. Favreau of Lamontagne's allegations on 14 August. An investigation was launched. Mr. Favreau informed Mr. Pearson of this matter on 2 September. In the meantime, Denis resigned, quietly. The RCMP reported on their investigation on 18 September, identifying Guy Rouleau as the probable "linchpin" in this affair. Here the matter would have died had it not been for the courage, competence, patience, and general vigilance of Erik Nielsen, Q.C., Conservative M.P. for the Yukon.

Mr. Nielsen came to me when he caught wind of what was going on. If he was going to embark on a private investigation of the Rivard-Denis bribery plot, he had to proceed carefully. Mr. Lamontagne had gone to the RCMP with his story because he feared Mafia reprisals. It was entirely within the realm of possibility that an attempt might be made to silence Mr. Nielsen if he were caught trying to expose the tentacles of Cosa Nostra activity within the Pearson administration.

Erik Nielsen finished his investigations on 20 November, and we had to ensure that he was provided an opportunity as soon as possible to state his case in the House. As it happened, with only a few weeks before the Christmas recess, the government faced two major problems. First, the flag committee had reported and a lengthy debate was expected. Second, unless the Main Estimates were completed (Justice, Defence, and Transport remained), the Ministry would have to request Interim Supply. The Honourable (now Senator) George McIlraith had succeeded Guy Favreau as Government House Leader on 30 October. A senior member of the House and a good parliamentarian, he knew the embarrassment his government would suffer if he had to ask for Interim Supply for the month of January, as seemed likely. The Pearson government would be in a position similar to that which had faced my government in 1963, a dangerous situation for a minority government. Our House Leader, Gordon Churchill, was fully aware of the difficulties facing the Government House Leader. He knew also that Mr. McIlraith would be knowledgeable of these matters. Thus, Mr. Churchill proposed delaying the impending flag debate, substituting instead the consideration of the Main Estimates, and setting the rigid time limit of five days for their completion; in return, he asked only that the estimates of the Department of Justice be taken up on Monday, 23 November. The other estimates might be brought forward at the government's convenience. Had the Cabinet rejected our offer, the business of the House would have been left in a state of uncertainty. They may have been suspicious, but they agreed. On Wednesday, 18 November, Mr. McIlraith announced the proposed plan; an order of the House confirmed it. Mr. Nielsen would have his chance.

Incredibly, though apparently given ample warning by various sources throughout Friday, Saturday, and Sunday, Favreau's Cabinet colleagues failed to rally to give him the support and guidance he so desperately needed. They knew that Nielsen would lead for us, but nothing was done to forestall him or blunt the edge of his attack. When Monday came, Favreau delivered a studiously prepared summary of his department's activities, policies, and plans. When he resumed his seat, Nielsen rose to unfold a story of alleged incompetence on the part of the Minister, of alleged bribery attempts in a narcotics case, of alleged involvement of persons closely associated with Cabinet Ministers and with the Prime Minister. The House was electrified.

Mr. Favreau denounced Nielsen's charges as a pack of lies. Cries of McCarthyism, muckraking, smears, and cowardice came from the government benches. The truth was apparent the next day when Prime Minister Pearson summarily fired Guy Rouleau as his Parliamentary Secretary. That afternoon, Mr. Favreau sought to extricate himself and the Liberal government from the crisis by agreeing to our demand for the appointment of a judicial inquiry. Chief Justice Frédéric Dorion of the Quebec Superior Court was appointed, and over the next few months would find proven every detail of the charges. For the moment, however, the government was on dry land, or should have been.

A question addressed to the Prime Minister on 24 November produced an unexpected result. Hansard records it thus:

Mr. Harkness: . . . Was he [the P.M.] informed by the Minister of Justice in regard to any of the other circumstances of this case prior to those circumstances being brought to the attention of this house yesterday?

Mr. Pearson: I was informed by the Minister of Justice of some of the circumstances shortly before his estimates came before the house. . . .

Mr. Harkness: . . . Does he mean he was informed yesterday or a week ago?. . .

Mr. Pearson: I think I was informed on the day before his estimates were brought before the house.

Mr. Favreau appeared stunned by Mr. Pearson's response. The truth was that the information had been conveyed to the Prime Minister not just a few days earlier but on 2 September, when the two of them had been together on a flight from Charlottetown to Ottawa. When Mr. Pearson was made aware that his reply was not in accordance with the facts, he waffled. Days elapsed before he finally acknowledged his error, not to the House of Commons but by a letter to Mr. Justice Dorion. He explained his "error" to the House only after he had been challenged on a Question of Privilege.

Some apologists for Mr. Pearson have advanced the view that because the flag debate precluded the normal question period, he had no opportunity to correct his position. This is, of course, contrary to a long-established and well-known custom of the House. Whenever any Member has reason to object to any previous proceedings that he considers unfair to him, or to correct statements of his that have been wrongly recorded, or to apologize for an error, the Speaker invariably permits him to rise on a Question of Privilege to state his case. This takes precedence over any other business. All that Mr. Pearson had to do at the opening of any day's sitting was to rise and explain.

The Dorion Report was tabled in the House of Commons on 29 June 1965. It concluded:

There cannot be any doubt either that lawyer Denis did offer to lawyer Lamontagne a sum of $20,000 to obstruct the course of justice. . . . I find no difficulty in reaching the conclusion that there is certainly "prima facie" evidence of an offence under the criminal code.

Of Guy Rouleau, the judge observed:

These facts clearly indicate that Mr. Guy Rouleau tried to use his influence as parliamentary assistant to the Prime Minister to secure the release of Lucien Rivard on bail. . . . an intervention of this sort, particularly coming from a person in authority, certainly constitutes a reprehensible act, because it comes into conflict with the normal course of justice; but it does not constitute an act within which are to be found the elements essential in the perpetration of a criminal act.

The Report continued:

On the other hand it is clear that Mr. Guy Lord did not wilfully commit a reprehensible act, but it is certain that he acted imprudently.

As to André Letendre:

There is no doubt that Mr. Letendre's intervention was reprehensible, but bearing the circumstances in mind, this step was taken without malicious intent, with the sole purpose of being agreeable to his friend, Guy Rouleau for whom he wanted to do a favour.

It was, however, the portion dealing with Guy Favreau that was crucial to a judgment of the Pearson government:

Considering that he did not require the R.C.M.P. to hunt for other facts that would have completed the information obtained up to that date;

Considering that he was placed in a position of being influenced by the relations that existed between himself and the persons mentioned in the denunciation formulated by Mr. Lamontagne;

Considering that he was called upon to hand down a quasi-judicial decision;

The Honourable the Minister of Justice before reaching a decision should have submitted the case to the legal advisers within his department with instructions to complete the search for facts if necessary and secured their views upon the possible perpetration of a criminal offence by one or several of the persons involved.

Mr. Justice Dorion also concluded that Prime Minister Pearson had been made aware of his Parliamentary Secretary's involvement on 2 September 1964. He had reached his conclusion despite Mr. Pearson's letter to him on 16 December denying this knowledge. The judge obviously found it difficult to understand a situation in which the Minister of Justice would tell the Prime Minister only of the involvement of the lesser of the individuals in the bribery plot, neglecting entirely to tell him of the involvement of the P.M.'s own Parliamentary Secretary. The judge must have found it curious, to say the least, that Mr. Pearson remembered none of this until forced to, and then only selectively. Mr. Pearson's letter did not constitute sworn evidence and, properly, could not be treated as such. If Mr. Favreau told the Prime Minister about Mr. Rouleau, then the Prime Minister did not give Parliament, the country, or Judge Dorion all the facts. If Mr. Favreau withheld what he knew about the Prime Minister's Parliamentary Secretary from 2 September to 23 November, then Mr. Favreau should have been dismissed on the spot. In either case, the Prime Minister should have taken action to deal with Mr. Denis. What did the Prime Minister do? When the report was handed down, he wrote another letter demanding the judge amend his report.

The casual attitude of Mr. Pearson to the Rivard business made people wonder if this was an everyday occurrence. It is true that in consequence of the Dorion Report Mr. Favreau lost his Justice portfolio. But by backing to the hilt the Prime Minister's incredible account of selective amnesia, he gained the Presidency of the Privy Council. The only visible effect these revelations had on the government was the letter Pearson sent to all his Ministers on 1 December 1964, outlining a "code of political conduct" to keep them and their staffs out of trouble.

Then, in the midst of the Dorion inquiry, on a rather balmy evening in early March, Lucien Rivard and another prisoner asked for permission to flood the skating rink at Bordeaux Jail. Naturally, permission was granted, despite the fact the rink contained half a foot of water. Using the hose for a ladder, they scaled the wall and escaped. Recaptured on 16 July, Rivard now faced Canadian charges. His extradition to the United States was proceeded with post-haste.

I was asked about this in an interview for CBC television's "The Nation's Business" on 21 July. I said, in part:

This is a strange sequel. For so long, a Parliamentary Secretary and Executive Assistants were doing everything they could to keep him from being extradited. After all, he was going to contribute $50,000 or $60,000 to the Liberal Party. An alleged $20,000 bribe was made. These people tried to prevent him being extradited; however, they did not succeed because of the honesty of Pierre Lamontagne, a lawyer in Montreal who could not be bought, and the courage of Erik Nielsen who stood up in the House of Commons and against jeers revealed the facts — indeed, he was met by the challenge of the then Minister of Justice [Mr. Favreau] that what he was saying was false, absolutely false, and that he was a coward to make the statement in the House of Commons. After all this came the findings of the Dorion Commission, which have left Canadians shocked, whatever their political party may be, that there could be such carryings-on in high places; that international crime and the Mafia had been able to work itself into the higher echelons of government.

Now that he has been recaptured, there is a great desire to get him out of the country. . . . They do not want him here before an election. They do not want him to give evidence. They say that later on, after he has been dealt with by the U.S., the charges that have now been withdrawn may be re-instated. All of that will be after the election, denying the people of Canada the information that should be available to them.

What do I suggest should be done? First, Chief Justice Dorion's rights as a Commissioner should be extended by Order-in-Council. His powers should make provision for an examination into the circumstances of Rivard's escape; whether that escape was connected in any way with the failure of those who were trying to defeat justice through bribery, and when that did not succeed the escape procedure was taken; and, also, the degree to which the Government, either in the high or low echelons, was aware of what was going on.

This man has a lot to tell. He could be brought before the Commissioner as a compellable witness. That is the first thing that should be done, so that the Canadian people may learn the true facts. Oh, I know what the Liberal Government is trying to do today. It is pretending that this is just an episode. It is not an episode of no importance when the moral fiber of a nation has been undermined; when internationally everywhere people are disturbed that such occurrences should take place in Canada. It is time to end the kind of pussy-footing on this subject that has been followed by the Government. . . .

What will we do when we assume office? We will get to the bottom of the mess. There will be no pussy-footing. . . . In other words, the time has come to outlaw outlaws in Ottawa. . . .

The posture of the government was incredible. Their defence, if Favreau's statements can be taken for that, was that Erik Nielsen should never have raised the matter and that I was evil incarnate for not denying his doing so. As to the episodic nature of the Rivard affair, how many episodes make a serial? One after the other, scandals were revealed: Banks, Rivard, Minaudo, Bonanno, Meunier, Asselin, Dupuis, the Lamontagne-Tremblay-Sefkind Brothers' furniture case. *The Times* of London was moved to comment on 10 July 1964: "There is a danger that until the question can be resolved, the issue of corruption in government will overhang Canadian politics like a cloud."

The federal wing of the Liberal Party in Quebec should have been shattered by the revelations relating to the influence of crime in high places. Unfortunately, Léon Balcer's parting gift to the Conservative Party was yet a further exercise in disunity. Following his performance in the flag debate, his attacks on my leadership built in crescendo to a demand, issued on 14 January 1965, in the name of the Quebec caucus of the Conservative Party, for "a meeting of the national executive of the party in order to fix a date for a national convention to decide upon the leadership of the party".

In his letter to the Party's national president, Dalton Camp (who had been elected at our 1964 Annual Meeting over Egan Chambers), Balcer charged me with nourishing an anti-Quebec backlash:

... It is our firm conviction, reached after the most careful consideration, that the Conservative Party can no longer carry on as a great national party under its present leadership and the policies which that leadership have engendered.

Balcer had begun his career in Parliament when elected from Three Rivers in 1949, under circumstances that led to proceedings to unseat him which were withdrawn only when the Conservatives agreed to a similar action in another riding. Rumoured a favourite of Premier Maurice Duplessis, he was a curiosity in a party that had that year elected only two Members from Quebec. The Toronto Warwicks made much of him. Despite his mean-spirited display when I was elected leader in 1956, I appointed him to my Cabinet the following year. Over the years, however, his activities at the organization level in Quebec were less than significant. The final comment on Balcer will remain forever the 1965 election. Without him, and despite him, we held even at eight seats and increased the party's popular vote by two per cent.

Basically, Balcer, so far as he believed any of the charges in his letter to Mr. Camp, was simply riding with the tide. Premier Lesage had gone off on his "maîtres chez nous" campaign; with the federal Liberals in disarray and Pearson under his thumb, he seemed to be making a popular success of it. The only party that offered the Quebec voter a real alternative was the Conservative Party. Balcer and his Liberal friends were now bent on eliminating this option. Balcer had had every chance to make his case in caucus. His public statements revealed a style most remote from what it had been, which gave rise to a suspicion among some Members that these had been extramurally prepared.

Erik Nielsen summed up admirably our position on the constitution in a memorandum to caucus on 1 March 1965. I quote but a small part of it here as an indication of the principles that underlay the party's approach to all federal-provincial matters:

. . . What is a constitution in a Federal State but the setting forth of the distribution of powers as between the Federal and provincial parts?

A constitution that does not do this is not a constitution; it is a pious hope.

An invertebrate constitution leads to an invertebrate national structure.

An invertebrate national structure leads to a loss of national identity and integrity and the absorption of our sovereignty. . . .

Are you going to have a situation where some provinces have powers that others do not?

Where the Federal writ runs in some provinces and stops at the boundaries of others?

Is that a nation?

Or is it a loose conglomeration of semi-autonomous states?

Is that what the people want?

If it is not what the people want—and I am sure it is not—that party which tamely subscribes to what it knows is wrong will write its own epitaph in history.

Our job is to stand for Canada. . . .

We will decentralize but not deconfederate.

We will recognize and deal with the problems.

But no adequate solutions can be proposed by a Federal Government shorn of the power to act. . . .

The Honourable Walter Dinsdale wrote to Balcer on 26 January 1965 to discourage him from precipitous action:

Thank you for yours of recent date providing background on the events giving rise to the startling press statements which have appeared regularly since the House recessed on December 18. You can imagine how distressing these have been to those of us sitting in the middle of Confederation here in the Province of Manitoba. It has reminded me of the thunderbolts that Dean Finlayson used to hurl from B.C. when George Drew was leading the Party.

I am glad to see that more recently the voice of moderation and good sense seems to be re-appearing in the Party councils. The Conservative Party has played musical chairs with leaders so often that it would almost appear that they have become addicted to the game. Certainly there should be no precipitate action until the Party Caucus has an opportunity to get together on the matter, especially at a time when the Grits are reeling from the relevations of the Dorion enquiry. . . .

Dr. Lawrence E. Kindt, then Member for Macleod, since deceased, expressed well the reality of our situation in a letter to Mr. Camp on 15 January 1965:

The people out here are up in arms and ready to fight anyone requesting a leadership convention. Mr. Balcer's personal campaign has damaged the entire Progressive Conservative Party across Canada.

Mr. Balcer's attitude and actions are losing us votes and playing directly into the hands of the Grits. Our goodwill and patience towards him and his difficult job in Quebec have been strained to the breaking point. No leader can satisfy everyone and we have all exerted every effort to maintain unity. Our present leader is generally right on the basis of principles. We have the best leader at the helm in the House of Commons, and so we don't need a leadership convention.

The Liberals fear the Right Honourable John G. Diefenbaker, Leader of the Opposition, more than anyone else, and they are constantly trying to destroy him. Mr. Pearson needs to cover up his party's faults by diverting attention. Therefore, this is no time for Conservatives to find fault or to change horses. The vote at the last P.C. Convention settled everything until after the next election, and so let's have no more talk from weak and disgruntled aspiring leaders about a leadership convention.

The meeting was called. E. A. Goodman and George Hogan beat the bushes by telephone, trying to drum up every executive member who was at all inclined to oppose me. In an effort to deprive me of caucus support, they scheduled their meeting for 6 February, a week before Parliament reassembled. I rescheduled caucus. It was getting tiresome, and I rather wearied of their game. The National Executive had no authority to call a leadership convention; even Camp admitted this. So why call the meeting, why jockey the dates? I will leave Mr. Camp, who in 1965 was still in the nuisance stage of his development and operations, until the next chapter.

I met with caucus on 5 February. It was a rousing meeting. The Honourable Paul Martineau represented the views of Léon Balcer, whose nerve appeared to fail him at the last moment. I found the handful who opposed me, led by Heber Smith, M.P. for Simcoe North, particularly offensive. It was with the support of caucus that I met the National Executive the next morning. There, I attempted to detail for them some of the home truths from the experiences of successive national leaders about leading the Conservative Party in Canada. I named the forces who had opposed me over the years and continued to do so. I ended with a plea for the Conservative Party, whose hopes of victory would be forever shattered if we failed to unite. My leadership was affirmed. Balcer was defeated.

In all, the experience left me depressed. I brooded on the situation and came finally to the conclusion that I would resign as leader. I decided that I simply had had enough. Over several days I drafted the letter announcing my decision. This I would give to caucus, to the National Executive, and to the press on 22 March 1965.

On Sunday, 14 March, I invited a few close friends and trusted colleagues to Stornoway to inform them of my decision. It would have been monstrously unfair to reward their years of support with any less notice of a decision that would affect each of them. These men included the Honourable Gordon Churchill, the Honourable J. Waldo Monteith, the Honourable Angus MacLean, Erik Nielsen, Richard Thrasher, National Director of the party, and Kenneth Binks, Q.C., of Ottawa, the party's National Secretary.

When an uninvited Member of Parliament arrived, my

first reaction was to ask him to leave. Instead, I confronted him directly: "Is it clear that there will not be any revelation?" "One hundred per cent," he replied.

In any other circumstance, I would not have considered secrecy so vital. But I had determined that I would use my last days as leader to perform a final public service. Whipper Billy Watson was seeking the Conservative nomination in East York. He had encountered opposition from some within the constituency association who claimed he did not have the right background to be an M.P. Mr. Watson had done more to help the crippled children of Canada than any other person I knew. My regard for him was very high. He felt, and I agreed, that it would be difficult for him to win the nomination unless I spoke in his favour.

It is another of those "ifs" of history. If the uninvited guest had not been present that Sunday morning, I would have been out within eight days. The fact is that the next morning he was busy soliciting support in caucus for the position of interim leader. This quickly came to my attention. When I arrived at my office, there was a letter from R. R. Southam, Conservative Member for Moose Mountain, protesting my unannounced decision:

It was with very great concern that I heard through a mutual friend and colleague yesterday that you were expressing grave doubts about your continuance as leader of our great party. Although I realize that you have had more than ample grounds and provocation for entertaining such thoughts, on the other hand I want to implore you to earnestly and seriously reconsider your position, if such was the case. I am positive, should you decide to resign at this crucial time in the history of our country, that Canadians everywhere would never forgive either you or our party for many years to come.

I was so aroused by the necessity of denying to the press my decision to retire, that I decided not to retire.

One person's immodest rush to advance his ambitions had undone what all the party's power brokers had not been able to achieve. I might add that Whipper Billy received his nomination.

CHAPTER TEN

※

WHY DID I CHOOSE TO FIGHT ON IN 1965? That year I celebrated my seventieth birthday. I had received the highest honour my country and my party could bestow upon me. At an age when most men had turned their thoughts to the quiet joys of retirement, why didn't I? The answer is simply that I had fought a lifetime to bring substance to my One Canada dream. Everything that my government had achieved in equalizing the opportunities for all Canadians in every section of this nation was being imperilled by the policies of the Pearson government and by the hostility of powerful interests within the Conservative Party, who did not want these changes entrenched. I was portrayed as a dangerous man for staying on to fight for all our rights.

The lines were firmly drawn on the battleground of "*Deux Nations*". All else was to become secondary or merely tactical. It was fundamental to me that the Conservative Party must not accept the idea that any Canadian province was a state within a state. I saw in the "Two Nations" concept, then widely advocated in certain parts of our country, the Canadian version of a principle advocated by the Southern States of the American Union in the first sixty years of the nineteenth century. I found shocking the prospect of Canada's division into constituent parts. I was reminded of Daniel Webster's declaration in the United States Senate on 7 March 1850:

Peaceable secession! Peaceable secession! The concurrent agreement of all the members of this great Republic to separate! A voluntary separation, with alimony on one side and on the other? Why, what would be the result?. . .What am I to be? An American no longer? Am I to become a sectional man, a local man, a separatist, with no country in common with the gentlemen who sit around me here, or who fill the other House of Congress? Heaven forbid!

I fought "Two Nations" every inch of the way from the appointment of the Royal Commission on Bilingualism and Biculturalism in 1963 to the attempt to convert the Conservative Party to this confederation heresy at its National Leadership Convention in 1967. As I wrote in Chapter Nine, for my convictions, for my refusal to accept any form of hyphenated Canadianism, I was portrayed as the instrument of an English-Canadian backlash, an anachronistic bigot who had missed the wave of the future. If only they could get rid of me! Prime Minister Pearson proclaimed that Canada needed a "strong Conservative party" (that is to say, a Diefenbakerless one). There was nothing that Quebec's Lesage feared more than a Conservative victory in the 1965 federal election. Ontario's Robarts, apparently, was of a similar mind.

To me, the Conservative Party was the party of Confederation. It could not be allowed to agree to the Balkanization of the country it had been so instrumental in creating. I recognized that French Canadians feared the loss of their identity through assimilation and absorption in the English-Canadian and American cultures. I appreciated also their wish, at the same time, for a fairer share in the economic life and progress of our country, from which they felt they had been excluded in the past. My contention was and is that Quebec could gain within the Confederation what it was impossible to gain outside it. The separation of Quebec would not change the fact of Quebec's cultural bombardment by the industrial society of North America, of which Quebec was and would remain a part. The survival of French Canada after a hundred years of Confederation, however, did not seem to be seriously in doubt, despite the highly charged emotional rhetoric of politicians, academics, and others whose statements consistently flew in the face of the basic facts. At the time of Confederation there were fewer than a million persons of the French race and culture in Canada. Now there were close to six million, excluding those who had emigrated to the New England States. Of those three million or more who lived in the United States, fewer than fifteen per cent had retained their mother language. My idea was that without Confederation there would be neither Canada nor French Canada.

In any event, I regard discussion of separatism's case as an exercise in futility, since Canada, as a free and sovereign nation, cannot under any circumstances contemplate the separation of one of its parts from the rest. This was not to preclude required changes—for example, in our tax structure or in the allocation of powers in our constitution. Believing in Canada and the necessity of its continuing existence, I accepted the necessity of paying the price of Confederation. To those who felt that the price of Confederation came too high, I could only point out that the wisdom of the Fathers had been manifest in the growth of a nation which had gained admiration around the world against tremendous odds of climate and in juxtaposition to the most powerful nation the world has ever seen.

With regard to the compact theory of Confederation, which has given those who would destroy the Canadian union much comfort, so far as there was a compact, it had existed *only* in the political deadlock and lack of progress on all fronts in Upper and Lower Canada (Canada West and Canada East), which made necessary a general British North American Confederation. Furthermore, the British North America Act is more than an ordinary constitutional or legal document; it is the Constitution of a great nation, the legal, spiritual, and fundamental essence and conscience of the Canadian way of life. To consider the product of the Fathers some one hundred years later in terms of a situation that existed only prior to Confederation, and then only in Central Canada, makes no sense to me.

Confederation had created a general government, with powers to legislate in the national interest, and provincial governments, with powers to legislate in matters of local or provincial interest. The original framework was designed to avoid the error of "States Rights" in the United States, which was seen as a major cause of the Civil War. Speaking in Canada's Confederation debates on 6 February 1865, the Honourable John A. Macdonald explained:

Ever since the union was formed, the difficulty of what is called States Rights has existed and this had much to do in bringing on the present unhappy war in the United States. They commenced, in fact, at the wrong end. They declared by their constitution that each state was a sovereignty in itself, and that all powers incident to a sovereignty belong to each state, except those powers which, by the constitution, were conferred on the central government and Congress. Here we have adopted a different system. We have strengthened the general government. We have given the general legislature all the great subjects of legislation. We have conferred on them, not only specifically and in detail, all the powers which are incident to sovereignty, but we have expressly declared that all subjects of general interest not distinctly and exclusively conferred upon the local governments and local legislatures, shall be conferred upon the central government. We have thus avoided that great source of weakness which has been the cause of the disruption of the United States.

Although this was modified to an extent by judicial decision, over the years the basic framework has remained intact.

In this connection, the words of Prime Minister St. Laurent in the House of Commons on 27 October 1949 are pertinent:

The position of our party is and always has been that at Confederation the sovereign powers of the Canadian nation were allocated, part of them to the central Parliament and part to the provincial Legislatures, with anything unprovided for in that specific allocation left within the general powers of the central Parliament; and it has been the view consistently held by the Liberal party that provincial powers should be respected. The corollary of this respect for all the portions of the national sovereignty allocated to the provinces is—our party has contended—that the powers allocated to the central authority can be exercised by that central authority through . . . the Members elected by the people to represent them in the central Parliament without any control by the provinces, or, I should say, by the premiers of provincial governments. . . .

I cite Mr. St. Laurent because his position stands in such stark contrast to the policy of withdrawal or abandonment of federal powers followed by his successors.

The Liberal Party's new position was spelled out by Mr. Pearson in a television interview on 19 April 1964 when he said:

When I said that Quebec had a special position . . . I was thinking of the special position of Quebec which, in my view, makes Quebec a province not exactly like the others. I was thinking of the special position of Quebec as the homeland of a people, the French-speaking people of Canada, and we must recognize

21. The "One Canada" speech to the Conservative Leadership Convention in Toronto, 7 September 1962.

29. That Mr. Diefenbaker is proud of the Scottish heritage he received through his mother is obvious in this photograph taken at the Glengarry Highland Games in 1975.

30. (*Upper right*) An autographed book for a young admirer.

31. (*Lower right*) One of the last photographs of Mrs. Diefenbaker.

surely in Ottawa and in other provinces that Quebec—the Province of Quebec, the provincial government of Quebec—has a special position in protecting and guarding the rights of French-speaking Canadians as guaranteed in our constitution.

This was, in essence, the "Two Nations" theory. It was also a theory which if carried out would lead to the progressive isolation of Quebec in Confederation and ultimately to its separation. Constitutionally, it is the federal government and not any one province which is the protector of the rights of minorities.

Thus, Mr. Pearson's theories struck at the very heart of Canada's constitutional structure. Issues, dormant or resolved many years ago, were resurrected. The results could not but be harmful to Canada's stature as a nation, to its economic well-being, to present progress, and to future achievement. I felt that no nation could long survive the internal disruption and division now in prospect, and at the same time resist the external pressures of continental homogenization which have always been there but which now would be more and more difficult to resist.

My aim was to put an end to those policies which only served to lend increasing respectability to the separatist movement in Quebec. By this I mean that separatism, in its progress from the bizarre and generally unsuccessful operations of Marcel Chaput to an accepted, if not entirely agreed with, part of the political spectrum of the province, was greatly encouraged by Mr. Pearson's practice of setting Quebec apart. It was not the bombings of 1963 and 1964 or the rioting or the rude reception accorded the Queen in Quebec City in October of 1964 that led an increasing number of individuals consciously to opt for separation. Instead, it was the ever-increasing role of the provincial government that led people to conclude that the federal authority was no longer relevant to their needs or futures.

Under the Pearson government, federal responsibility was too often abdicated, with the result that the Lesage government in Quebec moved in to fill the resultant vacuum. To begin with, the federal government had no right to surrender powers belonging to the federal Parliament. These powers were not the government's to surrender. They were, and are, accorded to Parliament under the British North America Act. The provinces by themselves have no right to act in federal matters, nor should agreements reached between the provinces relating to federal fields of jurisdiction have any validity. Only Parliament, under the Constitution, has the right to divest itself of its own powers. This it cannot properly do by simple resolution, but only by legislation which can be debated in detail and voted on, section by section and clause by clause. Constitutions might be amended and changed, but we thought it improper that this should take place behind closed doors and according to secret agreements between the Pearson and Lesage governments.

The question to be asked is, whence did the Liberal government derive its views? The so-called "Fulton-Favreau formula" for amending and Canadianizing the Constitution created a situation in which the provinces were to be given an open sesame in federal matters and the federal Parliament was to be subjected to provincial veto. By removing the dividing line between what was federal and what was provincial, under the guise of repatriating the Constitution, Mr. Pearson would facilitate the assumption by the provinces of powers similar to those claimed by "State Rights" advocates in the United States. I challenged the Fulton-Favreau formula, and I still do, because I fear the radical alteration of our national identity to a loose association of states, each possessing its own powers, in association with others, to legislate in matters affecting all Canadians. It proposed a crazy quilt of Balkanization to replace the Canadian Confederation.

As to Mr. Pearson's Bilingualism and Biculturalism Commission, I was convinced that its appointment and composition would encourage alienation and separatism. To begin with, the problems of biculturalism and bilingualism were both federal and provincial. This Royal Commission would be able to make recommendations only to the federal government. As I could not conceive of any party attempting to solve the problems of national unity through unilateral federal action, and at the expense of the merit system in the federal civil service, I thought the Laurendeau-Davidson Commission at best a dodge. At worst, I saw it giving rise to a popular false hope that solutions to the problems of Confederation would be achieved through a Commission of socialists and outspoken protagonists of particular constitutional changes. The only legitimate forum was a Dominion-Provincial Conference. Ultimately, whatever the views of the Commission, a Conference would have to be convened before any effective action could be taken, or so I thought. I contended this should be done immediately, so that all major ideological and regional points of view would find appropriate representation.

I had proposed such a conference myself in the House of Commons on 4 February 1963, in what amounted to the final policy pronouncement of my administration on this vital subject:

Canada under Confederation has grown and prospered. There have, however, arisen from time to time questions as to whether Canada as she approaches the close of the first century of Confederation has achieved the full measure of the vision of the Fathers of Confederation. It is with this thought in mind that the government has decided to propose the calling of a Federal-Provincial Conference and invitations to such a conference will be despatched to the governments of the ten provinces at once.

The scope of the conference will be of the fullest breadth. It will be asked to study ways and means of repatriating the Constitution; the problem of adequate representations in the public service, in Crown corporations and other government agencies; the recommendations of the Therrien Report [a subcommittee of the Glassco Commission on government organization]; the choice of a national flag and other symbols of our national sovereignty. In brief, the conference will be asked to examine biculturalism and bilingualism in a comprehensive manner.

We were ready to take action to deal firmly and positively with any danger which confronted the basis of the Canadian Confederation, in order that the Canada of tomorrow would be stronger, more united in her diversity, her strength drawn from the partnership of her two original cultures and enriched by the infusion of the people of many other races and colours.

On 29 April 1964 I wrote in reply to a high school student in Montreal:

First, as to Confederation, I believe it was an inspired conception that, over the years, produced a strong, free and prosperous nation. I conceive it to be the duty of all Canadians, from whatever racial stock they may spring, to cherish the spirit of Confederation, maintain its provisions and build on the vast possibilities for a full and rewarding life that it presents to men of goodwill. Confederation *is* Canada.

If Confederation is to be weakened or undermined, Canada will cease to be a nation. Having said this, you will know how I regard Separatism. Separatism is negative and destructive. It is barren alike of hope for the soul or inspiration for the mind. It is the ultimate defeat, the badge of unconditional surrender.

As to bilingualism and biculturalism, these are two necessary and inescapable facets of Canadian nationality. Canada was conceived of by men of two different but equally rich cultures, of two distinctive communities. Bilingualism and biculturalism are facts of Canadian life that cannot—and should not—be hidden or avoided. They are important, even vital, to Canada as a nation. But they are assets, not liabilities; positive factors, not negative ones.

They should be approached in the spirit of co-operation and mutual appreciation and never used as tools of narrow nationalism. They are too valuable to Canadians to be degraded by being used to further the ends of political expediency or as weapons in factional feuding.

The noted Canadian historian Professor W. L. Morton pleaded in a paper prepared for the Conservative Party's National Conference on Canadian Goals at Fredericton in September 1964 that we "Recall the nation to its senses by asserting that federal powers are even more necessary to Canada than provincial rights." This was my view. And, unlike the Liberals and some within the Conservative Party, I did not say one thing in Quebec and another in Toronto or Edmonton.

For example (if I may move ahead to the 1965 election campaign), on Tuesday, 26 October, during my third tour of the province, I had a major meeting in Quebec City. I did not indulge in answering the mendacious slanders used against me to guarantee French Canada's loyalty to the Liberal Party. I told my audience, "I was pictured in Quebec as your enemy, but I was your greatest friend. . . . Nothing means more to me than the unity of this nation. Nothing means more to any Canadian than that. I don't come to you in 1965 and say, 'Today I have certain views.' I have always held these views. . . . When I read these attacks upon me, I wonder whether we are living in a democracy or not." Among the attacks was one by the Honourable Bona Arsenault, Quebec Provincial Secretary, describing me, eulogistically no doubt, as being "worse than the atomic bomb, cholera and rats". I continued:

Let us have a constitution made in Canada for Canadians and by Canadians. That's my idea of Canadianism. . . . I oppose the Fulton-Favreau formula, because if that formula ever came into effect, it would emasculate the power of the central authority in Ottawa. . . . I make my appeal to the hearts of Quebec today and I say this: "If it hadn't been for the stand of the Conservative party, we would have that constitutional amendment today.". . . Canadians in every province want to have you, they want you to be in this nation. They want you to have equal partnership. We must join hands in equality.

I was not as surprised as the pundits who reported it that the crowds at my Quebec meeting far surpassed those of the Prime Minister three weeks before. Following Mr. Balcer's decision to cross the floor, I discovered that I was far from unwelcome in the Province of Quebec. Often, Balcer had discouraged me from speaking and had propagated the notion that I was anathema to French Canada. *La Presse*'s Gérard Pelletier had often declared that I was unwelcome, in fact detested, in *la belle province*. I had come almost to believe this myself until, at the urging of Clément Vincent, the Conservative Member for Nicolet-Yamaska, I spoke at Ste. Perpétue. The audience that evening was at least double the entire population of the village, some twelve hundred in all. To the astonishment of those who had said for years that I didn't know a word of French, I gave my entire thirty-minute speech in French, detailing our program for Eastern agriculture. The audience's response was overwhelming. The media dubbed it "le miracle de Ste. Perpétue".

Of course, those who supported me in Quebec were marked for damnation by the Liberal press. The Honourable Théo Ricard had replaced Balcer as Quebec caucus chairman. On 21 October 1965, the Liberal St. Hyacinthe newspaper *Le Clairon* carried this front-page column: "From day to day, old Dief. gets fat, takes on weight, puts

on a pot. His daily menu: A slice of French Canada sea-
soned with scandal sauce. That stuffs him, I tell you, that
stuffs him to the point that he has to associate himself to a
little guy from the riding to hold his fork . . .
because . . . that's the role [of] Mr. Ricard. . . . " It is perhaps sufficient to note the effect of this shabby propaganda: Mr. Ricard won the 1965 election in St. Hyacinthe-
Bagot by 3,437 votes.

According to some experts, one of my problems in the
1965 campaign was that Mr. Marcel Faribault, Montreal
financier, did not become a Conservative candidate. I first
met Faribault in 1962. He came to see me in Ottawa to
propose that he stand for election as a Conservative candidate in Quebec. Our discussion of the matter, however,
did not proceed beyond his demand for a $500,000 guar-
antee, payable at the rate of $50,000 per annum over ten
years. In 1965, Faribault again indicated an interest. Senator McCutcheon was most anxious that he run. Again
Faribault came to see me. He dismissed our earlier discussion as theoretical, a mere basis for negotiation. There
were certain additional stipulations this time. First, he informed me that he was the foremost Canadian authority
on external affairs, and would have to be Secretary of
State for External Affairs in the event that I formed a government. Second, as the leading French-Canadian Member, he would have to have the right of veto on *all* proposed legislation. Here, our discussion ended. The part
that interests me, however, is that those Conservatives
who touted Faribault must have been aware of his constitutional views. Did they then agree with his expressed
view that "the sole reason for the existence of a federal
government is the common good of the component
states"?

When the House of Commons adjourned on 30 June
1965, subject to recall on 27 September, I was convinced
that Mr. Pearson would call an election. Most of my col-

leagues did not agree. They judged that, as there was little likelihood of a Liberal defeat in the House, Pearson would carry on for at least another year, if only to live down the Dorion Report. So far as I could judge, however, the Liberal situation was likely to get worse, not better, and an election seemed the only avenue open to give Mr. Pearson a second chance. If the findings of Mr. Justice Dorion had tarnished what was left of a once-proud Liberal image, the allegations of Dr. Marcoux (see Chapter Eight), if brought before a Parliamentary Committee, would create a situation in which no Opposition Member would be able to support the government. If defeated by the censure of the Commons, the Liberal Party would be trounced in the resultant general election. For the moment, because of the much publicized internecine strife within the Conservative Party, the Liberals were riding high in both the Gallup and their private polls. Thus, it was apparent to me that we would be back to the hustings in the fall.

My principal task was to overcome past differences within Conservative ranks so as to present a united front to the Canadian people. To this end, I was prepared publicly to welcome back George Hees, who wished to run in Ontario's Northumberland riding; Davie Fulton in Kamloops; Richard Bell in Carleton; Frank McGee in York-Scarborough. I supported Douglas Harkness in Calgary North and Paul Martineau in Pontiac-Témiscamingue. I encouraged Dalton Camp and George Hogan to run in Toronto ridings. I accepted the support of Pierre Sévigny and Egan Chambers in Montreal. Finally, on the advice and solicitation of Wallace McCutcheon and John Bassett, and against the advice of some of my parliamentary colleagues, I appointed Eddie Goodman as National Campaign Director.

Our platform was drafted and approved in ample time, and I must give credit to the Honourable Alvin Hamilton for excellent work in overseeing the preparation of our policy papers. We had, to use our campaign slogan, "Policies for People—Policies for Progress". Most, of course, were an extension of policies and programs begun under my government between 1957 and 1963 and were thus based on sound experience. For example, we were committed to Medicare. We had, after all, set up the Hall Commission in 1961 to study health services. It was my government that brought hospital insurance to all Canadians. Now, we proposed to enlarge the same plan to cover all sickness, including mental illness, on exactly the same basis. We felt we could offer a national health plan including universal Medicare with proper priorities and efficient management.

On education, we proposed to more than double university grants, thus lowering tuition fees, and to bring new life to the federal-provincial programs for vocational schools, so that our youth would be trained for the new age of high skills and automation. To relieve the taxpayer, overburdened with education costs at the elementary and secondary levels, we proposed to allow, for federal income tax purposes, the deduction of municipal taxes, up to five hundred dollars. This would bring about a federal sharing of education costs with the provinces and municipalities, and would offer a national approach to the problems of education, without intrusion on the exclusive jurisdiction of the provinces over this matter.

On old age pensions, our senior citizens were unduly suffering under the spiralling cost of living. Because the Canada Pension Plan made no allowance for them, we proposed to provide one hundred dollars a month in old age pensions without a means test. This was a debt we owed to those who had built our country.

Other planks in our platform included:

N.H.A. mortgages for older homes to aid labour mobility; an end to the eleven-per-cent sales tax on building materials and production machinery (which the Liberals had imposed and which greatly added to the average Canadian's cost of living);

an aggressive foreign-trade sales program to build up world markets;

major port expansion to move Canadian wheat and other products;

the end of the sales tax on drugs (we felt there should be no penalty for being sick);

the establishment of more recreational parks in and near our cities;

urban planning research to assist all communities;

an Eastern farm policy, including a feed-grain agency, a guaranteed four-dollar-per-hundredweight payment for industrial milk to help the dairy industry, and catch insurance for our East Coast salt-fish industry;

a greater emphasis on the ARDA program than the Liberals had displayed;

a national power grid;

more roads to resources;

and the establishment of a Department of Youth to help young Canadians.

Certainly we were in a position effectively to counter the impression, so energetically fostered by the Liberals, and some Conservatives, that our party was disunited and not a practical alternative to the present government.

The election was called on 7 September. Canadians would go to the polls on 8 November. My early campaign schedule called for me to attend a political picnic in Oakville, Ontario, on the afternoon of 18 September before flying to Saskatoon that same evening. The next day, Sunday, I would drive to Prince Albert, where my nomination meeting would take place on the evening of 20 September. I would return to Ottawa the day following to attend to last-minute details. On Friday, 24 September, I would officially open my campaign in Halifax.

On the basis of past experience, I was not prepared to make more than one election appearance in Newfoundland. I had fought four past elections without ever making a breakthrough there. Neither was I prepared to have a large rally in Vancouver or in Kingston. Twice our meetings in Vancouver had been subjected to organized violence, and twice the Queen's University students had endeavoured to howl me down when I attempted to speak in their city. I wanted to avoid, if possible, the uglier aspects of past elections and to keep my campaign close to the people. In consequence of our success with the train in the 1963 campaign, I was determined, again over the objections of the party managers, to use it even more extensively in 1965.

My itinerary for Monday, 27 September, set my pace; in all, I would visit scores of Canadian cities, towns, and villages before election day, and make one hundred and fifty-seven speeches.

Monday, 27 September

12:10 a.m. (ADT)	Depart Moncton
4:10 a.m.	Arrive Campbellton (Remove cars from Train No. 59 and transfer to Train No. 3)
	Fernand Dubé, P.C. Candidate, and Roger Pichette will have group of people at Station prior to departure from Campbellton
8:00 a.m.	Depart Campbellton, N.B., Train No. 3
9:50 a.m.	Amqui, P.Q.
11:05 a.m.	Mont-Joli
11:25 a.m.	Depart Mont-Joli
11:58 a.m.	Rimouski
12:59 p.m.	Trois Pistoles
1:55 p.m. (ADT)	Arrive Rivière-du-Loup
1:15 p.m. (EDT)	Depart Rivière-du-Loup
2:15 p.m.	Ste. Anne
3:10 p.m.	Montmagny

4:10 p.m.	Arrive Lévis
4:30 p.m.	Depart Lévis
5:18 p.m.	Laurier
5:58 p.m.	Manseau
7:10 p.m.	Drummondville
7:50 p.m.	St. Hyacinthe
8:40 p.m.	Arrive Montreal
	Stay overnight

After whistle-stopping through northern New Brunswick and Quebec to Montreal, I returned to Ottawa by car through the ridings to the north of the Ottawa River. The next day, the campaign train took me to Toronto for a major meeting, thence to Windsor, London, and the Hamilton–St. Catharines area. Returning to Toronto, I flew to Winnipeg for a large rally, where I again picked up the campaign train and whistle-stopped through Manitoba, Saskatchewan, and Alberta, with speeches at many points en route. After the Calgary meeting, I flew to Prince George, and thence to Victoria. From there I flew into the Okanagan Valley, which I covered by car before rejoining my train at Kamloops. The train brought me back to Winnipeg. I went on to Port Arthur and Fort William by air.

If there was a turning-point in the 1965 campaign, it came with our meeting at Fort William on 18 October. Local organizers had expected a maximum of fifteen hundred people. Soon all the seats in the arena were taken up, all the standing-room too. An adjoining building had to be quickly opened to make room for the overflow of a thousand or more. One of my major points that evening was the Conservative Party's pledge to enact consumer-loan legislation to ensure a reduction in the rates of interest paid on instalment buying. Studies had shown usurious rates of interest, ranging from eighteen to thirty per cent, and in one case even eighty per cent. We had behind us the experience of the Farm Improvement Loans legislation. We were prepared to do the same for urban dwellers.

On Tuesday, 2 November, the final day of my whistle-stop campaign, the "Conservative Special", as my train was called, moved through southern Ontario, with thousands of people turning out at the fifteen stops en route. The warmth of our reception was reflected there, as it was all over the country, by signs which read, "He cared enough to come". In Montreal, on 3 November, over four thousand people attended a rally in the Maurice Richard Arena, over a thousand more than had attended the Prime Minister's rally the night before. When the Honourable Pierre Sévigny, who appeared unannounced and marched up to the stage to shake my hand, turned to the audience and said, "Stand up and show Mr. Diefenbaker how you're with him," the audience got to its feet. There was no repetition of the fist-fights that had marred the Pearson rally. On Thursday, 4 November, an overflow audience packed Edmonton's Jubilee Auditorium. Ignoring a death threat, I took my stand. I told the crowd that the time had come for Canadians to declare whether they believed in a socialist state or in the principles of private enterprise, tempered to assure the public interest. According to newspaper reports, the crowd broke into applause forty-two times during my speech. I asked the voters to "join humbly and with God's help to build a better Canada. I look ahead with eyes undimmed to that Canada, my Canada, your Canada."

I had great fun in the campaign, twitting the Prime Minister, who seldom ventured forth from his Liberal fortress in Ottawa. On 28 October, he testily declared that the voters could expect another election in a year or eighteen months if another Liberal minority government was formed on 8 November. Fortunately, this remark was tape-recorded by a Toronto newsman. Shortly after that, when the Prime Minister was asked to elaborate on the statement, he denied ever making it. When the recording was played back, he said he didn't mean what he had appeared to say. It was, as I explained to the amusement of my audiences, a case of: "I didn't say what I said when I said it. What I meant to say when I didn't say it was that I wouldn't have said what I said when I did say it." On a more serious note, the major questions concerning Mr. Pearson's national stewardship were left unanswered. Never did the Prime Minister provide any satisfactory answer as to why he felt obliged to demand of Canadian electors a majority government. Never did he answer the charges of corruption in high places. I was surprised, even amazed, when he was able to salvage his situation in Quebec by recruiting the socialists Marchand, Pelletier, and Trudeau as Liberal candidates.

On election day, 8 November 1965, I visited my committee rooms in Prince Albert, talked with party headquarters in Ottawa, and made a rather sentimental journey to the old Land Titles Office where Father had registered our homestead claim in 1904. Later, the reporters who had accompanied us on the campaign presented Olive with a purse and gloves as a token of their personal esteem. After dinner, I listened to the results at a special headquarters set up in the dining section of my railway car. With me was Senator Allister Grosart, who flew in for the final crucial hours. Newfoundland was, as expected, bad. In the three Maritime Provinces we added five seats. In Quebec we held our own. In Ontario the result was, to say the least, depressing. The Prairies remained solid; we actually increased our victories by one when Pearson's Minister of Agriculture, the Honourable Harry Hays, went down to defeat in Calgary South. In British Columbia, even with Mr. Fulton's return, we lost one seat, to drop to three. We had ninety-seven seats in all, two more than in 1963, but not enough.

I had done my best. I cannot imagine that I could have campaigned harder or longer. That little bit of help required to put us over the top was simply not forthcoming. Had the Honourable Duff Roblin, Premier of Manitoba, been a candidate, I believe nothing could have stopped us.

Duff Roblin, in 1965, was at the height of his political career. He had been a member of the Manitoba Legislature since 1949. As leader, he upset a long-established Liberal government in 1958 to form the first Conservative administration in over forty years. In 1959, he won a resounding victory. In 1962, he had been returned to office without difficulty. He was forward-looking and progressive, a good speaker and fluently bilingual. Nationally, he was considered one of the most promising young politicians in the land.

On 9 September, I received a telephone call from Gordon Churchill indicating that Premier Roblin was seriously interested in running federally. I authorized him to tell Mr. Roblin that if we were successful in the election, he would be guaranteed a Cabinet position; if we remained in Opposition, I felt sure that, in due course, he would be a front runner for the leadership. This was not unreasonable, considering that he was in his forties while I was in my seventies. All this I personally confirmed in an airport conversation with Premier Roblin on Saturday, 18 September. He had received considerable encouragement from caucus, and there was general support for his candidacy across the country. He thus agreed to become a candidate, and it was arranged that on the Monday following, when I would be passing through Winnipeg again, he and I would announce it. He was to name the Honourable Sterling Lyon his successor as premier, who would be sworn in on the Monday afternoon.

At the time I was not aware of the messages and emissaries arriving in Winnipeg from Toronto with contrary advice. I found out a year later that Dalton Camp and George Hogan had arrived on the Sunday to argue Roblin out of running. Consequently, on the Monday he informed me the time was not right for him to leave Manitoba politics. He would do everything he could to help, but he would not run. Destiny was knocking on his door; had he not changed his mind, conceivably he would have been Prime Minister of Canada. "The Moving Finger writes; and having writ, / Moves on: nor all your Piety nor Wit / Shall lure it back to cancel half a Line, / Nor all your tears wash out a Word of it."

Ontario's Premier Robarts pledged me every assistance in early September, "full-throttle support" he called it. Initially, Robarts' support seemed as good as his promise. The Conservative Party's "Unity Rally" in Toronto on 1 October was a resounding success. I wrote to a supporter in Vancouver about this on 5 October:

All the meetings were wonderful, but perhaps the most important was the one in Toronto. The Varsity Arena was jammed, over 7000 inside, and something over 20000 outside. Three Premiers were present, Robarts, Stanfield and Roblin, and Shaw from Prince Edward Island was represented by his Minister of Agriculture. Everyone agreed that it was an outstanding success, and all the prophets are predicting that we will regain many of the seats we lost in Ontario, and perhaps take some that we don't usually get. Altogether I am very pleased with the progress to date.

Three weeks before the election, I had a meeting with Premier Robarts. We exchanged estimates on the election outcome. I told him what I thought. As things turned out, I was three or four under the number we received in the other provinces. When it came to Ontario, he predicted forty-five seats. This number of actual victories would have put us in. From that point on, Robarts did nothing to assist us, except for the final day of the campaign in

Ontario, when he came along on the train. I later discovered that he had been less than co-operative from the beginning, refusing to make any sponsorship-type statements for television and radio broadcast and even refusing to allow the use of a photograph of the two of us in campaign literature. Of the twenty-three ridings considered possible turn-overs in Ontario, we won only three: Carleton, Hastings South, and Northumberland. Nine thousand more votes nationally would have brought the Conservative Party to power.

Beyond Premiers Robarts and Roblin, whose roles I have described, and Premier Stanfield of Nova Scotia, who worked as hard for the party as anyone could, it is difficult for me to assign responsibility for things that went well or wrong during the campaign. Camp and Hogan I have mentioned in connection with the Roblin decision. They were soon engaged in elections of their own in Toronto Eglinton and York West. Thus, their capacity for general mischief was limited by their desire to stake out their own political futures. Unlike 1963, when Camp was National Director, our campaign advertising was not channelled through his agency. As to Camp's role as National President, even he may have understood the incongruity of his running as a "leaderless" Conservative, for nowhere was my name mentioned in either the Camp or the Hogan campaigns.

I do know that often my instructions to our national campaign headquarters in Ottawa were not translated into effective action. The responsibility for this must rest with either Goodman, who was in charge, or Flora MacDonald, who was at headquarters and was often in touch with Camp. It is true that McCutcheon's "small boy" (he called him that), Lowell Murray, was around, but he was of no importance. As to Dr. Jim Johnston, who assumed the tasks of Conservative Party National Director in the autumn of 1965, he is one in whom I had then and have now every faith.

When I was asked about the party leadership on election evening, 1965, I replied: "Some of you people have been making these predictions over the years. Regularly the pundits and prophets have predicted my demise. I allow the pundits and the prophets to enjoy themselves while I continue to serve the Canadian people. There were times when the prognosticators said there was no hope. I knew differently. I approached the future in the same spirit I had followed in the past, my country always first, my Canada, your Canada."

As I viewed the coming session in the days following the election, it was obvious that the Conservative Party would be stronger in this new Parliament, that no other party so widely represented all parts of Canada. The Liberal Party, still in a minority position, was non-representative on the Prairies and scarcely representative in the Maritimes. Three of the ten provinces were without a Liberal Member. As to Mr. Pearson's prospects, the degree of support the government would be able to secure in the House would rest on its ability to produce constructive measures to meet Canada's problems, which had been badly neglected in the previous two years. The Pearson government had brought about an unnecessary election on the pretence that it needed a majority, without which, the Prime Minister declared during the campaign, he could not, indeed would not, carry on. It did not get that majority.

As to Mr. Pearson's threat to call yet another early election, I said in Prince Albert on election evening: "Constitutionally, he has no such right. Before he can take any such stand he must draw to the attention of the Governor General that there is a second party that believes it could form an administration, a strong administration, and carry on the Government of Canada without having an election hanging over the Canadian people."

The 1965 election had cost the Canadian taxpayer some thirteen million dollars, and there was a widespread popular belief that another election should not take place. Therefore, if defeated in the House, Pearson would have the bounden duty to advise the Governor General to call on the party holding the next-largest number of seats. In response to my remarks, the Liberal press immediately engaged in a propaganda effort to convince Canadians that votes of non-confidence in the House of Commons were not justifiable. In fact, there is no other way open to an Opposition to bring about changes in government policies; if amendments were not moved, the government would simply mock an Opposition advocating any action not supported by its vote. 2,499,378 Canadian citizens had supported the Conservative Party; they were not to be ignored.

I was not impressed by the reasons offered for the resignation of Finance Minister Walter Gordon on 11 November. That he should accept full responsibility for the government's failure to gain a majority in the election was absurd. Actually, the Pearson Cabinet, in allowing him to resign, voted non-confidence in themselves. The whole government bore his responsibility. To have a single Member bear the blame was a travesty of responsible government, and much like the Soviet system of self-incrimination and disgrace, rather than anything in the annals of parliamentary democracy.

While en route to Ottawa by train on 12 November, I wrote to my friend Dr. Lorne Connell in Prince Albert, who died two days later:

We are approaching Ottawa where big events have been taking place. The Minister of Finance resigned because he gave the Prime Minister wrong advice. . . . the Prime Minister and his Cabinet should resign for having acted on the advice. However, this Government does not follow regular parliamentary practices. Gordon has been offered as a sacrificial goat.

It will take some time before the true facts come out. What has been revealed so far is a travesty of parliamentary usage.

Olive and I hope to have a few days' holiday now but when we will be able to get it is hard to say. I would like to take her to Massachusetts where she might for the first time see the view of Plymouth Rock where her ancestors landed in the Mayflower company. . . .

Mr. Trudeau, the present Prime Minister, elected as a Liberal in 1965 in Montreal Mount Royal, had commented on the Pearson minority victory in 1963: "I am only concerned with the anti-democratic reflexes of the spineless Liberal herd. Power beckoned to Mr. Pearson; he had nothing to lose except his honour. He lost it. And his whole party lost it too." In 1963, it had been United States nuclear weapons. In 1965, it was the "Social Credit Six" revelations. Dr. Marcoux lost his seat, and with it the opportunity to press his charges.

When the Twenty-seventh Parliament opened on 18 January 1966, it was as if the Twenty-sixth Parliament had never ended. The government, with the assistance of the Honourable Lucien Cardin, who had replaced Guy Favreau as Minister of Justice following the Dorion Report, was in the midst of a new scandal. This one involved one George Victor Spencer, charged and convicted without trial of low-level espionage activities on behalf of the Soviet Union. Spencer had been fired from his Post Office job without pension, and was living out his last days with terminal cancer under RCMP surveillance. Under pressure from the NDP and the media on this question, Cardin kept digging the government deeper and deeper into a grave-sized hole. Without going into unnecessary details (they are chronicled elsewhere), the government's position became so confused that I pressed for an inquiry into the matter on 31 January. Cardin refused,

Pearson refused, Marchand refused, until 4 March, when the NDP's David Lewis moved a motion to reduce the estimates of the Department of Justice by $17,000, the amount of Mr. Cardin's ministerial salary: it was in effect a non-confidence motion. The Prime Minister immediately retreated, leaving another of his French-Canadian Ministers high and dry. It was in the midst of this heated debate that Justice Minister Cardin revealed the Prime Minister's secret, deadly weapon, which he called the "Monsignor" case.

I have never accepted Mr. Pearson's alibi that the Munsinger case was revealed by accident. This was deliberately done and had been planned for some time. Shortly after the exposure of the Rivard scandal in November 1964, the Prime Minister requested from the RCMP information bearing on matters in which Ministers of the Crown under my administration had been involved. The Commissioner produced the report on Munsinger. I have no intention of going into the details of this report. The matter was investigated by the RCMP, and their report was brought to my attention through Justice Minister Fulton. I reviewed the file in detail. There was no evidence of any security violation. It is worthy of mention that the RCMP pursued their investigation over a six-month period, recording every detail of Mrs. Munsinger's liaisons. There were personal indiscretions involved, but no more. I was satisfied that this was the case. It was my decision to make as Prime Minister, and I made it.

On 4 December 1964, a special messenger delivered a letter from Mr. Pearson to my home in Ottawa. It read:

In discharge of my constitutional duty as Prime Minister, I am writing this letter to you as a Privy Councillor and former Prime Minister.

I have been much concerned, not only about allegations made recently in a particular case, the Rivard case, but, even more, about an attitude toward the operation of the law that certain evidence in this case discloses. This attitude is not widespread but the Rivard case illustrates the need to take thorough action to remove it.

The problem has not sprung up suddenly. In order to assess the need for corrective action, I have asked for a full report of instances in the last ten years or so in which political intervention was involved in investigations. This information will enable me to see how such matters could and should be dealt with.

One case (the Munsinger case) has given me very grave concern. It affects the security of the country. In 1960-61, a Minister who occupied a position of great responsibility in the Government was involved in a liaison which clearly endangered security.

I have been greatly disturbed by the lack of attention which, insofar as the file indicates, this matter received. The Minister was left in his position of trust.

I have decided that I cannot, in the public interest, let the matter lie where it was left and that I must ask the R.C.M. Police to pursue further enquiries.

I recognize that the file before me may not disclose all the steps that were taken. In view of this, it is my duty to write to you about the matter in case you might be in a position to let me know that the enquiries that were pursued and the safeguards that were taken reached further than the material before me would indicate. That material now indicates that the Minister of Justice brought the matter to your attention and that no action was taken.

Because national security is involved, this is the most serious and disturbing of the matters that have been brought to my attention. But I assure you that all incidents during the last ten years are being thoroughly examined and will be followed up without fear or favour if and when the evidence requires it.

If there is further information you can provide about the Munsinger case, I will be grateful if you will let me know.

I was confined to my bed with pneumonia when I received Pearson's letter. I discussed it with Gordon Churchill and I decided that I would make my reply orally and in person. This I did the following week, on Friday, 11 December. I recall that it was about noon when I arrived at the Prime Minister's East Block office. I was surprised that Mr. Pearson did not rise to greet me. He just sat there, behind his desk.

I kept a note of what I said to the Prime Minister that day. I told him that I certainly would agree that a full examination should be made regarding political intervention in the operation of the law and that any investigation that he chose to have made by the RCMP would of course be welcomed. I thought the whole field of security should be looked into. I assured him that at no time during my period of office was there, to my knowledge, any failure in the field of national security. I did consider, however, that the fullest examination should be made of the circumstances revealed in the evidence taken before the United States Senate in the Committee of the Judiciary and Internal Security submitted in connection with the Embassy in Washington and particularly the evidence of the hearings among which would be that contained in Volume 96, 14 August 1951. This matter had concerned me greatly when it came to my attention.

Basically, the Prime Minister's letter was an attempt to blackmail Her Majesty's Loyal Opposition into silence on the scandals rocking his government. The point of my reference to the U.S. Senate Committee hearings was to remind him about the Elizabeth Bentley testimony, which had implicated Pearson himself. I remember that Pearson got to his feet. He walked over to me and, in his most ingratiating way, said: "We should not talk to each other like this, John." I rejoined: "I didn't write the letter that you sent to me, Mike." I added, "And neither did you." Mr. Pearson admitted that the letter had been drafted for him. He then added, "You know I am not a politician, I am a diplomat." I replied that I had heard a diplomat defined "as a person who lies away from home". I turned to leave and added, "You are no diplomat." I heard no more about the Munsinger case until January 1966.

It is a fact that I have never played the kind of politics that Mr. Pearson was endeavouring to play. I recall one of my colleagues coming to me in early 1961 with a proposal that we eliminate the obstruction of a certain Member by exposing his past. I told him in no uncertain terms that I was shocked to hear such a tactic would even be considered by a Member of the Conservative Party. I had known about this for years. One did not club a man, no matter how aggravating he was, with a past for which he had paid. Parliament was too noble an institution for that kind of action.

On 13 January, I received a clear warning to cease discussing the Spencer case when Mr. Pearson stated in the House:

Consideration will be given as to whether there should be the kind of inquiry that has been suggested for this particular individual [Spencer] or, indeed, whether that inquiry should be extended to other cases of individuals, examination of which might throw light on our security methods generally.

On 23 February, his warning assumed a broader tone:

Not only did I study the details of this case [Spencer] . . . but I examined other security cases in the last ten years . . . certain cases which were of very direct and immediate concern to the government of the day, which was the government preceding this government.

Mr. Cardin's references were even more direct. For example, on 28 February, he said:

. . . is the Rt. Hon. gentleman saying that prosecutions were proceeded with in all security cases that came to his attention between 1957 and 1963? I am sure the Rt. Hon. gentleman is not saying that and with reason.

I was not about to be intimidated. I had nothing to fear. Neither had Mr. Fulton, to whom Guy Favreau issued a personal warning that unless we relented on the Spencer affair, the Munsinger case would be brought forward. Accordingly, I was hardly surprised when Cardin dropped his so-called bomb on 4 March.

Hansard records that the Prime Minister encouraged Cardin in his revelation. The disclosure of the name Munsinger set off a chain reaction. A number of people in the media had known about her. Robert Reguly of the *Toronto Star*, who had located Hal Banks in New York, uncovered Mrs. Munsinger, alive and well in Munich, within twenty-four hours and flashed the news to the world.

On Wednesday, 9 March, Cardin held a press conference. He declared that the Munsinger case was worse than the Profumo scandal in Britain. He also implicated all those who had been in my government by using the plural "Ministers", which, when challenged, he refused to retract. On Friday, 11 March, he charged that I had failed to seek advice from the law officers of the Crown and that I had mishandled the case.

The whole business would have been ridiculous had it not been for its intent to dredge, to sludge, to smear, to destroy me with the dirtiest of McCarthy-ite tactics. To take Cardin's charge that I had mishandled the case, what was I supposed to refer to the Crown's law officers? There had been no security violation.

The Prime Minister should have put a quick end to Cardin's irresponsibility. He was familiar with the facts. He had had them in his office for some fourteen months. If Pearson had failed to support him, however, Cardin would resign, and all his Quebec colleagues as well. The government would be finished. Thus, his bid to finish me through the appointment, on 14 March, of a Royal Commission to "investigate" the Munsinger affair, under Mr. Justice Wishart Flett Spence of the Supreme Court of Canada.

The circumstances of Spence's appointment were hardly a secret. Justice Spence had a solid Liberal background before his appointment and was an old school chum of the Honourable Paul Martin, Pearson's Secretary of State for External Affairs. I know that the Supreme Court judges had decided between them that under no circumstances would any of them become a commissioner on a matter of such political import. I asked Paul Martin in the House if in his discussion with Justice Spence he had alluded to a forthcoming vacancy for Chief Justice. This was, of course, denied. However, I have never followed the course in Parliament of asking questions just to see my name in Hansard. The question served its purpose.

The Spence Commission provided a spectacle not seen since the abolition of the Star Chamber in 1641. I commend to the reader who is interested in this travesty of the judicial process the analysis of Thomas Van Dusen, who was my Executive Assistant at the time, in Chapters Thirteen through Sixteen of his book *The Chief*. I fully anticipated the nature of the Commission's findings, published on 23 September 1966. I refuse to elevate this sordid episode by discussing its detail. I will say only that its proceedings were so lacking in fairness, disregarding even the most elementary rule of evidence, I felt obliged to withdraw my counsel from its proceedings on 18 May. Mr. Justice Spence did exactly the job the Liberals hoped he would. The hearings of his commission, sometimes open, sometimes closed, had given the press a field day. His report had the same effect. The Commission Report gave Dalton Camp the edge he needed in his new campaign to force me out as leader of the Conservative Party.

What Prime Minister Pearson failed to realize when he created the Munsinger scandal was that the goddess of vengeance is a lady of voracious appetite. My reputation did not suffer any permanent effects. Neither did Mr. Fulton's. The explanation for this is simple: we had done no wrong. Those who did suffer were Messrs. Pearson and Cardin. Lucien Cardin subsequently retired completely from public life, his political usefulness as a Minister ended. Mr. Pearson, although he tried, was never able to provide a satisfactory explanation for his actions.

On 19 May, as a prelude to events later in the year, Dalton Camp, who had resumed his active function as National President after his unsuccessful attempt to get elected to the House of Commons, spoke at a private meeting at that sanctum sanctorum of Ontario Conservatism, Toronto's Albany Club. He called for a "Leadership review". Encouraged, and in anticipation of the Spence Report, Camp went public on 20 September. He made the same "Leadership review" speech to the Toronto Board of Trade. Davie Fulton, Douglas Harkness, Marcel Lambert, Ged Baldwin, Heath Macquarrie, Gordon Fairweather, Jean Wadds, Gordon Aiken, Richard Rohmer, Finlay MacDonald, James Doak, and others joined his "pilgrimage". The Conservative Party's Annual Meeting in November would provide them their chance.

I found it particularly significant that the Honourable Stanley Randall, Ontario's Minister of Economics and Development, announced a few days after Camp's speech that he was in complete agreement with Camp's demand for a leadership review. I expected no more from Premier Robarts, although I was somewhat mystified by the statement of the President of the Ontario Conservative Association, Mr. Elmer Bell, Q.C., that the Ontario organization would adopt complete neutrality on the question of national leadership. Thus, when I spoke to the Ontario annual meeting in Toronto on 30 October, I made a completely unprovocative speech, carefully worded to cause no further division or dissension in the party. As things turned out, the Camp people had decided to use this meeting as something of a dry run for the National Annual Meeting in November.

A group of individuals, all young and occupying a very visible place in the audience, had been assembled for the sole purpose, apparently, of sitting on their hands during my speech. This was supposed to be a Conservative meeting, yet no one condemned their rudeness, neither the President nor any senior member of the Executive of the Ontario Association. The neutrality assumed by Mr. Bell was thrown aside three or four days later when he came out publicly for Camp. The effect of this was evident in the choice of delegates-at-large from Ontario to the national meeting. With scant exception, qualification was determined by their support of Camp. So flagrant was this that Mr. Arthur Maloney, Q.C., was denied an appointment, his offence apparently being that he intended to contest the presidency against Camp.

In Quebec, Camp's most important success was the conversion of Paul O. Trepanier, the party's new provincial president, to his anti-Diefenbaker crusade. Because local Conservative organizations existed only on paper in many of the constituencies in Quebec, the selection of delegates to the Annual Meeting was open to vast manipulation. Although Camp talked about the pressing "need to reform our political party system", the scene was set to return the Conservative Party to its pre-1956 dark ages.

In Nova Scotia, Premier Stanfield supported Camp. Stanfield explained that he felt obliged to repay Camp's work for him in provincial elections. I thought this an improbable rationalization; Camp's advertising agency had prospered on contracts from provincial Conservative governments. It surprised Mr. Stanfield, however, when

Finlay MacDonald, one of Camp's allies on the National Executive, was defeated by my friend and supporter Maurice Flemming for the position of provincial president. In Manitoba, Premier Roblin gave Camp his blessing, with the result that, despite the determined efforts of loyal men like the Honourable Stewart McLean and the Honourable Harry J. Enns, the majority of the Manitoba delegates were for Camp. In British Columbia, most of the delegates were Fulton supporters.

Gordon Churchill had sent Camp the following telegram on 22 September:

Your immediate resignation as national president should be submitted to the national executive. You have flagrantly abused the privilege of your position in making a public attack on our Leader.

You have no authority from the membership at large for your action. For a national president to attempt to undermine and disrupt his party under the specious guise of attacking the leadership of the Liberal party as well is too obvious a subterfuge.

As a private member of the Party you may speak your mind as you see fit. As national president you have a duty to strengthen the Party not weaken it.

You have taken advantage of your temporary position in a manner that admits of no excuse or explanation. Your resignation should be made effective today.

Camp, of course, did not resign. He had long since made it clear that he held elected Members of Parliament in contempt. This "great democrat" considered the party's National Executive far more competent than caucus to give direction to the party; our M.P.s were to be no more than puppets.

One by one, the troublemakers of the past declared for Camp. I was not surprised. McCutcheon, Goodman, Ernest Jackson, Harry Price could not have worked harder or with more intensity if they had been campaigning against an opposing political party. John Bassett, however, was in a class by himself. Less than ten days before he turned against me at the Annual Meeting, he had insisted that I go to Toronto to be present at the dinner he was giving for Lord Thomson of Fleet. Over the next several days, I had a number of telephone conversations with Bassett. He was going to "devastate Camp", to use his expression. The Annual Meeting was to begin on the following Monday, 14 November. He said he had already written an editorial for the front page of the Toronto *Telegram* to appear on that day. It did not appear. He called me to say it would go the next day. I am still waiting.

I was to make a major address to the meeting on the Monday evening; Camp was to open with his report as President, I was to follow as National Leader. Earlier in the day I had spoken to the Conservative Women, where my remarks received a most enthusiastic reception; I was scheduled also to speak to the meeting's wind-up banquet, which, in the event, was cancelled. About half an hour before that never-to-be-forgotten Monday night meeting, Tom Van Dusen reported that there was some trouble being planned by Camp and others of that ilk. When Olive and I entered the Château Laurier's Convention Hall, I sensed what had taken place. As we moved towards the platform, everyone within my range of vision sat in silence. The gathering had been packed by the Camp crew.

I later learned that their troops had been brought in to fill the front portion of the auditorium some three hours before the meeting was to begin. Harkness, Mrs. Wadds (Earl Rowe's daughter), Heath Macquarrie, and others were charged with maintaining discipline among the crew. Their strategy was as follows:

1) Don't stand when Diefenbaker enters, and don't applaud his entry.

2) Don't applaud during his speech.

3) Heckle and boo him frequently.

4) Don't give him an ovation when he finishes.

5) When Camp takes the rostrum, stand to give him a rousing ovation, shouting, "Go, Camp, Go."

I looked around the platform as Joel Aldred introduced me. Premier Stanfield appeared to be not displeased with the cold reception I was receiving; he was chatting amiably with Dalton Camp. Premier Robarts had entered on cue, just moments before me. As Camp completed his report with the hypocritical words "tolerance to all and malice to none", Robarts walked onto the stage and shook his hand. This gave apparent substance to the rumour spread the next morning by certain members of the Ontario Executive that Premier Robarts had advised me Monday evening that he could no longer support me as National Leader. No such conversation, or anything that could be so interpreted, had taken place, but the fact that it was false in no way detracted from the benefits that flowed to Mr. Camp from its circulation.

When I rose to speak, I discovered just how thorough Camp had been. For the regular podium, one had been substituted that would not hold my notes! Throughout, my remarks met with boos and jeers. I could not see a friendly face. I heard Pat Nowlan say: "Shut up and sit down!" I could not believe that I was speaking to a Conservative meeting. I was attempting to give an account of the last two years of my stewardship. I did not hold the view that my leadership should go on forever. I told them that. I doubt if anyone could hear me over the din. I stated that I was not going to turn the Conservative Party over to the forces of reaction and inaction. I wanted to know what had prompted the change in Camp's assessment of my leadership. To a chorus of boos, hisses, and ruder noises, I quoted some of his laudatory statements of less than a year before. "The Night of the Knives", Bob Coates called it. Had it not been nationally televised, Canadians would never have believed it.

The only cheering note during that entire meeting came from John Bassett, who, entering late, walked in front of the platform, and gave me an "O" sign with this thumb and forefinger. The next day, I discovered that he too had lined up with Camp and Goodman. Following my speech, Goodman and another spent considerable time arguing with him that he should do everything to get rid of me. At first he demurred. Finally, he agreed. I have often wondered about Bassett: how he could explain his somersault. His son Doug is a fine man and has remained my friend. John Bassett had run as a candidate in 1962 in Toronto-Spadina. He had done a great deal for the people of Italian and Jewish origin there, and considered himself very popular and was sure that he would win. Indeed, during the campaign, he informed me that in the Italian areas he was known as "Giovanni Bassetti, the candidati Conservatori". When the votes came in he was roundly defeated. He had to blame someone. Obviously, given his appreciation of his many talents, he was not going to look to himself. He blamed me then.

I had marched in the ranks of the Conservative Party for almost half a century and never did I think that I would live to see the day when this great party would be reduced to ashes by such methods! The Liberal scandals of the "Tenth Decade" died when Pearson retired as leader; Camp's conduct has continued to haunt the Conservative Party. The people were not deceived; as Harvey Kane, President of the Winnipeg North Conservative Association, said, they understood that without loyalty the Conservative Party had nothing. I haven't the slightest doubt that Camp saw himself as my successor. Whatever slight chance he may have had disappeared on the night of 14 November 1966. Assassins are hired, as required. His re-election as National President on 16 November was significant only in terms of his already diminishing support.

It was Arthur Maloney who touched the responsive chord at the Annual Meeting and throughout Canada when, in his nomination speech, he challenged Camp's tactics:

I have no obligation to our national leader, I have no obligation to him whatsoever except one, which by reason I suppose of my Renfrew County upbringing is really to me, terribly important. And that is the single obligation that we all owe, each and every one of us to the man we picked as leader, loyalty and respect.

That means among other things that in regard to the Right Honourable John George Diefenbaker, sometime Prime Minister of Canada, present leader of the opposition and the national leader of the Conservative Party of Canada, when he enters a room, Arthur Maloney stands up! When the day comes that he decides to lay down the mantle of leadership which we gave him, he will do so in a blaze of glory.

The consequence was not victory for Maloney, but near defeat for Camp. The difference was only fifty-eight votes. I doubt, however, that Camp understood the implication of the result. The election of Flora MacDonald to the office of National Secretary over Ken Binks, a staunch and devoted friend of many years, was of little importance, for by the time the vote took place the delegates were leaving the meeting in droves and in disgust.

On Thursday, 16 November, just before noon, while Camp and Goodman were tending their final "Leadership review" business, I went over to the Château Laurier, unannounced, to bid farewell to friends and supporters who were leaving. The response was overwhelming. I saw none of those people who had jeered me down so short a time before. Those who gathered in the lobby to welcome me were Conservatives, tried and true. With Arthur Maloney by my side, I told them that, rumours to the contra-

ry, I was not dead yet. I quoted Sir Andrew Barton, an El-
izabethan soldier:

> *Fight on, my men ...*
> *I am wounded but I am not slaine*
> *I'll lay me down and bleed awhile*
> *and then I'll rise and fight againe.*

When I was asked if I was going to resign, I said, "No."
Seventy-one Conservative Members of Parliament requested that I continue as leader. Forty were prepared to
form a break-away party if I resigned. I owed my parliamentary colleagues too much to ignore their wishes; nor
could I run out on the overwhelming numbers of Conservatives whose messages urged me to stay.

The Annual Meeting had passed a resolution calling for
a leadership convention before January 1968. I favoured
getting it over with as quickly as possible, if not in February then at least in March, so as to end the uncertainty
that was bound to affect our performance in the House of
Commons. Camp favoured November. Although he had
pledged at the Annual Meeting to discuss this matter with
me, he did not, with the result that Eddie Goodman
served in his stead. Early September in Toronto was the
unsatisfactory compromise.

I had absolutely no intention of running to succeed myself, but I kept my counsel, waited, watched, and listened
in vain for just one of the nine men who announced their
candidacy to succeed me to give some encouragement to
the view that a strong federal government was necessary
and vital to the future of Canada. Had any one of them
done so, to him I might have been able to give my blessing. But in every case, while protesting care and concern
about national unity, there was nothing but promises to
give more and more to the provinces. They fell in line
with the ideas of the Conservative Thinkers' Conference
held at Montmorency in August, which, far from helping

our party, had simply tried, in a desperate effort, to fabricate in four days policies which would get votes, regardless of the fate of our country. Ignored was the fact that the conference did not speak for the Conservative Party. Indeed, many of those "thinkers" boasted publicly that they were not Conservatives. It was yet one more example of ruthless and ambitious people attempting to use a great party for their own ends.

I have been asked why I finally decided to stand for re-election as leader in realization that I would be defeated. The answer is that this so-called Thinkers' Conference adopted, at the urging of Marcel Faribault, a resolution supporting the Two Nations theory, the absolute reverse of everything I had stood for in life, and the reverse of everything the Conservative Party had stood for, from Macdonald to me. Subsequently, on 6 September, this resolution was brought before and passed by the platform committee at the Leadership Convention; the 150 who voted for it there represented less than seven per cent of the convention's 2,350 delegates.

I made my views perfectly clear when I spoke to the convention on the evening of Thursday, 7 September. I had advised my friends and supporters that I would not stand. "Two Nations" eliminated all choice. The telephone calls and telegrams that flowed in after my Thursday night speech assured me that my course was a right one. Nominations had to be in by ten o'clock the next morning. I was determined that this Two Nations resolution would not be accepted by the convention. It could not come before the convention, however, until twelve o'clock noon on Saturday. Therefore, to preserve my right to fight this resolution by a vote of the convention, my nomination was put in a scant fifteen minutes before the Friday deadline. I realized that I would be clobbered in the voting, as I told my friends and supporters, but as no other candidate was prepared to pit himself against this monstrous course, it was up to me. It would have been interpreted as gross weakness on my part to have voiced my opposition to the heresy of Two Nations and then to have refused to stand against it as a candidate. The probability of defeat is no justification for surrender to a false principle.

I wish that I could give credit to all the people who helped make my eleventh-hour candidacy less disagreeable than it otherwise would have been. This I obviously cannot do. My staff as Leader of the Opposition, however, deserve a special mention for their unswerving loyalty and ability; people like Major Gregor Guthrie and Dr. Sant Singh and those others mentioned elsewhere in the text were invaluable to me. Also I was greatly encouraged during that Centennial summer of 1967 by the establishment of the Youth for Diefenbaker Movement, led by three young men, two in their twenties and one but fourteen. The latter, Sean O'Sullivan, was, in the 1972 general election, to become the youngest person ever elected to the House of Commons, where, until his decision to leave politics for the church, he served with distinction. Sean, along with William Hattan and Keith Martin, did a wonderful job in establishing that the disgraceful conduct of those at the 1966 Annual Meeting was not representative of Canada's Young Conservatives, and that the One Canada concept knew no generation gap in its appeal.

In order to bind the party, the Two Nations resolution had to pass the convention as a whole. It never came before the convention. Gordon Churchill and Joel Aldred were the men who forced the Convention Chairman, E. A. Goodman, and the Policy Committee Chairman, William Davis, now Premier of Ontario, to a reluctant realization that if the Two Nations resolution were not tabled, there would be a long-drawn-out and acrimonious debate that would break the party whatever its outcome. But more important in defeating Two Nations was my Thursday-night speech to the convention.

People have asked me how long it took me to prepare that speech. I answered, "My entire life." It was the testament, the sum, of my experience in public life. I believed in it so strongly that I was prepared to endure the ignominy of defeat in order to force a retreat on the Two Nations issue. I told my party and my nation:

... This is the message that I give to you today—"Le Canada français a besoin du Canada, le Canada a besoin du Canada français." That has been my attitude throughout the years.

We are a party with a great tradition, a party of great principles. In this convention, we hold communion with those who have gone before. We change not principles, we change programs to meet modern conditions, using as a basis principles which brought this party into existence. These principles have served our country before and since confederation. Our purpose must be to leave a memorial of greatness to future generations. ...

In the last four years, we have seen a Government "frittering around" in their relations with the provinces. They brought about what they called "cooperative federalism". It was neither cooperative nor federalism. ... In capitulation to compromises they brought about opting-out, two pension plans, two flags, two student loan plans. They have even, by unification of the armed forces, opted out with the defence of this nation! What are they building? Ten separate governments with vast authority? To Quebec, they have promised everything under the sun. They have opted this out and opted that out. It's time that French Canada started opting in rather than opting out. ...

Principles are the heart and soul of the party. Policies divorced from principles are dangerous. ...

When in office, we maintained the constitution, we equalized opportunities in the various provinces, we developed northern Canada, we entered into the greatest development plan this nation had ever seen, we abolished discrimination under the law. We stood for one Canada. . . .

We expanded social security. We thought of the veteran, the older people, the sick and the crippled. I was criticized for being too much concerned with the average Canadians. I can't help that; I'm one of them! . . .

When in power, we gave young Canadians opportunities, we raised standards, we gave them new hope, hope that they in this nation under free enterprise, protected against injustice, would be able to make their full contribution in their day and generation. We did something more. We ended discrimination. . . .

Now I want to speak particularly to French Canada. . . .

I am going to make an appeal to you and your conscience. The rights of Canadians, whether of the parent races or otherwise, must not be placed on the auction block for political gain, or to use a colloquialism, "put up for grabs". I stood against the Prime Minister when he announced the "two nations" idea. . . .

The adoption of the two nations concept would segregate French Canada. I am not going to agree, whether it's popular or not, to take the stand, to erect a Berlin Wall around the province of Quebec. That is what this proposition will do. Its proponents say that, to understand it, requires knowledge of the meaning of "nation"; that while it is the same word in both languages, the meaning of "two nations" is different in French than in English. Laurier said, "This is one nation." Cartier said, "This is one nation." Langevin, Bourassa, St. Laurent said the same, all through the years. We are asked today to go back to the period between 1841 and 1867 to two Canadas. . . . I am pleading with you. I am looking into the hearts of Canadians everywhere. I know what discrimination is. I know how much easier it would have been if my name had been my mother's name. But, from the earliest day when it was unpopular, I raised the standard of equality in this country. Let us be Canadians. Let us not deny equality to those whose surnames are not of the parent races. I don't believe that the true heart of French Canada wants the two nation idea. It is a minority who yell so loud they give the impression of being a majority. . . .

In 1957, I promised French Canada their constitutional rights and they got them. But I did not promise, and no party has the right to promise, to add any additional rights without agreement by the peoples of all the provinces. . . .

A leader has to take responsibility. He has to have courage. It is easy to point out the easy road. I could have done that on the subject of nuclear proliferation. In 1963, I refused and today that policy is accepted internationally. I have never asked for sympathy, nor do I now. Leaders have to take action which they believe will serve the nation. Is there any reward while one lives? I wish you could read my correspondence, my letters from across this nation in the last week or so. Humble people who generally do not speak out have written and sent telegrams. Their sentiments cannot be purchased. . . .

Canada faces a crisis the gravity of which calls for statesmanship. I must tell you, in all frankness and without equivocation, I cannot accept the two nation policy. I implore you. You make that decision for me when you decide on that policy because I cannot and shall not accept it. I am not going to go back 100 years and more to borrow a policy that has proven to be wrong, to get votes in 1967. The sub-committee and committee on policy has accepted the two nations principle. I hope that the convention will repudiate it before we leave here. . . .

It has been my purpose in life to maintain the basic foundation of the constitution, to make the diversity of our national origin a source of pride to all; to have Canadians realize the richness of its many cultures. Men and women of this Convention! Don't move backwards. There is no one who can show me that suddenly, in 1967, "nation" in French means different from what it means in English. . . .

God has been good to me. Mine has been a long life

and I feel privileged to have had the opportunity to continue serving Canada in the House of Commons. The Canadian people, without regard to political affiliation, have given me their affection. I bear no ill-feeling to those who, in the past, opposed me. But I stand today, as I have always stood, for principle:

Freedom and Equality for all Canadians, however humble their lot in life and whatever their racial origin. One Canada, One Nation.

APPENDIXES

APPENDIX I

The following is a list of Acts passed by the Diefenbaker Government from 1957 to 1963.

First Session, Twenty-Third Parliament, 6 Elizabeth II

Assented to October 24, 1957

CHAP. 1. Appropriation Act, No. 6, 1957.

Assented to November 7, 1957

2. Advance Payments for Prairie Grain prior to delivery thereof, An Act to provide for.
3. Old Age Security Act, An Act to amend.

Assented to November 21, 1957

4. Blind Persons Act, An Act to amend.
5. Disabled Persons Act, An Act to amend.
6. Old Age Assistance Act, An Act to amend.
7. War Veterans Allowance Act, An Act to amend.

Assented to November 28, 1957

8. Unemployment Insurance Act, An Act to amend.

Assented to December 5, 1957

9. Appropriation Act, No. 7, 1957.

Assented to December 20, 1957

10. Buffalo and Fort Erie Public Bridge Company, An Act to amend an Act respecting.

First Session, Twenty-Fourth Parliament, 7 Elizabeth II

CHAP. 2. Unemployment Insurance Act—Temporary Extension to Seasonal Benefit Periods.

Assented to May 20, 1958

3. National Housing Act, 1954, An Act to amend.

Assented to June 5, 1958

4. Appropriation Act No. 3, 1958.

Assented to June 26, 1958

5. Canada Agricultural Products Standards Act, An Act to amend.
6. Hospital Insurance and Diagnostic Services Act, An Act to amend.

Assented to July 25, 1958

7. British Columbia Coast Steamship Services Operated by the Canadian Pacific Railway Company, An Act to provide for the Resumption of.
8. National Parks Act respecting boundaries of Cape Breton Highlands National Park, An Act to amend.
9. Yukon Act, An Act to amend.

Assented to August 7, 1958

10. Appropriation Act No. 4, 1958.
11. Animal Contagious Diseases Act, An Act to amend.
12. Canada-Belgian Congo Income Tax Convention Act, 1958.
13. Canada-Belgium Income Tax Convention Act, 1958.
14. Canadian Farm Loan Act, An Act to amend.
15. Prairie Farm Assistance Act, An Act to amend.
16. Prairie Grain Advance Payments Act, An Act to amend.

Assented to August 13, 1958

17. Canadian National Railways Financing and Guarantee Act, 1958.
18. Criminal Code, An Act to amend.
19. Indian Act, An Act to amend.
20. Lake of the Woods Control Board Act, 1921, An Act to amend.

Assented to September 6, 1958

21. Appropriation Act (Special), 1958.

CHAP. 22. Broadcasting Act.

23. Campobello-Lubec Bridge Act.

24. Canadian Citizenship Act, An Act to amend.

25. Children of War Dead (Education Assistance) Act, An Act to amend.

26. Customs Act, An Act to amend.

27. Customs Tariff, An Act to amend.

28. Emergency Gold Mining Assistance Act, An Act to amend.

29. Estate Tax Act.

30. Excise Tax Act, An Act to amend.

31. Financial Administration Act, An Act to amend.

32. Income Tax Act, An Act to amend.

33. Judges Act, An Act to amend.

34. Lakehead Harbour Commissioners Act.

35. Loan Companies Act, An Act to amend.

36. Maritime Coal Production Assistance Act, An Act to authorize certain amendments to the Agreement with the Dominion Coal Company Limited.

37. National Capital Act.

38. Parole Act.

39. Penitentiary Act, An Act to amend.

40. Railway Act, An Act to amend.

41. Returned Soldiers Insurance Act, An Act to amend.

42. Trust Companies Act, An Act to amend.

43. Veterans Insurance Act, An Act to amend.

44. Appropriation Act No. 5 (Main Supply), 1958.

Second Session, Twenty-Fourth Parliament, 7-8 Elizabeth II

Assented to February 25, 1959

CHAP. 1. Appropriation Act No. 1, 1959.

Assented to March 20, 1959

2. Appropriation Act No. 2, 1959.

3. Appropriation Act No. 3, 1959.

4. Fisheries Improvement Loans Act, An Act to amend.

5. National Defence Act, An Act to amend.

6. National Housing Act, 1954, An Act to amend.

CHAP. 7. Northwest Territories Act, An Act to amend.

8. Public Servants Inventions Act, An Act to amend.

9. St. Lawrence Seaway Authority Act, An Act to amend.

10. Trans-Canada Highway Act, An Act to amend.

Assented to June 4, 1959

11. Appropriation Act No. 4, 1959.

12. Customs Tariff and The New Zealand Trade Agreement Act, 1932, An Act to amend.

13. Excise Act, An Act to amend.

14. Old Age Security Act, An Act to amend.

15. Parliamentary Secretaries Act.

16. Representation Act, An Act to amend.

17. Veterans Rehabilitation Act, An Act to amend.

18. War Service Grants Act, An Act to amend.

Assented to July 8, 1959

19. Bretton Woods Agreements Act, An Act to amend.

20. Canada-Finland Income Tax Convention Act, 1959.

21. Canadian Forces Superannuation Act.

22. Canadian National Railways Financing and Guarantee Act, 1959.

23. Excise Tax Act, An Act to amend.

24. Export Credits Insurance Act, An Act to amend.

25. Farm Improvement Loans Act, An Act to amend.

26. Federal-Provincial Tax-Sharing Arrangements Act, An Act to amend.

27. Freight Rates Reduction Act.

28. Judges Act, An Act to amend.

29. Length and Mass Units Act, An Act to amend.

30. Prime Minister's Residence Act, An Act to amend.

31. Prison and Reformatories Act, An Act to amend.

32. Public Service Pension Adjustment Act.

33. Queen Elizabeth II Canadian Research Fund Act.

34. Royal Canadian Mounted Police Superannuation Act.

35. Seeds Act.

36. Unemployment Insurance Act, An Act to amend.

37. Veterans' Land Act, An Act to amend.

38. Weights and Measures Act, An Act to amend.

Assented to July 18, 1959

CHAP. 39. Coal Production Assistance Act.

40. Combines Investigation Act and the Criminal Code, An Act to amend.

41. Criminal Code, An Act to amend.

42. Crop Insurance Act.

43. Farm Credit Act.

44. Humane Slaughter of Food Animals Act.

45. Income Tax Act, An Act to amend.

46. National Energy Board Act.

47. New Brunswick Indian Reserve—Agreement between Government of Canada and Government of Province of New Brunswick.

48. Newfoundland Additional Grants Act.

49. Newfoundland Fisheries Laws respecting Exportation of Salt Fish, An Act to repeal.

50. Nova Scotia Indian Reserve—Agreement between the Government of Canada and the Government of the Province of Nova Scotia.

51. Pigeon River Bridge Act.

52. Public Lands Grants Act, An Act to amend.

53. Queenston Bridge Act.

54. Royal Canadian Mounted Police Act.

55. Appropriation Act No. 5, (Main Supply), 1959.

Third Session, Twenty-Fourth Parliament, 8-9 Elizabeth II

Assented to January 28, 1960

CHAP. 1. Prairie Grain Loans Act.

2. Prairie Grain Provisional Payments Act.

Assented to March 9, 1960

3. Appropriation Act No. 1, 1960.

4. Department of Justice Act.

Assented to March 31, 1960

5. Appropriation Act No. 2, 1960.

6. Appropriation Act No. 3, 1960.

7. Canada Elections Act, an Act to amend.

CHAP. 8. Indian Act, an Act to amend.
9. National Energy Board Act, an Act to amend.
10. National Housing Act, an Act to amend.

Assented to May 27, 1960

11. Appropriation Act No. 4, 1960.
12. Export and Import Permits Act, an Act to amend.
13. Federal-Provincial Tax-Sharing Arrangements Act, an Act to amend.
14. Feeds Act.
15. Fisheries Laws of Newfoundland, an Act to repeal.

Assented to June 9, 1960

16. Appropriation Act No. 5, 1960.
17. Australian Trade Agreement Act, 1960.
18. Canada-Netherlands Income Tax Agreement Act, 1957, an Act to amend.
19. Nanaimo Harbour Commissioners Act.
20. Northwest Territories Act, an Act to amend.
21. Oshawa Harbour Commissioners Act.
22. Trans-Canada Highway Act, an Act to amend.
23. Windsor Harbour Commissioners Act, an Act to amend.
24. Yukon Act, an Act to amend.

Assented to July 7, 1960

25. Canadian National Railways Financing and Guarantee Act, 1960.
26. Canadian National Toronto Terminals Act.
27. Customs Tariff, an Act to amend.
28. Emergency Gold Mining Assistance Act, an Act to amend.
29. Estate Tax Act, an Act to amend.
30. Excise Tax Act, an Act to amend.
31. International Boundary Commission Act.
32. International Development Association Act.
33. LaSalle-Caughnawaga Bridge Act.
34. Old Age Security Act, an Act to amend.
35. Railway Act, an Act to amend an Act to amend.
36. War Veterans Allowance Act, 1952, an Act to amend.

Assented to July 14, 1960

37. Criminal Code, an Act to amend.

CHAP. 38. Public Service Superannuation Act, an Act to amend.

Assented to August 1, 1960
39. Canada Elections Act.
40. Canada Shipping Act, an Act to amend.
41. Department of Forestry Act.
42. Freight Rates Reduction Act, an Act to amend.
43. Income Tax Act, an Act to amend.

Assented to August 10, 1960
44. Canadian Bill of Rights.
45. Combines Investigation Act and the Criminal Code, an Act to amend.
46. Judges Act, an Act to amend.
47. Judges Act, an Act to amend.
48. Appropriation Act No. 6, 1960 (Main Supply).

Fourth Session, Twenty-Fourth Parliament, 9-10 Elizabeth II

Assented to December 2, 1960
CHAP. 1. National Housing Act, 1954, an Act to amend.
2. Railway Operation Continuation Act.

Assented to December 20, 1960
3. Appropriation Act No. 7, 1960.
4. National Productivity Council Act.
5. Small Businesses Loans Act.
6. Technical and Vocational Training Assistance Act.

Assented to March 9, 1961
7. Canadian National Railway Company, Construction of a line of railway in Prov. of Quebec, from Kiask Falls Subdivision to vicinity of Mattagami Lake.
8. Halifax Signal Station, an Act to repeal certain laws relating to.
9. Indian Act, an Act to amend.
10. Pension Act, an Act to amend.

Assented to March 29, 1961
11. Appropriation Act No. 1, 1961.

CHAP. 12. Appropriation Act No. 2, 1961.

13. Canadian and British Insurance Companies Act, an Act to amend.

14. Coastal Fisheries Protection Act, an Act to amend.

15. Fire Losses Replacement Account Act, an Act to amend.

16. Foreign Insurance Companies Act, an Act to amend.

17. Income Tax Act, an Act to amend.

18. Tariff Board Act, an Act to amend.

Assented to June 1, 1961

19. Canada-United States of America Estate Tax Convention Act, 1961.

20. Coal Production Assistance Act, an Act to authorize certain Amendments to the Agreement made with Bras d'Or Coal Company Limited.

21. Criminal Code (Race Meetings), an Act to amend.

22. Farm Improvement Loans Act, an Act to amend.

23. Fisheries Act, an Act to amend.

24. National Design Council Act.

25. Representation Act, an Act to amend.

26. Vocational Rehabilitation of Disabled Persons Act.

Assented to June 8, 1961

27. Appropriation Act No. 3, 1961.

28. Canadian National Railways Act, an Act to amend.

29. Freight Rates Reduction Act, an Act to amend.

Assented to June 22, 1961

30. Agricultural Rehabilitation and Development Act.

31. Army Benevolent Fund Act, an Act to amend.

32. Canada Shipping Act, an Act to amend.

33. Export Credits Insurance Act, an Act to amend.

34. Government Property Traffic Act, an Act to amend.

35. Control of Narcotic Drugs, an Act to provide for.

36. Farm Credit Act, an Act to amend.

37. Food and Drugs Act, an Act to amend.

38. Judges Act and the Exchequer Court Act, an Act to amend.

39. War Veterans Allowance Act, 1952, an Act to amend.

Assented to July 13, 1961

40. Appropriation Act No. 4, 1961.

CHAP. 41. Canadian National Railways Financing and Guarantee Act, 1961.
42. Combines Investigation Act and Criminal Code, an Act to amend.
43. Criminal Code, an Act to amend.
44. Criminal Code (Capital Murder), an Act to amend.
45. Customs Tariff, an Act to amend.
46. Excise Act, an Act to amend.
47. Excise Tax Act, an Act to amend.
48. Financial Administration Act, an Act to amend.
49. Income Tax Act, an Act to amend.
50. Industrial Development Bank Act, an Act to amend.
51. Loan Companies Act, an Act to amend.
52. National Energy Board Act, an Act to amend.
53. Penitentiary Act.
54. Railway Act, an Act to amend.
55. Trust Companies Act, an Act to amend.

Assented to September 29, 1961

56. Canadian National Railway Company, construction of a line of railway in Province of Alberta and in Northwest Territories from Grimshaw, Alta., in northerly direction to Great Slave Lake in N.W.T.
57. Civil Service Act.
58. Federal Provincial Fiscal Arrangements Act.
59. Fitness and Amateur Sport Act.
60. National Centennial Act.
61. National Housing Act, 1954, an Act to amend.
62. Natural Resources Transfer (School Lands) Amendment Act, 1961.
63. Transport Act, an Act to amend.
64. Appropriation Act No. 5, 1961 (Main Supply).

Fifth Session, Twenty-Fourth Parliament, 10-11 Elizabeth II

Assented to February 7, 1962

CHAP. 1. Appropriation Act No. 1, 1962.

Assented to February 15, 1962

CHAP. 2. Blind Persons Act, an Act to amend.

3. Disabled Persons Act, an Act to amend.

4. Old Age Assistance Act, an Act to amend.

5. Old Age Security Act, an Act to amend.

6. Veterans Insurance Act, an Act to amend.

7. War Service Grants Act, an Act to amend.

Assented to February 23, 1962

8. Canadian National Railway—Construction of a line of railway from Optic Lake to Chisel Lake and Purchase from the International Nickel Company of Canada, Limited, of a line of railway from Sipiwesk to a point on Burntwood River near Mystery Lake—all in the Province of Manitoba.

9. Canadian National Railway—Construction of a line of railway from Whitecourt, Alberta in a westerly direction for a distance of approximately 23.2 miles to the property of Pan American Petroleum Corporation.

10. Children of War Dead (Education Assistance) Act, an Act to amend.

11. Civilian War Pensions and Allowances Act, an Act to amend.

Assented to March 23, 1962

12. Appropriation Act No. 2, 1962.

13. Canadian National Railway, Construction of a line of railway in the Province of Quebec between Matane and Ste Anne des Monts.

14. Export Credits Insurance Act, an Act to amend.

15. Farm Improvement Loans Act, an Act to amend.

16. Fisheries Improvement Loans Act, an Act to amend.

17. Representation Act, an Act to amend.

18. St. Lawrence Seaway Authority Act, an Act to amend.

19. Small Businesses Loans Act, an Act to amend.

Assented to April 5, 1962

20. Appropriation Act No. 3, 1962.

21. Canadian Wheat Board Act, an Act to amend.

22. Judges Act, an Act to amend.

Assented to April 18, 1962

23. Appropriation Act No. 4, 1962.

CHAP. 24. Appropriation Act No. 5, 1962 (Interim).

25. Canada Grain Act, an Act to amend.

26. Corporations and Labour Unions Returns Act.

27. Customs Act, an Act to amend.

28. Representation Act, an Act to amend.

29. Veterans Land Act, an Act to amend.

First Session, Twenty-Fifth Parliament, 11-12 Elizabeth II

Assented to October 25, 1962

CHAP. 1. Appropriation Act No. 6, 1962.

Assented to November 1, 1962

2. Export Credits Insurance Act, an Act to amend.

Assented to November 29, 1962

3. Appropriation Act No. 7, 1962.

4. Combines Investigation Act and the Criminal Code, an Act to amend.

5. Estate Tax Act, an Act to amend.

6. Excise Tax Act, an Act to amend.

7. Farm Credit Act, an Act to amend.

8. Income Tax Act, an Act to amend.

Assented to December 20, 1962

9. Appropriation Act No. 8, 1962.

10. Atlantic Development Board Act.

11. Canadian National Railway—construction of a line of railway in the province of New Brunswick, from Nepisiguit Junction to the property of Brunswick Mining and Smelting Corporation Limited, a distance of approximately 15 miles.

12. Canadian World Exhibition Corporation Act.

13. Coal Production Assistance Act, an Act to amend.

14. Federal-Provincial Fiscal Arrangements Act and the Federal-Provincial Tax-Sharing Arrangements Act, an Act to amend.

15. Food and Drugs Act, an Act to amend.

16. National Health and Welfare Act, an Act to amend (Department of).

17. National Housing Act, 1954, an Act to amend.

APPENDIX II

✳

DECLARATION OF LOYALTY

Ottawa, November 15, 1966
We, the undersigned Members of Parliament of the Progressive Conservative Party, request that the Right Honourable J. G. Diefenbaker continue as Leader of our Party

Wally Nesbitt
J. W. Monteith
Lewis Brand
Lawrence E. Kindt
Harry A. Moore
Hugh M. Horner
Ernie Pascoe
R. R. Southam
P. B. Rynard
George R. Muir
Hugh John Flemming
Eric Stefanson
Theo Ricard
Edward Nasserden
Michael Starr
John Loney
Harold W. Danforth
Ron D. McLelland
W. H. A. Thomas
Melvin J. McQuaid
W. Skoreyko
Stan Korchinski
J. A. Irvine
*Lloyd Crouse
Frank Fane

William Scott
R. "Bud" Simpson
Deane R. Gundlock
Jack H. Horner
Gordon Churchill
Donald MacInnis
Albert Horner
Erik Nielsen
Roger Regimbal
Bob Coates
Reg Cantelon
R. E. McKinley
Ken More
G. Chatterton
Rod Webb
J. N. Mandziuk
Walter Dinsdale
Bob McCleave
Russell MacEwan
J. Angus MacLean
D. M. Code
John Bower
*A. Cadieu
Terry Nugent
Eric A. Winkler

David V. Pugh
J. McIntosh
Jack Bigg
Reynold Rapp
Elmer Forbes
J. R. Keays
M. T. McCutcheon
George Hees
W. H. Jorgenson
Alvin Hamilton
J. Chester MacRae
J. Ellwood Madill
A. Douglas Alken-
    brack
James N. Ormiston
Paul Beaulieu
Cyril F. Kennedy
L. Watson
Bob Muir
Cliff Smallwood
G. D. Clancy
*Percy Noble

*Telegrams attached.

(The list of those who did not sign is revealing, and is included to keep the record complete.)

Gordon H. Aiken
Martial Asselin
Gerald W. Baldwin
H. Ray Ballard
Richard A. Bell
Thomas M. Bell
Siegfried Enns
Gordon Fairweather

J. Michael Forrestall
E. Davie Fulton
Lee Grills
Heward Grafftey
Alfred D. Hales
Douglas Harkness
W. Marvin Howe
Marcel Lambert

David MacDonald
Heath Macquarrie
J. Patrick Nowlan
L. R. Sherman
Heber E. Smith
Georges-J. Valade
Jean Wadds
Eldon M. Woolliams

INDEX

Trepanier, Paul O., 274
Tribune, The (Winnipeg), 7-8, 182
Trudeau, Pierre Elliott, 8, 15-16, 189, 260, 266
Truman, Harry S., 42, 96, 183-4
Two Nations theory, 242-4, 247, 281-6

unemployment, 111, 116, 126, 127
Unemployment Insurance Act, 186
Union Nationale Party, 132, 179
United Arab Republic, 74, 201, 203
United Nations (UN), 8, 71, 72, 73, 74-5, 76; and Cuban crisis, 79, 83, 86, 88
United States, 10, 63, 73, 82, 83-4, 103-4, 115, 118, 120, 122, 123, 133-4, 142, 151, 175, 182, 185, 188, 202, 214-15, 218, 227, 233, 242, 245, 246, 248, 269; and Britain, 94-9, 101, 102-4, 105-6; and Cuba, 77-80, 81-92, 98; and cultural imperialism in Canada, 15; and defence relations with Canada, 1-4, 7-30, 32, 36-7, 43-4, 46-108, 124, 154, 160, 185, 266
Urton, Jack, 191

USSR 14, 21-2, 29, 34, 35, 46, 53, 56, 63, 72-3, 75, 81, 84-5, 95, 96, 100, 102, 104, 107, 266; and Cuban crisis, 77-80, 81-3, 86, 87, 88, 90

Van Dusen, Thomas, 272, 276
Vanier, Georges, 148, 187, 193, 194
Vincent, Clément, 252

Wadds, Jean, 272, 276
Walker, David J., 139, 165, 170, 171, 199
Wardell, Michael, 182
Warren, J. H., 97
Watson, William "Whipper Billy", 240, 241
welfare. *See* social justice
Welsh, Keith, 4
Wigglesworth, Richard B., 68
Wilcox, G. L., 39
Winnipeg Free Press, 10

Young Progressive Conservatives (YPC), 152-3, 181
Youth for Diefenbaker Movement, 282